THE

COAST

PREVIOUS WORKS BY JOSEPH J. THORNDIKE

THE VERY RICH: A HISTORY OF WEALTH

THE MAGNIFICENT BUILDERS

St. Martin's

Press

New York

JOSEPH J. THORNDIKE

THE
COAST

A JOURNEY

DOWN THE

ATLANTIC

SHORE

ILLUSTRATIONS BY FRANK RICCIO

Design by Jaye Zimet
Maps and illustrations © 1993 Frank Riccio

Parts of Chapter 6 (Cape Cod) were originally published in *American Heritage* magazine.

Library of Congress Cataloging-in-Publication Data

Thorndike, Joseph Jacobs, 1913–
    The coast : a journey down the Atlantic Shore / Joseph J. Thorndike.
        p.   cm.
    "A Thomas Dunne book."
    ISBN 0-312-08700-4
    1. Atlantic Coast (U.S.)—Description and travel.   2. Thorndike, Joseph Jacobs, 1913–   —Journeys—Atlantic Coast.   I. Title.
F106.T49   1993
917.504'43—dc20   92-41223
                                                                            CIP

First Edition: April 1993
10 9 8 7 6 5 4 3 2 1

For Jane

my friend and fellow traveler

CONTENTS

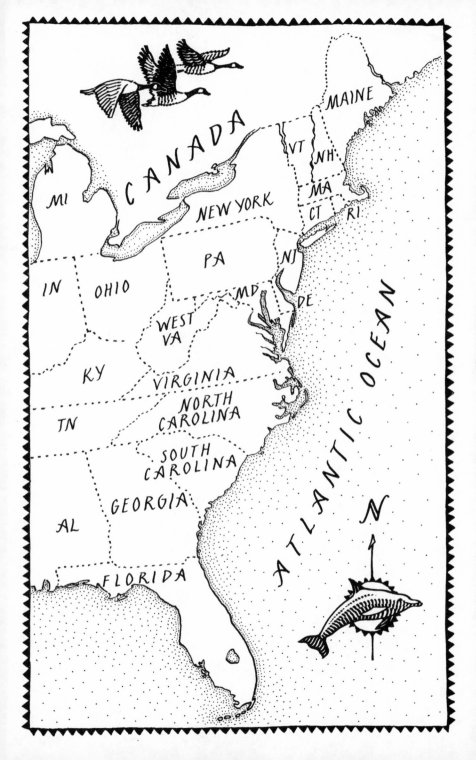

INTRODUCTION

WHEN I moved to Cape Cod some years ago, I decided, on a whim, to walk around the shore of the Cape. I did not make it all the way, partly because there are too many harbors and marshes and other breaks in the sandy coast. But I did retrace the journey that Thoreau made in 1849 along the Great Beach, and I saw how things have changed since then. I could understand why so many people are drawn, as he and his companion were, to "the shore of the resounding sea, determined to get it into us." I could also see, to a greater or lesser degree, the problems that now beset the coast—overcrowding, over-building, overfishing, erosion, pollution, and the closing of beaches to the public. However, Cape Cod, in both its history and its geography, is too much a special case to stand for the whole Atlantic shore of the United States. I decided, therefore, to have a look at the rest of the long coast, in all its natural and man-made variety, from Maine to Florida.

This book is a record of journeys taken at different times, over several years, to different sections of the coast. In some areas, the time of my visit was chosen to fit the season—Maine in summer, Florida in winter. In others, it was dictated by an event—for example, South Carolina after Hurricane Hugo. For clarity, however, I have organized it as a continuous description of the coast from north to south. That explains why the seasons change, not always in proper order, from chapter to chapter. The geographical order, I hope, will make it easier to see the coast as a whole and to see how it is faring almost five centuries after European explorers reported finding it.

Some like to think that Saint Brendan, an Irish monk half lost in myth, was the first voyager from the Old World to see the coast of what is now the United States. Others favor Medoc, a twelfth-century Welsh prince, or earlier nameless Carthaginians, Phoenicians, or Egyptians. Very likely, the first were the Vikings, but no one has placed them with certainty west of

Newfoundland. Columbus was too far south and John Cabot was too far north. So to Ponce de Leon, who discovered Florida in 1513, goes credit for the first authenticated sighting of our Atlantic shore.

Most of the rest of the coast, from the Carolinas to Maine, was first seen and explored by Giovanni da Verrazano, sailing under French colors, in search of the Orient. When he landed in 1524 on the Outer Banks of North Carolina, somewhere south of Cape Hatteras, he looked right across the continent, or so he thought, and saw another ocean beyond. In fact, what he looked across was Ocracoke Island and what he saw beyond was Pamlico Sound, not the Pacific.

As the Atlantic shore of what is now the United States took shape on the charts of European mapmakers, it was seen to be a coastline of geologic variety hardly matched anywhere in the world. The northern section, from the present Canadian border to the southern part of Maine, is a jagged front of promontories and inlets, set off by hundreds of rocky islands. The rest of the New England coast is the complicated work of the last glacier, with sandy shores broken by rocky headlands and marshes. From New Jersey south to Florida, the prevailing pattern is that of long, thin coastal barriers—some of them islands and some of them spits—backed by sounds, lagoons, and great inland-reaching bays. But that pattern is varied in North Carolina by the far-flung arc of the Outer Banks and in Georgia by clumpy sea islands, just seaward of wide salt marshes. Finally, the coast ends in the coral reefs of the Florida Keys.

It was not what some European visionaries, misled by early reports of naked Indians on lush Caribbean islands, had imagined—a land of plenty, something like the Garden of Eden, where "natural man" plucked bountiful food from trees. Nor was it El Dorado of the Spanish conquistadors, strewn with gold and silver for the taking. But it was a coast to make Europeans feel at home, whether they came from rocky Scotland or marshy Norfolk or sandy beaches in Portugal.

Sir Walter Raleigh's expeditions to Virginia excited the Elizabethan court with reports of the exotic flora, fauna, and native inhabitants—all brought vividly to life in the watercolors of an expedition artist and governor, John White. Later, Capt. John Smith sailed along the coast from Virginia to Maine, noting especially what would be of use to settlers: the tall trees (for building, for firewood, and for ships' masts), the animals whose furs could be sold in Europe, and especially the fish. His map of New England shows a school of fish fairly erupting out of the water to make a mound on the surface of Massachusetts Bay. His report was glowing:

> Of all the foure parts of the world that I have yet seene not inhabited, could I have but the meanes to transport a Colonie, I would rather live here than any where: and if it did not maintaine itselfe, were we but once indifferently well fitted, let us starve.

Some came ill-prepared and some starved, but for Europeans during the centuries that followed, America was a land of promise, free of the ancient legal and social fetters that bound men's lives in the Old World.

So powerful was that appeal that in the course of time the fine harbors of the Atlantic Coast were to be the receiving points for the greatest mass migration in history. The sea-lanes that stretched from those ports became the busiest in the world, plied by the greatest ships. For four centuries, this coast has been the interface of the Old World and the New, the starting place for new lives, new ventures, new fortunes.

This historic role has not been fulfilled without damage to the coast itself. For ten thousand years, before the coming of the Europeans, the Indians had lived lightly on this shore. They felled a few trees, cleared fields for their plantings, set weirs for fish, paddled their log or bark canoes. They had not the means to leave much mark on the land, nor did they understand the doctrine, proclaimed in the white man's Bible, that the earth and all its creatures had been created for the sole use and benefit of Adam's race. Thus, at the beginning of the seventeenth century, a virtually untouched coast lay ready for the impact of the ax, the plow, the gun, and, in time, the pile driver, the bulldozer, the cement mixer, the oil tanker, the sewer pipe, the pesticide, the plastic bottle, the dune buggy, and the nuclear power plant.

The early settlers were struck by the vast forest that ran like a green headband along the land's edge and stretched far beyond the western horizon. Except in Scandinavia, Western Europeans had not seen such forests since the Middle Ages. By the seventeenth century, England was chronically short of wood for building or burning or for making ships and masts—especially masts for the ever-larger fighting ships. Before long, the Admiralty was sending agents through the American forest to mark the tallest trees with the king's broad arrow, reserving them for masts. The settlers went at the rest of the forest with axes, and in later times lumber companies finished the job. The great forest resource was stripped as fast in the nineteenth century as the continent's petroleum resource has been sucked up in the twentieth.

Wood, of course, is a renewable resource. Along sections of the northern coast where trees have grown back, they are mostly fir and spruce, however, with some oak, birch, and maple. Of the great white pines that stood as much as two hundred feet tall, only a few tiny stands remain.

In place of the forest—and largely with the yield of the forest—we, the settlers' descendants, have fashioned a new headband for the coast, a fringe of man-made structures running all the way from Maine to Florida. In the great harbors, they make a solid wall against the sea. On the open shores, they stand in rows, often for miles without a break. In some sections, hardly a waterfront lot remains unbuilt upon.

When developers ran out of dry land, they turned to the salt marshes—muddy wastelands, as people then thought. Around harbors such as Boston and New York, the draining and filling of marshland pushed city limits well out beyond the original shorelines. No wetland was safe. By the time we recognized that wetlands are the nurseries of all kinds of fish and shellfish and the refuge of seabirds, half of the coastal states' salt marshes had been lost.

Unlike the marshy shore, the sandy shore resists man's efforts to change it. By tearing up the vegetation, he may turn a treed or grassy shore into barren sand, but he cannot impose his will, against nature's, on the sand itself. On many stretches of the coast, owners have tried to protect or build up their beaches by seawalls and groins. These may stop erosion for a time and even trap some sand, although often at a neighbor's expense, but sooner or later the ocean has its way. If a beach is moving landward, as the Great Beach on Cape Cod has been moving at the rate of three feet a year since records have been kept, nothing will stand in its way. The hotel owners of Miami Beach found that out when they erected miles of seawall, only to lose all the sand in front of it. Now the city, state, and federal governments have spent $68 million to restore the beach, but no one knows how long it will stay.

While the coast itself, except for the marshes, can generally withstand the assault of man, the creatures of the shallow offshore waters cannot. Until this century, no one supposed that the supply of shellfish on the Atlantic banks was anything but inexhaustible. Yet on the coast of Maine, where the Indians left piles of oyster shells twenty-five feet high, oysters now sell for fifty cents apiece. Trawlers loaded with electronic fishing gear bring in half as many cod and haddock as they did without that gear twenty years ago.

In assessing the damage that we have done to the coast, mostly in this century, it is not easy to think of things that we have done to counterbalance the harm. The best to be said is that we have stopped doing some of the worst things. We have generally stopped destroying coastal wetlands. We are making some progress in cleaning up the polluted rivers and sand flats. We have spruced up some of the old, dilapidated harborfronts. Perhaps we have learned the folly of trying to stop sandy beaches from moving.

The bright side of the picture is that, except for the wetlands, the damage is not irreversible. Unlike the soil of the western Plains, the rocks and sand of the coast have not blown or washed away. The fish will come back if the overfishing is stopped. The shellfish will recover if the pollution is controlled. Where the sand cover has been destroyed, the trees and grasses will grow again if they are planted and protected.

In traveling along the shore, it is always a joy to come upon a section that has been saved, often in the nick of time, from developers. First among the saviors of the coast is the National Park Service, with its seven eastern national seashores. Much less recognized is the U.S. Fish and Wildlife Service, guardian of a string of refuges, all up and down the Atlantic flyway, that began with Theodore Roosevelt's effort to protect the pelicans on one small island in Florida. Other stretches of the coast have been saved by private organizations such as the Nature Conservancy and the Audubon societies, as well as by many local conservation groups. Quite a number of especially fine spots, once private estates, have been given to the public by the owners or their heirs.

Some, though not all, of the states have also shown foresight in preserving sections of the coast as parks or public beaches. But for many towns and cities, the same cannot be said. Too often, the local establishments of politicians, landowners, builders, lawyers, and real estate brokers, all claiming to be for economic progress, have joined hands with outside developers to despoil their own communities. The familiar story is that citizens wake up to find their harbors fouled, their streets clogged, their trees cut down, their shores blighted by ugly buildings and often blocked off.

The Atlantic Coast has never lacked friends. Over the years, various parts of it have attracted writers and artists who, through their work, have made those places their own. Thus, as we shall see, the rocks and spray of the Maine coast belong to Winslow Homer, the long, lonely beach of Cape Cod to Thoreau, the eerie Georgia marshes to Sidney Lanier. Every cove and headland is someone's favorite place. And now that the perils to the coast are well understood, many who cherish it are working to halt the forces of damage and to reclaim its beauties.

Indeed, the greatest peril to the coast today may be that it has too many friends, too many people who want their part of it. After four centuries of continental expansion, the strip of land that faces the Atlantic is still by far the most populous part of the country. Today, more than half the people of the United States live within an hour's drive of the shore, and on fine summer weekends it sometimes seems as if all of them are headed for the water's edge.

Therein lies the crunch. At the same time that more and more people want to get to the shore, more and more of the shore is being closed to them. If, in time, we learn to restore and protect the coast, whose coast will it be? Everyone's or only the shorefront property owners'?

Until this century, no one had much trouble getting to the shore, for swimming or picnicking or fishing or just sitting on the sand. But, in fact, as we now learn, only 6 percent of the Atlantic seaboard is publicly owned and available for recreational use. Along the rest of the shore, there spring up year by year an ever-increasing number of PRIVATE—NO TRESPASSING signs.

The soaring price of seashore in recent years has made the problem acute. In a typical waterfront community, a graph of land prices will show them rising, tier by tier, as they approach the shore and then shooting straight up as they reach the actual coast. Such a chart makes it seem as if the ocean is closed off by a wall of money, and so indeed much of it is. Recent buyers who in some places have paid $300,000 for a hundred feet of waterfront do not take kindly to the idea of strangers coming between them and their ocean.

Enclosure is the legal term. It calls to mind the hated process whereby English and Scottish landlords in the eighteenth century fenced in the common lands and evicted their tenants, many of whom migrated to America. Now it is the shorefront that is being enclosed. The British landlords were within their legal rights, and so, generally, are the waterfront owners today. As a Massachusetts court ruled in 1814: "the owner of the adjoining land may, whenever he pleases, inclose, build, and obstruct to the low-water mark, and exclude all mankind." Massachusetts is one of five Atlantic coastal states in which property rights run to the low-water mark; in most of the rest they run to the high-water mark. The rights descend from Colonial grants made by the king of England. They run counter to an even older legal tradition, formulated in the Code of Justinian, that the shore belongs to everyone. The two legal principles are on a collision course.

If this were the sixteenth century and our ancestors asked me for advice from the perspective of the twentieth, I would have a few suggestions about the coast: Don't cut down all the trees. Don't fill in the wetlands. Don't pollute the water. Don't try to catch all the fish. Don't build on shifting sands. And keep the coast open to all.

In a sense that transcends royal grants, we all have a vested interest in the coast. Between the closing of the Bering land bridge and the coming of air travel, all our ancestors crossed the ocean to reach this hemisphere. And even as we settled the broad continent, we remained a maritime people. Now, as the population figures show, we are drawn increasingly to the coast, hoping to find that it has not changed for the worse. The Romans had it right: The seas and the shores of the seas are a public trust.

THE COAST

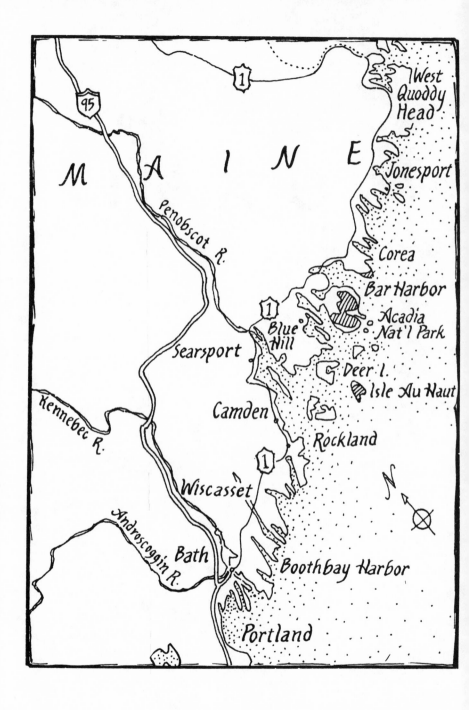

WAY DOWN EAST

WEST Quoddy Head Light stands on the tip of a rocky headland, bright and cheery in its red and white candy stripes. The day is sunny here, but out over the ocean, where the cold Labrador Current meets the warm Gulf Stream, the fog has been forming. As it rolls toward the coast, the first thing to disappear is Grand Manan Island, fifteen miles away in Canadian waters. At the lighthouse, a sensor has its unblinking eye trained on the fog bank, and when visibility falls to less than three miles, it triggers the first blast of a foghorn. The last thing to vanish is Sail Rock, a jagged hunk of granite three hundred yards offshore. After Sail Rock disappears, it is only minutes before the fog holds Quoddy Head in a cloud so thick that a stranger can get lost, as I did a little while later, walking from the lighthouse to the visitors' parking lot. Quoddy Head, the northern tip of the

1

Atlantic Coast of the United States, is fogbound on an average of fifty-nine days a year.

For the first time in almost two hundred years, West Quoddy Head Light has no keeper. It was automated in 1988, as part of an ongoing Coast Guard program that has left only one light—that in Boston Harbor—still under on-site human control. The keeper's cottage is not empty, however. Its present occupant is David Jones, a genial, stocky man whose roots lie deep on this promontory. His grandfather was keeper of the light in the days before ships carried LORAN to tell them where they were, before the Coast Guard had helicopters instead of dories to rescue shipwrecked sailors. David Jones's parents were married at the lighthouse, he told me, and he has never strayed far from its sweeping beam. At present, he is assistant manager of the Quoddy Head State Park, which adjoins the Coast Guard station.

If there is any place on the coast that can take whatever the wild ocean hurls against it, the granite fist of West Quoddy Head would seem to be it. If the sea rises several feet in the next hundred years and floods coastal cities, as some oceanographers think it may, the effect will hardly be noticed on this high cliff where the tide normally rises fourteen feet twice a day. When Cape Cod is a mere stub of its present self, a few thousand years from now, Quoddy Head will, in all likelihood, remain almost unchanged. When the sand of the barrier islands of New Jersey and North Carolina has been washed out from under all their boardwalks and cottages, Sail Rock will probably still have its distinctive gaff-rig profile.

Still, nothing is quite impervious to the power of the ocean. "Look over there," says Raymond Thompson, the park manager, pointing to a wide scar where the promontory has been swept clean of soil and vegetation, the trees left flat and dead. "The Groundhog Day storm of 1978 did that," Thompson says. Below us, I could see that the cliff itself was indeed being eroded, not suddenly as a sandy bluff may be collapsed but a bit at a time as water finds crevices in the rock and builds up pockets of pressure until little pieces break off and fall to the shore. The talus of small stones at the foot of the cliff gave proof that in the unending battle of the sea against the land, the land never wins.

When Raymond Thompson was a young man, he was all set for a good job as a crane operator during construction of a hydroelectric plant at Passamaquoddy Bay. The plan was to build a dam across the mouth of the bay, which has a twenty-four-foot tide, and generate electric power. It was a favorite project of President Franklin Roosevelt, whose summer home was on Campobello Island, just across a channel from Quoddy Head. But the plan died with Roosevelt. Probably the scheme made no economic sense in those days. But when the price of oil shot up in the seventies, local people hoped that its time had come. No such luck. It is still on hold, awaiting yet another energy crisis. "Not in my time," says Thompson.

Instead of running a crane, Thompson spent most of his working life as a lobsterman. Fishing and lobstering are the chief occupations of this northeast coast, and both are in trouble. The lobster catch has been fairly steady but here, as all along the coast, it took four or five times as many traps in the 1980s as it did in the 1950s to catch the same number of lobsters. At his home near the lighthouse, Robert Olsen, another old lobsterman, told me that at the age of seventy-five he still set seventy traps, but only because that was his life. "It doesn't pay for the gas," he said.

All the old-timers who go down to Quoddy Head to keep an eye on the state of the ocean have memories of better days. Harold Wasson went to sea as a boy, sailing out of Lubec on his father's schooner. On one voyage, his father fell ill and Harold got his first command, taking the vessel into New York with a cargo of lumber. He was twenty-one at the time. Later, he sailed his own ships, but the coastal trade was dying. In 1937, he captained the last three-masted schooner to sail out of Lubec.

Wasson's wife experienced her own share of the region's declining fortunes. For years, she worked in one of the plants at Lubec where small herring were processed and canned as sardines. Unaccountably, the herring catch dwindled and, one by one, the canneries closed. Wasson remembers the day when his wife's cannery shut down. "She had tears streaming down her face," he recalls.

The towns and most of the houses bear the marks of long depression. But here and there, you can see signs of a different economic future. The house next to that of Olsen, the old lob-sterman, looks new and freshly painted. It belongs to Marc Goodrich, a retired engineer from Pennsylvania. He told me how he came to build it: "My wife and I decided we wanted a place on the Maine coast for vacations and later for retirement. We spent two summers searching the coast, beginning at the south and moving north. Finally, we got to the northern end and bought this land next to the lighthouse." If there is a bright spot in the economic landscape of this threadbare coast, it is the appearance of summer visitors who come on vacation and sometimes stay for good. The Goodrich house is the northern tip of an ocean-seeking migration that has filled up the Atlantic Coast all the way from here to Florida. I would see a lot more of it.

Looking at the map of North America, one may wonder what reason of history or geography made Quoddy Head the northern extremity of the eastern United States coast. The search for an answer takes us back to a French expedition that arrived off this coast in the late summer of 1604. The name of its leader was Pierre du Gast, the Sieur de Monts, a noble in the court of King Henry IV, but the name known to history is that of his young geographer, Samuel de Champlain. Charged by the king with establishing a base for colonization of the American coast between the St. Lawrence and the Hudson, they chose to set up camp on an island in the St. Croix River, twenty miles up from Quoddy Head. Champlain had time to scout the coast only as far south as Penobscot Bay before winter set in. Marooned on St. Croix Island by floating ice, without fresh food or even wine (which froze and burst its bottles), the French spent a winter so grim that by spring almost half of them were dead of scurvy and other ills.

In the spring, Champlain set off in a pinnace with the Sieur de Monts to explore the coast farther south. His reports and charts of the coast and its harbors, as far south as Cape Cod, were so clear and accurate that explorers used them for many years to come. If his superiors had taken advantage of them, the shores of the Gulf of Maine might have become New France instead of New England.

But nothing could persuade the Sieur de Monts to spend another winter on that forbidding shore. The French retired to the gentler shore of Nova Scotia and decided to make their thrust up the St. Lawrence valley. Having set out to extend the French dominion down the Atlantic Coast, they ended up by setting the southern limit of that dominion.

In later years, from their base in Canada, the French made several attempts to establish colonies in Maine, but each one was wiped out by the English. The best the French could do was to use the Abnaki Indians in a guerilla war against the English until finally, on the Plains of Abraham at Quebec in 1759, they lost their Canadian empire. A quarter of a century later, in the Treaty of Paris that ended the American Revolution, the boundary between the United States and Canada was drawn right where the French had stopped in 1604, at the St. Croix River.

St. Croix Island, where the French spent their terrible winter, is now an international historic site, albeit a rather frustrating one for the tourist. You cannot get to the island from either shore unless you have your own boat. On the Maine side, a park ranger invites visitors to look through a telescope that is focused on a small monument marking the site of the French camp.

From Quoddy Head, the coast of Maine stretches 220 miles to the border of New Hampshire—in a straight line, that is. Geographers cannot agree on how long it is if you follow it around the edges of every bay and promontory. Estimates range from 2,500 to 3,500 miles. The length depends, for one thing, on whether you measure it at high tide or at low; on a coast where the tides range from ten feet to twenty, the difference is considerable.

This is what geologists call a drowned coast. At times during the last Ice Age, the mainland extended far beyond the present shoreline, making meadows of what are now fishing banks in the Gulf of Maine. But beneath the weight of an ice sheet more than a mile thick, the land sank beneath the sea. When the glacier began to retreat, some fifteen thousand years ago, the land rose again, but not as high as it had been before. Then, as the ice cap of the whole northern hemisphere released its water, the seas rose and came flooding back into the valleys and among the hills of the coast. The present capes and points were once ridges on the landscape; the islands were hilltops.

The stretch of coast from Quoddy Head to Mount Desert is not the most beautiful part of Maine. Its hills are not as high, its vegetation not as vivid, its soil even thinner than farther south. The country way down east is spare and muted, though the sandy soil is good for one thing—blueberries. Ninety-five percent of all the wild blueberries harvested in the United States are grown on these barrens.

The unlikely captain of the wild blueberry industry is Dr. Amr Abdel-Fattah Ismail. I found him at the headquarters of the Maine Wild Blueberry Company at Machias, a short ways downriver from Bad Little Falls. Clad in blue pants and a blue sweater, sitting on a chair with a blue cushion in an office with a blue rug, he looked every inch (about seventy-five of them) and every pound (about three hundred of them) a blueberry king. The son of an Egyptian general, Ismail had never seen a blueberry before he came to this country thirty years ago to study agriculture. He was "just a kid from downtown Cairo," he says, and his plan was to go back and manage the family farms. Instead, he married an American girl from Smith, took a teaching job at the University of Maine, and found himself in charge of a blueberry research project.

At that time Maine's low-bush berries, which grow in the wild and have to be picked by hand, were losing market share to the larger, high-bush berries which may have less taste but are easier to harvest. Ismail, working first at the university and later as executive vice-president of Maine Wild, developed new methods of cultivation and pest control, and new uses in cereals, muffins, and soft drinks. Within fifteen years, the wild blueberry harvest had tripled.

The berries are processed in a modern plant where they are shot through a freezing tunnel at a speed of seventy miles an hour and a temperature of forty degrees below zero. But they are still harvested by crews of pickers with small hand rakes. Sometimes, when the season is late, the opening of school is delayed so that the students can join housewives from the towns and Indians from Canada to get the crop in. "It's part of the way of life here," says Dr. Ismail.

For the traveler, this coast has a special attraction. It is a landscape out of our past. When you start down the highway from Lubec, you look twice at the route marker to reassure yourself that this is really Route 1, the Atlantic coastal highway that so many motorists know farther south as a commercial strip of gas stations, fast-food restaurants, motels, and auto dealerships. In northeast Maine, Route 1 is a two-lane road running for the most part through open country, with few roadside signs and light traffic. Except that the side roads are paved and many of the new dwellings are trailers, you are seeing what you might have seen from a Model T in 1925.

The side roads lead down to coastal villages that cluster tightly around the shores of small, protected harbors. The houses are small, nondescript in their architecture, snugly built against the chill of long, damp winters. At low tide, when the sea level drops by ten or twelve feet, the harbors shrink in size and the docks stand awkwardly on tall, spindly piles. If Route 1 has the aspect of 1925, the fishing villages are not far removed in appearance from 1875.

One such village is Corea, at the tip of the Gouldsboro peninsula. I had heard about it from a sailing friend who once found refuge there. Corea has no facilities for visiting pleasure yachts. Not many sailors venture so far down the coast, and those who do usually keep going. But my friend was caught in a sudden storm in waters famous for their hidden rocks and thick fogs. When he telephoned ashore to Corea, he had to wait until the harbormaster called around and located a lobsterman whose mooring was not in use. In the tightly packed harbor, he tied up safely with hardly a foot to spare between his bow and the next boat. His only mistake in judgment, he told me, was in offering to pay for the mooring; he was brusquely refused. That seemed proof enough that Corea was not part of the modern sailing world.

Louise Dickinson Rich lived at Corea in the 1950s and wrote a lively, affectionate book about it entitled *The Peninsula*. There were thirty boats in the harbor then. Last year, according to Joel Strout, who manages the Lobster Cooperative where the catch is landed, there were fifty-six boats during the summer but still only thirty-one in the fall. The other twenty-five belong to less-serious lobstermen who knock off when the weather gets cold. The hard core stick it out through the month of December. In midwinter, some of them switch to scalloping or go on unemployment until spring.

Half a dozen lobstermen, just off their boats, were warming up at Joel Strout's stove. The coast was changing, they said, and they didn't like it. "It's these outside people," one of them said. "They're buying up the whole shore. They get a piece of land on the water and the first thing they do, even before they start a house, is to put up a Private Property sign.

"We've always used the shore where we needed to," said another man. "So have the fishermen and the clammers and the wormers. But these new people think they own the shore."

If you ask a lawyer, he will tell you that, yes, they do. Private property in Maine runs down to the mean low-water mark. Under the state constitution, others may use the dry shore for purposes of "fishing, fowling, and navigation," but they may not pass over private land above the shore to get to it. That is the state law and it is sometimes enforced by private owners with more than signs. Someone quoted an aggrieved clammer: "You think twice about crossing private property when you have looked down the barrel of a shotgun."

The fishermen have their own unwritten law. It says that a man has a right to get to his boat, no matter whose land he has to cross, and that he can use the shore for landing his catch or fixing his gear or whatever his work requires. The unwritten law has its own sanctions, as one lobstermen related: "There were some fishermen down the coast who had always used a particular road to get to their boats. A stranger bought the property and didn't want them there, so he parked his car across the road to block it. Well, the fishermen drove up an old truck of their own and locked him into his own drive." Other new property owners have learned that it is not wise to antagonize the fishermen and then leave their property unattended in the winter. "There have been some mysterious fires along the coast," said one lobsterman darkly.

During most of the year, the lobsterman gets up while it is still dark and is out of the harbor before the sun comes up. He is gone for most of the day in all weather, often out of sight of land or any other boat. Lobstering is still, for most of the men who pursue it, a one-man, one-boat operation. While the boats that drag for fish have gotten ever larger and their gear more complicated, the lobster boats have stayed much the same and so have the lobster traps. Lobstering is the last stand of the solitary fisherman.

It might seem that, with gasoline engines and hydraulic

haulers to pull up the traps, the work would be easier and the profits greater than they were in the old days, but it has not worked out that way. The nineteenth-century lobsterman had to row a dory and pull up his traps by hand, but he did not have to go very far offshore and he could usually count on a good catch in every trap. Now he must sometimes go twelve or fifteen miles out and must set many more traps—four or five hundred of them. He checks half of them every day and often finds many empty.

This is a coast on which it was once possible to tell how well-off a schoolboy's family was by looking into his lunch box. If he had a meat-loaf sandwich, his family was relatively affluent; the poorer children ate lobster. By the late 1980s live lobsters were bringing three or four dollars a pound at the dock and perhaps eight or ten dollars by the time they got to a retail market.

Remarkably, Maine's annual lobster catch remained almost steady through most of this century—a little under or a little over 20 million pounds. But the supporting statistics gave cause for alarm. In 1900, about 17 million pounds were taken by 3,100 lobstermen in 156,000 traps; in 1985, about 18 million pounds were taken by 9,000 lobstermen setting 2 million traps.

What to do? Some said there are just too many lobstermen with too many boats and too many traps. Some said the lobsters were being taken too young—before they had a chance to reproduce—in order to satisfy a market that likes them to weigh a pound or a pound and a quarter (the size that most people order in restaurants). Some said they were eaten in ever-greater numbers by seals, which are protected by law. Many blamed the draggers, which sweep the bottom in deep water and bring up lobsters in their fishnets. Lobsters that are undersize (three and a quarter inches, measured by the length of the carapace or body shell) and egg-bearing females are supposed to be thrown back, but sometimes they are not. This coast, with its unnumbered coves, sparse population, and frequent fogs, has long been a smugglers' haven. Just as food supplies were smuggled to the British in Canada at the time of Jefferson's Embargo Act of 1807, and liquor was landed during Prohibition, and bales of marijuana in recent times, there is some suspicion that illegal lobsters may find their way ashore.

Most people agreed that the thing to do was to take some

of the pressure off the lobster stock and let it gradually recover. One way would be to limit the number of licenses or the number of traps or the length of the season. Another plan, already being phased in, is to raise the size limit; just an extra eighth of an inch would give more lobsters a chance to reproduce.

Such plans are on hold for the time being because, to almost everyone's surprise, the lobster catch jumped to 28 million pounds in 1990 and to 30 million in 1991. Fishery experts do not know quite what to make of it. Some look for a cause in the sharp decline in the stock of codfish, a voracious consumer of baby lobsters. Others, however, say that the lobstermen have been setting more traps in the deep offshore waters where the breeding stock congregates. That could spell more trouble ahead.

Lobstermen resist all controls because they know that while controls may work in the long run, the first effect might be to reduce the catch and push some marginal lobstermen over the edge. Besides, they find it hard, temperamentally, to accept the idea of regulation. Anne Johnson, the marine biologist of the Maine Audubon Society, who has been working with the state on fishing policy, understands their reluctance. "After all," she says, "the reason they are lobstermen is that they don't like any interference with their work. They are natural loners."

Yet the world of the lobsterman is not the closed world that it used to be. While the little harbor of Corea looks very much as it did when Mrs. Rich wrote about it, the feeling of isolation has eroded. There are new faces in town, belonging to "away" people who have bought up a great part of the coast for summer homes or just for speculation on the price of shorefront property (up 200 percent in three years before the recession). If you listen to the talk at the Lobster Cooperative when the boat owners come in to warm up around the stove, one voice will have the accent of a "Bert and I" record, while another might as well be from Boston. It is no longer taken for granted that a son will follow his father to sea. He may go off to college and never come back to stay, while someone else's son may come up from suburbia to take up lobstering.

Why, with all its problems, do so many stick with this hard and lonely work? Mrs. Rich put that question to two of the lobstermen she knew in Corea. One of them, Lewis Conley, who was thirty-five at the time, answered, "It's the thing I know

best. It's the only work I can do where I can be my own boss."
The other, Junior Jordan, who was twenty-two, said simply,
"Because I love it."

Thirty-five years later, I inquired after them in Corea. Conley, I learned, had just recently retired after half a century of
lobstering and had moved away. Lawrence Jordan, Jr., was still
at work—in fact, he was out in his boat at the time and not
expected back before dark. In the years since Mrs. Rich had
talked to him, his father had died of a heart attack while out in
his own boat. His two daughters had married nonfishermen. His
son had become a high-school teacher in Eastport. His wife, Joy,
who runs the office of the Lobster Cooperative, told of a rare
occasion when he had taken her out in his boat. "It's just like
Christmas," he told her. "When I pull up those traps, it's just
like opening Christmas presents."

THE MAINE ISLANDS

FROM Corea, you have only to go up one peninsula and down the next and across a bridge to find yourself on Mount Desert Island (spelled as in an atlas but pronounced, as many natives insist, as on a menu). Here, like a luxury yacht run aground among the lobster boats, is the grand, faded seaside resort of Bar Harbor. Mount Desert was a true island, unconnected to the mainland, and Bar Harbor was a fishing village like all the others on this coast when the painter Thomas Cole "discovered" it in 1844. Cole was followed by Frederick Edwin Church and other artists of the Hudson River School, who opened the eyes of their New York patrons to the rugged beauties of the Maine coast. Church brought his lawyer friend Charles Tracy and Tracy brought his son-in-law J. P. Morgan, and the rest of Society followed.

The multimillionaires of the Gilded Age came by steamer

from New York and Boston, or in their yachts, or after 1884 by rail in their private Pullmans. They lined the shore with "cottages" of fifty or seventy rooms, built of cedar shingle and stone, with a profusion of turrets, balconies, gables, verandas, and terraces. There was nothing like it north of Newport.

Bar Harbor's heyday lasted from the 1880s to the great crash of 1929, when the owners fell victim to stock-market losses, the income tax, and the servant problem. Some of the mansions were burned down in a great fire that swept part of the island in 1947. Others have been given to institutions or opened to tourists. A few of the mansions and more of their gatehouses are still lived in by the old families.

Bar Harbor is a good place to contemplate the contradictory effects of wealthy occupation on the coast. To begin with, a visitor finds it difficult to see the coast at all. It lies just out of sight beyond the fences, gates, and hedges of one fine estate after another. Big money seized this shoreline a century ago and, with the help of compliant local officials, walled it off from public use. Unless you are a guest of one of the landowners, there is not much to see in Bar Harbor.

Yet the same wealthy summer residents—or some of them at least—took the lead in turning most of Mount Desert Island, behind its fashionable fringe, into a national park. Through the efforts of such notables as President Charles W. Eliot of Harvard, George Vanderbilt, and John D. Rockefeller, Jr., the mountainous, forested interior of the island was saved from the lumber companies and forced upon a somewhat reluctant federal government. Acadia National Park is a hiker's joy, with its evergreen forests, sparkling lakes, and the bare-topped mountains that led Champlain to name this island Ile des Monts Déserts. It draws more visitors per acre than any other national park in the country.

Mount Desert is only one, though the largest, of the seemingly countless islands that are scattered off the Maine coast. Attempts to count them lead only to argument. How big does a ledge have to be to be given the status of island? What about fingers of land that become islands only when the tide comes in? Or others that break the surface only when the tide goes out? "More than 3,000" is the figure used by the Island Institute at Rockland.

The essence of an island is that you can reach it only by boat. Some of the Maine islands, such as Mount Desert, lie so close to the mainland that they have been connected by bridges and have thereby lost their standing as islands in all but name. When people come by car instead of by ferry, and supplies come by truck, as on Deer Isle or Beals Island, there is not much feeling of islandness left. On the other hand, some islands such as Monhegan lie far out to sea, just visible on clear days as gray shapes on the horizon. When storms stop the ferries and fog grounds the planes, they might as well be small continents to themselves.

In the last century, you could take one of the many steamers that plied this coast, carrying passengers and cargo from port to port. They are all gone now, put out of business by the automobile and the airplane, as well as the rising costs of labor and insurance. You can go by ferry to some of the larger islands, or you can take the mail boat around the islands of Casco Bay or Penobscot Bay. Or you can take a week's cruise, along the coast and among the islands, on one of the big sailing ships that leave from Portland, Rockland, Camden, and other ports.

One of the best islands to visit, wild but accessible, is Isle au Haut (in local franglais, Aisle-uh-Hoe), which is part of Acadia National Park but eight miles out to sea and reached quite separately by ferry. I heard about it from my friend Jane who was spending the summer at Blue Hill and who had agreed to join me in exploring some sections of the coast. We left by the morning ferry from Stonington, an old working lobster port now showing the first signs of touristy cuteness. Some of our fellow passengers carried backpacks (and permits from the Park Service) for camping overnight. One couple was planning to stay in style at a bed-and-breakfast place recently opened in the keeper's cottage of the old lighthouse. The rest of us returned, after a day of hiking on forest trails and over coastal boulders, by the afternoon ferry, glad to have seen a large island still pretty much in its natural state.

When you look at any of the islands from a distance, cloaked as most of them are in blankets of spruce, you may think you are looking at scattered chunks of a primeval world, never touched by man. But that perception is misleading. Many of them have a human history going back before Columbus, perhaps even before the Vikings. Several tribes of the Abnaki Indians made their summer camps on these islands, where their crops were safe from most of the mainland predators and they themselves were safe from other tribes. When European fishermen began coming to the Maine coast, they often established their own bases on the islands, for much the same reasons. On the islands, the fishermen could set up their drying racks for the fish without much fear of trouble from unfriendly Indians or animals.

Even when the fishermen shared an island with Indians, they generally got along peacefully. Like the Indians, the fishermen were only seasonal campers and, unlike the farmers who came after them, they had no desire for permanent, exclusive land rights. Only when year-round settlers arrived did trouble ensue, as events on Matinicus Island illustrate.

In the early years of the eighteenth century, Ebenezer Hall, who had settled on Matinicus, fed his cattle by harvesting hay on nearby Green Island. Then, as now, Green Island had a large population of seabirds, whose eggs and young were gathered for food by local Indians. All was peaceful until Hall began burning the island over to improve his hay harvest. By that time, Maine had been claimed as a colony by Massachusetts, so the Indians petitioned that commonwealth to stop Hall from destroying the bird colonies. Getting no satisfaction in that quarter, they ambushed Hall in 1724 and scalped him.

The busiest time for the islands came in the early and middle years of the nineteenth century. At that time, when almost everything that moved for any distance along the coast of Maine did so by water, the islands were more readily accessible than all but a narrow fringe of the mainland. While the inland forests were still largely untouched, most of the islands were cleared and their hardwood sold for lumber. On the cleared land settlers planted crops, cut hay, and pastured sheep or cattle. By 1820, almost every sizable island had its flock of sheep.

With the coming of roads and railroads and the decline of shipping, the islands lost their special advantages in all but the heaviest of the products they had to offer: their very bedrock itself. Quarries were opened up to cut Maine granite for the building boom that followed the Civil War.

One of the most vigorous quarrying operations was carried on by General Davis Tillson, late of the Union army. In 1873, he bought Hurricane Island in Penobscot Bay, just offshore from Rockland, and brought in European immigrants to do the work. If any of the southern slaves whom he had helped to free had set foot on Hurricane Island, they would have had cause to wonder whether much, except the climate, had changed. The general paid his cutters ten dollars a week and paid it in credit at the company store, which was the only one around. Labor unions, liquor, and voting for Democrats were strictly forbidden. His Italian workers called him Bombasto Furioso; the locals called him Lord of the Isles. From his quarries came pink granite for the Boston Customs House and Museum of Fine Arts, the St. Louis Post Office, and the Treasury Building in Washington, D.C.

The granite trade petered out before World War I, as Vermont marble came to be used for monumental buildings and concrete replaced granite in commercial structures. The workers drifted away from Hurricane Island, the post office closed, and in 1917 the last inhabitant died. For almost half a century, the island lay scarred and derelict. Then in 1964, it came to life as the site of the Outward Bound School. At that super-rugged summer camp, boys—and recently girls, as well—test their courage and endurance by scaling the walls of the old quarries and diving at dawn into the icy waters of Penobscot Bay.

Except for taking care of summer people and their houses, about the only economic activities left on the islands are fishing and lobstering. As the summer population has grown, the year-round population has slowly declined. Only fourteen of the islands have winter residents, and of those only five still have schools. Children who must go to the mainland for their education are likely to make off-island friends, get off-island jobs, and marry off-island husbands or wives. Many do not come back to stay.

At the Island Institute, Philip Conkling and his associates are trying to reverse the trend before the island world becomes one big summer colony. With backing from the state and some private owners, they are trying to identify economic activities that could do well on the islands. One project is to bring back the sheep. "Islands are great places for sheep raising," Conkling says. "There aren't any predators and the sheep can't run away, so there is no need for fencing." An experimental herd has been established on Allen Island, owned by Betsy (Mrs. Andrew) Wyeth.

Mussel culture is another potential source of profit. Since gourmets convinced a skeptical American public that *moules* are as delicious as the French always said they were, the market has grown rapidly. Islands offer plenty of low-tide sites, free from the risk of pollution that occurs on parts of the mainland.

Another newly valued creature is the sea urchin, that nasty little ball of spines that lies in wait for unwary waders on southern beaches but mercifully tends to stay a little ways offshore in the north. Lobstermen on Orr's Islands were surprised in 1987 to find that they could sell them for thirty-five cents a pound to the Japanese, who eat the raw roe on a bed of rice. On a good day, an "urchineer" can harvest a ton of the little creatures, with a value of seven hundred dollars. Not many local people have tried the delicacy, but one woman who did so was moderately pleased. "It's more something you have to get over in your mind than in your mouth," she told a reporter.

At Jonesport, on the mainland coast, I had seen some of the urchins at the first stage of their journey to Tokyo. Wayne Peabody, a genial lobsterman, was watching his son Steve unload crates of the odd-looking "sea eggs" from boat after boat and stack them in a waiting truck. "I tried it once," said Peabody, "but that was enough." He showed me a finger swollen to twice its normal size by a chance encounter with an urchin while he was handling his lobster lines. Since sea urchins do not walk into traps as lobsters do, the best way to get them is to dive down and pick them off the bottom. A young man who had just come ashore with his drysuit and shoulder tanks said that, for trained scuba divers, this was a bonanza. "They're coming in from all over the coast," he said.

In the long run, perhaps the most promising island enterprise is aquaculture. With the sharp decline in the fish catch all along the Atlantic Coast, the market for farm fish is ready and waiting. A major problem, however, is that fish raised in pens tend to pollute the surrounding water. In Cobscook Bay, at the northeastern end of the Maine coast, where exceptionally high tides help to flush out the fish waste, a large salmon farm is in operation. But along most of the coast, shellfishermen see the fish pens as a threat to the lobster grounds and clam flats. Why not, then, put them on islands, which are constantly cleaned by the ocean? Another Institute experiment on Allen Island is a small fish farm designed to see whether aquaculture would pay off for the individual fisherman.

One of the most ambitious projects to preserve an island economy is under way at Frenchboro on Long Island in Blue Hill Bay. Faced with a declining year-round population and the prospect of closing its only school, the islanders raised enough money to build seven houses and offer them on bargain terms to young off-island families who would join the lobstering community. By the spring of 1989, six families were in residence, along with a teacher who started out with seven children in four grades in the one-room schoolhouse. The first long winter, on an island where the ferry comes only twice a week, proved too much for some of the newcomers, but others took their place. With seventeen new residents, the population of Frenchboro was up by 31 percent.

The idea of living on an island, alone with one's family or perhaps only with nature, self-sufficient or nearly so, away from the great world, is one that appeals to a good many people. Henry Wadsworth Longfellow, who summered with other literary folk on the Isles of Shoals, had it right: "[Some] islands have one house and one barn on them, this sole family being lords and rulers of all land and sea girds. The owner of such an island must have a peculiar sense of proprietorship and lordship; he must feel more like his own master than any other people can."

The tug of year-round island life is still there. A few respond to it, as any real estate broker will tell you, but only a handful stick it out for more than one winter. From a sailboat on Eggemoggin Reach, I saw an island with a lighthouse, no longer in use, and a keeper's cottage. It was only a few hundred yards from a mainland dock, easily reached by a launch, and yet in its isolation, I thought, a little kingdom of its own. Others must have thought so, too, because I was told it had changed hands three times in as many years and was up for sale again.

Summer is a different matter. Almost every island that has enough rock to put a house on, and any kind of decent anchorage, is somebody's summer home. Many families feel stronger ties to their weather-beaten vacation places than they do to their year-round homes. Their children grow up with memories of fairly primitive living conditions, sparkling sunny days and dripping foggy ones, the flashing of lighthouses and the clanging of buoys, clambakes and camp fires, fishing, sailing, and, with a shiver, swimming. For most people, this is a place to be *on* the water, not in it.

People who do not own their own islands are not so lucky. Less than 5 percent of Maine's islands are open to the public and many of those are mere scraps of rock, the leavings of a state auction ninety years ago. At that time, the state thought to raise some money by auctioning off several hundred islands that were still publicly owned, for whatever they would bring. It was a shortsighted move, because the boom in vacation property was just around the corner.

Individually owned islands are not the only ones closed to the public. Almost five hundred, including some large ones, are controlled by conservation organizations, whose first concern is usually for the wildlife, especially rare and endangered species. Many of their holdings, donated by private owners, are encumbered with provisions that the owner's family continue to live there, or that the property be kept forever wild. The conservation people, feeling beholden to the donors, and sometimes legally bound, may then see fit to keep their islands off-limits to visitors.

The Maine Audubon Society, which also holds title to property on both the islands and the mainland, takes a different view. Its wildlife refuges are open to the public, not only for nature walks but for hiking, picnicking, and other recreational uses. "So long as there are reasonable restrictions," says Anne Johnson, the Society's marine director, "the birds and the people get along fine."

With most of the mainland coast built up, and so much of it closed to public use, the islands may be the last resource still available to those who are looking for some kind of solitude by the sea. With that in mind, the Island Institute in 1987 came up with the idea of an Island Trail, rather like the Appalachian Trail and other mountain paths. A survey of the islands still owned by the state found forty that were large enough and good enough for recreational use. An Island Trail Association, led by David R. Getchell, Sr., then negotiated rights for members to land or camp on some of the private islands. The result is a trail that twists along the coast, in and out of bays, from Portland to

Machias. You can follow it by motorboat or sailboat, but for the in-group of offshore adventurers the craft of choice is the sea kayak.

Environmental correctness is the watchword of the Island Trail. On some of the islands, camping is limited to the rocky shore because the fragile vegetation will not bear walking on. Some are so tiny that there is room for only one or two tents. Fires should be built below the high-tide line, so that any traces will be washed away; blackened stones should be tossed into deep water; portable camp stoves are better. And everything should be carried out—*everything*, including human waste. As an added precaution, some members of the Association "adopt" individual islands and police them to make sure that they look as if no one has been there. "The Trail is not for yahoos," says Annette Nagel of the Institute, firmly.

The islands of the North Atlantic Coast have always been nesting grounds for hundreds of species of birds. Over the years, they have been prey to both Indian and white hunters who raided their nests for eggs in the spring. The birds managed to survive those attacks, but in the last years of the nineteenth century some of them were almost done in by an unholy combination of market hunters and milliners. It was the Gilded Age, when fashion dictated elaborate women's hats with crowns of feathers and sometimes even stuffed birds. One day in 1896, Dr. Roy Chapman Andrews, director of the American Museum of Natural History, during a stroll on Fifth Avenue, counted forty hat-borne species, including Wilson's warblers, pileated woodpeckers, Acadian owls, bluebirds, pine grosbeaks, and northern shrikes, along with a profusion of herons, egrets, terns, and gulls. By the time the slaughter was ended by federal law, at least one species, Eakins' curlew, had been wiped out and several others driven from the American coast.

Nowadays, under equal protection of the law, some species thrive at the expense of others. In many of their established nesting grounds, the terns are fighting a losing battle with the larger and more aggressive gulls. The gulls not only crowd them out but they will eat almost anything, including the eggs and young chicks of the terns. In order to keep the tern colonies from being wiped out, the U.S. Fish and Wildlife Service, with the reluctant support of the National Audubon Society, sent teams to certain islands to poison the gulls. To some of their outraged members, who deplored such interference with nature, the Society pointed out that man has already tipped the balance in favor of the gulls by making them welcome at ever-growing city dumps.

Since 1907, the Atlantic puffin, once common along the New England coast, has nested only on two remote islets. Now, after eighty years, the National Audubon Society is trying to reestablish a puffin colony on Eastern Egg Rock in Muscongus Bay. In 1974, fifty-four chicks were brought from Newfoundland and raised by biologists schooled in the ways of parental puffins. The chicks were placed in long, narrow burrows dug into the rocky earth, where they were safe from gulls, then stuffed full of fish for a month, and then abandoned until they got hungry enough to leave the burrows and flutter into the water. When they were grown, they flew off, as puffins do, not to return for three or four years, when they would be ready to have chicks of their own. In the following years, the experiment was repeated. It was a red-letter day in 1981 when the first puffins came flying back to Eastern Egg Rock.

The puffin is one of nature's playful inspirations, like the dolphin and the panda, that arouse a response of instant delight. It is a chunky little bird that stands straight up on its legs, in the manner of a penguin, and sports a large red triangular beak that makes it look like a seagoing parrot. Puffins have special appeal to people who don't know much about birds. Even if you can't tell a gull from a tern, you can instantly recognize a puffin. If you can see one, that is.

At Boothbay Harbor, we boarded a double-decker cruise boat, under charter to the Maine Audubon Society, and headed out into Muscongus Bay. There are more lobster pots in Muscongus Bay, it is said, than anywhere else on earth. Slowly, the captain threaded his way through a bobbing mine field of buoys, each bearing the colors of some particular lobsterman.

As we bore down on Eastern Egg Rock, with eighty-odd pairs of eyes and almost as many binoculars ready, it became apparent that puffin watching was not as simple as, say, whale watching. The rock and the air above it were alive with birds, but most of them were gulls and terns. Below them, in lesser numbers, were smaller, stockier birds that stood up on the rock or flew low and dived beneath the water. The difficulty was that puffins were far outnumbered by their relatives, the black guillemots, which stand, fly, and dive the same way, using their stubby wings like fins to swim under the water. It ought to be possible to tell the puffins by their bright red beaks, but when they were in the air they always seemed to be flying away from us and when they landed on the water they quickly ducked under it. "There's a puffin," our guide would cry as a little bird sped away. ". . . I think it was."

We were not the only puffin watchers at sea that day. Another boatload of eighty-odd birders was off our starboard bow and when the cry of "Puffin" went up, both boats would jockey for position to give their passengers the best view. With skill, a collision was avoided. Within a few minutes, several definite sightings had been called by our guide and confirmed by a Boston lady, a birder of unmistakable authority, who was sitting on my right. As for me, I was relieved to think that I would not be called upon to testify before some Audubon tribunal that I had actually seen a red beak on some of the birds that flew past.

Shortly, we left Eastern Egg Rock and made our way to Wreck Island, where we got very satisfactory views of blue herons and ospreys—a consolation prize for inexperienced birders like myself.

As of now, the puffin population of Eastern Egg Rock is barely holding its own from year to year at a level of about twenty pairs. One season, it suffered a major setback when a mink turned up on the island, having apparently swum out from the mainland, and ate up some of the new chicks before it was captured. In the nesting season, gulls are an ever-present menace to both eggs and chicks. The rest of the year, out over the open ocean, the puffins face other perils, ranging from storms to plastic debris (which may choke or entangle them) and pollutants such as oil and chemical wastes. Each spring, the biologists wait anxiously to see how many birds will come back. If the puffins ever outnumber the puffin watchers on a good summer weekend, the Audubon Society will call its experiment a sure success.

CHAPTER THREE

THE ROCKY COAST

MAINE is a big state, filled with bear, moose, trout, potato fields, cold blue lakes, Mount Katahdin, and the International Paper Company. Much of that inland empire is still forest. More than half the people of the state live in a strip along the coast that is no more than ten miles wide. In the eighteenth and nineteenth centuries, this was the stage for Maine's great maritime enterprise of shipping and shipbuilding. It is the only part of the state that three out of four summer visitors see today.

Northeast of Mount Desert, I had traveled along a coast that is spare, open, and still "unspoiled." But as I started south from Mount Desert, I landed with a jolt in the late twentieth century. Suddenly, Route 1 was its familiar, garish self—the classic American commercial strip, lined with car lots and fast-food restaurants. Does the American roadside have to look like this? Some states, including Maine, have banned billboards on

23

highways, but not many municipalities have tried to control how roadside businesses look. They may have the power, through zoning and licensing regulations, to control the size and illumination of on-site signs and even, in certain places, to pass upon the appearance of private buildings. But local business people, with products and services to sell, do not often take kindly to such efforts at "beautification." Generally, the looks of the roadside are left to the still-developing aesthetic sensibilities of marketers such as Exxon and Burger King.

I was glad to leave Route 1 and turn off to Blue Hill, a town judged by Stuart Little and his creator, E. B. White, to be the prettiest place anywhere. Indeed the whole Blue Hill peninsula is picture-postcard country, all blue water and green islands and cup-shaped harbors and coveys of racing sailboats. It is so attractive that even the shopkeepers are afraid of being "discovered." At the general store, I heard a rather gushy lady from Ohio, who was buying a lobster T-shirt, tell the sales clerk how she loved Blue Hill.

"I'm going to tell all my friends about it," said the shopper.

"Please don't," murmured the clerk.

The question leaps to mind: How come the developers have left this peninsula alone? The answer, at least in part, is that much of the shore is owned by families of means who have been there a long time and are jealously protective of it. One lady told how she and her sister played a sort of detective game when they were young. Their family owned a big house above the harbor, overlooking the most unpronounceable of yacht clubs—Kollegewidgwok. "We would sit on the veranda," she said, "with our reference books. When a boat appeared in the channel, I would read its name through binoculars and look up the owner in *Lloyd's Register of Yachts*. Then my sister would check him out in the *Social Register* to see if he was all right."

Such vigilance makes for a rather closed society, but it does protect the coastline. A developer on the Blue Hill peninsula is about as popular as a speedboat in Blue Hill Bay.

With my friend Jane, I went looking for the offices of *Woodenboat* magazine and its subsidiary enterprise, the Woodenboat School. On a dead-end road leading down to a point, we passed the entrance three times before spotting a tiny sign half-hidden among the leaves. *Woodenboat* is the brainchild of Jon Wilson, who came up from Connecticut in 1971 with the beard and cast of mind of a hippie. His assets were a love of wooden boats and some experience in building them. After finding a shack to shelter himself, his wife, and their baby, he built a boat shop and then built some boats and then, having scraped together a capital of $14,500, launched a magazine.

Anyone on Madison Avenue could have told him that the whole thing was folly. The sum of $14,500 would not pay the cost of a market test to find out whether anyone wanted such a magazine, let alone the costs of production, circulation promotion, and advertising sales. But what Wilson had was a magazine that struck instant sparks among people who, in an age of aluminum and fiberglass, retain a passion for wooden boats. Now, *Woodenboat* is a thoroughly professional operation with an affluent readership and a high renewal rate—twin keys to success in the magazine business—and sidelines in books, videos, boat plans, and catalog sales. The staff now occupies a mansion on an estate overlooking Blue Hill Bay. Across the lawn, in a brick barn, is the school where apprentices learn to build elegant little skiffs, prams, and canoes. When we left them, they were getting ready to row and paddle across the bay to an island for lunch.

The little boom in small-boat building recalls a time when two very different traditions of nautical construction met on this coast. When the first explorers arrived from Europe, the Indian artifact that intrigued them above all else was the birchbark canoe. They had seen dugout canoes farther south on the coast but nothing like these lightweight, maneuverable craft made from the bark of the white birch that grew only in the northern forests. Champlain saw later what they could do on the St. Lawrence River, whose rapids he was trying to negotiate with a wooden skiff: "We had scarce gone three hundred paces when we were forced to get out, and some sailors had to get into the water to free our skiff. The savages' canoe passed easily."

The Abnaki Indians, who had come to live on this coast soon after the time of Christ, were a branch of the Algonquian people who occupied the eastern forests from Canada to the Carolinas. They grew crops, caught fish in weirs, and made clay pots. But they were something of a disappointment to the French adventurers, who had hoped to find in their territory the shining city of Norumbega.

According to reports that had reached Europe during the preceding century, Norumbega was the capital of a rich Indian kingdom where nobles clad in fine furs with gold and silver trimmings walked among crystal towers. Verrazano's map of 1529 gave seeming substance to the rumors by attaching the name Oranbega to the region of Penobscot Bay. Then David Ingram, a British sailor who had been stranded on the shore of the Gulf of Mexico in 1567 and had walked, amazingly, through the forest to Maine (and who thereafter supported himself by tall tales of his travels), claimed that he had actually seen the crystal city on the banks of the Penobscot River.

In the Abnaki language, *norumbega* means "a quiet place between two rapids," and that was what Champlain found, just downriver from the present site of Bangor, when he sailed up the Penobscot River. In his report of the voyage, he laid the Norumbega legend to rest: "I am convinced that the greater part of those who mention it never saw it, and speak only by hearsay."

The fate of the Abnakis, like that of other eastern Indians, was to be devastated by European diseases and eventually to be dispossessed. By the end of the French and Indian Wars they were reduced to a few remnants in isolated spots. They did not quite vanish, however. In the nativist enthusiasm of the 1970s, they were roused by some of their own leaders and by white lawyers to claim their ancestral lands. For a few heady years, the courts entertained claims by two of the Abnaki tribes, the Penobscots and the Passamaquoddys, to more than half the land area of Maine. In the end, they were awarded $81.5 million in damages. They have used their wealth wisely to buy a big cement plant and various local enterprises, as well as timberlands and blueberry fields.

For a while, the Penobscots also made a good thing of running high-stakes beano games on Indian Island in the river at Old Town. The enterprise attracted crowds of visitors but ran afoul of a state law that limits gambling prizes to one thousand dollars. The Indians claimed that the games were "an internal tribal affair" and thus exempt from state regulation, but a judge decided against them. "Beano," he ruled, "has played no part in the Penobscot Indians' historical culture." With lower stakes the casino is still doing well.

The coast where the Indians had spent their summers for

many centuries was not unknown to Europeans before the explorers found it. Long before Champlain, perhaps even before Columbus, sturdy little boats from France, England, and Portugal had been crossing the North Atlantic to the Grand Banks and returning with loads of cod and haddock. Their captains knew what oceanographers have since confirmed: The cold waters flowing down from the north are much richer in nutrients than southern waters. Spreading out across the shallow, sandy banks of the continental shelf, they support some of the world's most abundant fishing grounds.

Like fishermen everywhere at all times, those who fished the Atlantic banks did not talk much about where they had been. They left it to Champlain and his fellows to spread the word that this coast had what was needed for permanent settlement: a gulf full of fish, limitless forests for lumber, and deep, protected harbors.

The English got the same report from their redoubtable Capt. John Smith. After sailing up from Virginia to make his own survey of the coast, he advised his compatriots to forget about the Spaniards and their preoccupation with precious metals and instead to heed the example of the Dutch, who had founded their affluence on herring. "Never," he wrote, "could the Spaniard with his Mynes of golde and Silver pay his debts, his friends, and army, halfe as truly, as the Hollanders still have done by their contemptible trade in fish."

Jane joined me for a day's trip through the coastal towns where the early colonists settled. Beginning in the seventeenth century, they cut down trees along the shore and made them into pinks, snows, brigs, and pinnaces for fishing and coastwise trading. By the end of the seventeenth century, sloops and schooners were sailing to the Caribbean and across the Atlantic, with crews of local boys who commonly went to sea in their early teens. Because Maine ports were far from the centers of trade, many of the larger ships that were built there in the nineteenth century sailed away, never to return, taking their captains and crews with them.

We stopped for lunch in Rockport, where Maine's long history of shipbuilding came to an apogee with the launching of the clipper *Red Jacket* in 1853. Accounts tell how the schools closed, bands played, and the whole town made holiday. On its first transatlantic voyage, the *Red Jacket* set a record from New York to Liverpool—thirteen days, one hour, and twenty-five minutes—that has never been matched by a commercial sailing ship. It was the first full clipper built in Maine, and the last. The beautiful ships turned out to be money-losers and their time came to a sudden end.

Searsport came into its own in the closing decades of the age of sail, between the Civil War and the turn of the century. By that time, many other ports were building steamships, but Searsport stayed with sail and with two designs in particular. One was the down-easter, a small version of the square-rigged clipper, broader of beam, slower, but more economical for many bulk cargos than steamships. The other was the schooner, carrying the fore-and-aft sails that required smaller crews than square sails. In the latter half of the nineteenth century, the schooner evolved into a vessel with three, four, five, six, and in one case seven masts.

In 1889, Searsport was home to seventy-seven captains. By then, the seas were safer, thanks to lighthouses and better navigational instruments. Hostile vessels and pirates were seldom encountered. Crews were not driven as hard. In that Indian summer of the age of sail, captains fixed up comfortable cabins and took their wives on long voyages. Children were born at sea or in distant ports, sometimes coming home with given names such as India, Mindoro, and Ceylon.

Searsport today presents a rather dispiriting aspect, with fine old houses turned into antique shops, and vacant lots filled with flea markets. It is easy to understand why the city has been split by a controversy over a plan to build a cargo port, with a deep-water channel for container ships. The city fathers and business elements say that it would bring money and jobs to a region that has been drowsing since the age of sail. The Sierra Club and other environmentalists are against it because it would tear up ninety acres of clam flats.

If Searsport has fallen victim to antique "treasure and trash," as one sign proclaims, Camden is struggling to maintain an appearance befitting its preeminence as a social summer resort. Old and new money have combined to fill the lovely harbor with expensive yachts, together with half a dozen graceful windjammers that take passengers on week-long cruises. It is difficult, however, to reconcile Society with Tourism. The main street is a jam of small, cute shops and big, hard-breathing tour busses.

A few days later, Jane and I drove down the long peninsula south of Rockland and caught the ferry to Monhegan Island, eleven miles offshore. Monhegan has long been a landfall for voyagers from the Old World. Verrazano probably sighted it in 1524 and John Smith caught a boatload of fish there in 1614. Some think it was visited much earlier by oceanic adventurers who left their marks on its small sister, Manana Island, just across from Monhegan's harbor.

The belief that Vikings visited North America is cherished by true believers all along the Atlantic Coast. Claims have been made for at least fifty sites in Maine alone. The Vinland described in Norse sagas could indeed have been some part of Maine, for grape vines grow there. But it could equally well have been Nova Scotia or Cape Cod or Rhode Island, all of which have had proponents among the Viking relic hunters. The westernmost site recognized by archaeologists is L'Anse aux Meadows in Newfoundland, where a Norse settlement was unearthed in 1960.

Viking buffs are hard to discourage, however. Some years ago, one of them took latex copies of the marks on the stone cliff at Manana Island and sent them to Dr. H. Barraclough Fell at Harvard. Fell is a professor emeritus of marine biology, a recognized authority on the classification, evolution, and behavior of echinoderms. But he is known to a wider public as a student of prehistoric sites, stones, and inscriptions. Professor Fell brushed aside the Viking theory but came up with something much farther out. The inscription, he said, was an example of a Celtic script known as Hinge-Ogam, dating from 400 B.C. He translated it as follows:

Ships from Phoenicia. Cargo platform.

This was interpreted as a message to Phoenician sailors that Manana was a place to pick up a cargo, presumably fish.

It is wonderful how a careful, accredited scholar in one field can be liberated from academic restraints when he gets into something else. When H. Barraclough Fell writes of prehistoric markings under the name of Barry Fell, he seems to have dropped some of his scholarly scruples along with part of his name. Of course, no one can say for sure that the Manana markings are not what Dr. Fell says they are, but so far his reading has not met with acceptance by professionals in the field. Some geologists think they are just cracks in the stone.

As we stood looking at the marking on the rocks, the first wisps of fog began drifting over Manana Island. Soon the inscriptions, if such they were, would be lost in the fog, as prehistoric voyagers, if any there were, are lost in the fog of time.

It is more rewarding, we found on another trip, to look for Indian remains. One thing we can be sure of is that, no matter how many voyagers may have reached this continent from the other side of the Atlantic, there were natives here to greet them. At burial sites that date from at least as early as 3,000 B.C., archaeologists have found the remains of a people who used knives and spear tips of flint and buried their dead with a distinctive red clay that they must have brought two hundred miles from the region of Mount Katahdin, the only place where it is found. After the Red Clay People, the historical record is blank until the appearance of another people around 1500 B.C. The most distinctive marks of their occupation are huge piles of oyster shells, as much as thirty feet high, on the bank of the Damariscotta River. The Oyster Shell People, like the Abnaki a thousand years later, evidently came down from the forest in summer to enjoy the abundant shellfish of the coast. We found the scene of their feasting just downriver from the Route 1 bridge over the Damariscotta in Newcastle.

We continued on down Route 1, stopping at Wiscasset for a look at two old hulks that lie rotting on the flats, clearly visible from the bridge that crosses the Sheepscot River. They are the four-masted schooners *Hesper* and *Luther Little,* veterans of the coastwise coal and lumber trade. They were grounded in the river half a century ago and there they remain, chance memorials to Maine's maritime past.

Since Route 1 generally follows the post road of early days, you do not have to look very far to see the most enduring fruits of the oceanic enterprise. These are the rows of fine houses that stand on, or just off, the main streets of the major coastal cities. Some have been turned into local historic sites or antique shops or bed-and-breakfast hostelries, but because of Maine's long economic siesta most of them stand where they were built. They are not as grand as those of Boston or Salem. Their owners are not as renowned as the Hancocks or Derbys. Their architects have not left such famous names as Bulfinch and McIntire. But they are handsome, spacious houses, built by craftsmen who learned their woodworking skills in the shipyards.

Our last trip took us to Bath and its fine Marine Museum, which comprises several historic shipowners' mansions, as well as a restored shipyard. Bath's maritime history did not end with the age of sail. After the Civil War, the city plunged into the new era of iron ships and steam power. Today, after a century of building ships for the navy and the merchant marine, the Bath Iron Works is the state's largest employer.

Back in Blue Hill, before starting south by myself, I looked into a book entitled *Tales of the New England Coast* by Holman Day. He had this to say:

Of old, muskets drove the Abnakis off the coast of Maine. Today money is driving away another race. . . . Half the states of the nation are represented in these summer colonies. Cove and cape, the coast is pretty well monopolized by non-residents. "No Trespass" signs are so thickly set that they form a blazed trail.

The year of that complaint was 1909. I wondered how the author would feel today.

Mr. Day was alarmed in particular that the usurpation of the coast by summer vacationers would drive out the "Queer People" who found refuge in lonely spots on the promontories and islands. One such eccentric whom he knew was Ossian Dustin of Newcastle, who lived alone in a hut with a dirt floor on an income of fifty dollars a year, which he earned by cutting wood and doing odd jobs. He spent most of his time searching for Captain Kidd's treasure in the region of Cod Lead Nubble. Most often, he searched by night, using a treasure rod tipped with cow's horn and studded with bits of metal and whalebone. As Dustin explained, the powers of evil tried to divert him from the treasure whenever he got close, but he expected that his charms would eventually prevail. He was one of many fortune hunters who have dug for pirate treasure on the New England

Coast. While their quest has not been successful, it holds as much promise as the search for Celtic inscriptions.

To get back to Mr. Day's complaint about the seizure of the shore by summer people, the cause for concern is five times as great today because that seems to be about how many more summer homes there are now than there were in 1909. "We can't afford to live here anymore" is the common complaint of old residents faced with rising prices and rising taxes. Some of them, to be sure, sold out at prices that gave them a nice windfall profit on their land. Some of them also saw those prices double and triple after they sold.

When roads are crowded, parking lots filled, the coastline closed off, and the clam flats polluted, summer people are often viewed as the culprits. But in Maine communities, as elsewhere, the pressures for development have come mostly from local land-owners, builders, and real estate agents who want to turn empty land into houses, condominiums, offices, or shopping centers. Indeed, the people "from away" are often the first to oppose headlong growth and the first to support zoning laws, which have been almost nonexistent in many communities. Critics describe their attitude as "Pull up the gangplank, we're on board." It is kinder to say that, unlike the local power brokers, they are not looking to make money and they want to preserve the attractions that brought them there.

Maine's rocky coast—which means all of the coast from the Canadian border south to Portland—is still in better shape than any other long stretch of the Atlantic seaboard. The pressure of development came later here, giving the state government time to learn from bad examples farther south. While the towns have been generally lax about zoning, the state has enacted some stringent laws, requiring, among other things, that new houses be set back one hundred feet from the water, that septic systems not drain into the ocean, and that most of the trees be left standing along the shore. In other respects, the shore is its own best protection: Because it is rocky, it is not endangered by erosion, as sandy beaches are. Even the closing of so much of the shore to the public seems less of a burden on a coast where beaches are exceedingly rare and the water exceedingly cold.

Portland is a special case. Maine's largest city and chief port, it has problems of a different order, common to most of the major ports on the American coast. During most of this century, its waterfront was a place of crumbling wharves, dingy canneries, and dilapidated buildings, all relics of the maritime era. But since World War II, urban waterfronts have become fashionable. Portland's story is that of Boston, on a quarter the scale and twenty years later. The old Port Exchange district has been restored and gentrified with apartments, restaurants, antique stores, and trendy shops.

What tends to be crowded out in the push of development are the fishermen's docks, ship-repair yards, and marinas. In order to save them, the city is now being forced to zone parts of the harbor for water-related activities.

The rockbound coast is generally said to end at Cape Elizabeth, at the southern tip of Casco Bay. But just southeast of Cape Elizabeth is one last thumb of granite known as Prout's Neck. If you have in your mind a lasting image of the rockbound coast, this, more than likely, is where it came from. Prout's Neck was the home of Winslow Homer, whose paintings fixed the image of the Maine coast in people's minds as surely as Gilbert Stuart's portraits fixed the image of George Washington.

Most of Prout's Neck was bought in the 1880s by Winslow Homer's father, Charles Homer, Sr. His idea was to live there and also to develop it as a summer colony for selected Boston friends. At the tip of the point, he built a big shingled house, known as the Ark, where the family gathered in the summer. By that time, Winslow was well along in a career that had begun as an illustrator of the Civil War. During summers at Gloucester, Massachusetts, and two seasons at the fishing village of Tynemouth on the North Sea coast of England, he had developed his love for marine subjects. Then by happy chance, he found himself in a place that suited both his taste for a solitary life and his attraction to the sea. Behind the Ark, he built a simple studio, heated by a coal stove, where he lived for the rest of his life— alone, for he never married.

He was not really a recluse. In the spring, he often went with his brother Charles to a hunting and fishing club in the Adirondacks where he painted upcountry scenes as fine as his seacoast work. In the winter, he sometimes went to Florida or Cuba to paint the southern waters, the palm trees bending in tropical storms, and fishermen in the Gulf Stream.

If he did not welcome visitors to his studio, that was because he needed privacy for his work. To one acquaintance who had hoped for an overnight invitation, he wrote, "I have never yet had a bed in my house. I do my own work. No other man or woman within half a mile & four miles from the railroad or P.O. This is the only life in which I am permitted to mind my own business." In his studio, a later Mrs. Charles Homer pointed out to me a sign that he had stuck in his garden near the door: SNAKES, SNAKES AND MICE. Droll, but purposeful.

Outside his studio, he was on good terms with the local people, some of whom he used as models. Almost a lifetime later, a lady who had lived nearby recalled how, as a girl of eight, she had followed Homer when he went out to paint. So long as she said "Good morning" and not another word thereafter, the artist allowed her to stand beside him and sketch the same scenes.

Beginning in Homer's time and continuing since then, Prout's Neck has been divided up and sold to various owners, and they have built houses along the shore where he painted. But the shore is not entirely closed to the public, as it is in so many other "exclusive" enclaves. By design of the Homers and the Libbys, who owned the point before the Homers, a Marginal Way, a hundred feet wide, was reserved along the shore. It was meant for use of the property owners jointly, but, in legal fact, it is open to anyone.

Open, but not easy to get to. Like so many other nice places that might draw visitors, Prout's Neck is a parade ground of NO TRESPASSING signs, and access paths to the Marginal Way are unmarked, not to say camouflaged. However, if you avoid the lurking patrol car, park furtively, as I did, and go on to the end of the point, you have only to walk past a small monument (commemorating a gift of land to the Audubon Society) to reach the Marginal Way. Once found, it is easy to follow. Wear rubber soles because some of it is over slippery rock.

Perhaps it is just as well that the path is not more readily accessible, because it is literally a footpath, just wide enough for one person. If it were more heavily traveled, the fragile vegetation on either side would be trampled and some of the natural charm would be lost. But for anyone who wants to see the rockbound coast exactly as Homer did, this is the place to go. Here is Cannon Rock, which he painted repeatedly, in different lights, seas, and seasons. Here is High Cliff, where waves driven by winter storms climb forty and fifty feet up the face of rock. Here is the view of the Ark and the painter's studio looming up through the mist as they do in his picture, *The Artist's Studio in an Afternoon Fog*, that hangs in the art gallery of the University of Rochester. You could make a study of the hydrology of the Maine coast just by studying Homer's paintings.

Before leaving Prout's Neck, you should take a look to the southwest, across Saco Bay. You are standing on the last point of the rocky coast. Beyond lies a totally different shore, low, smooth, sandy, and crowded.

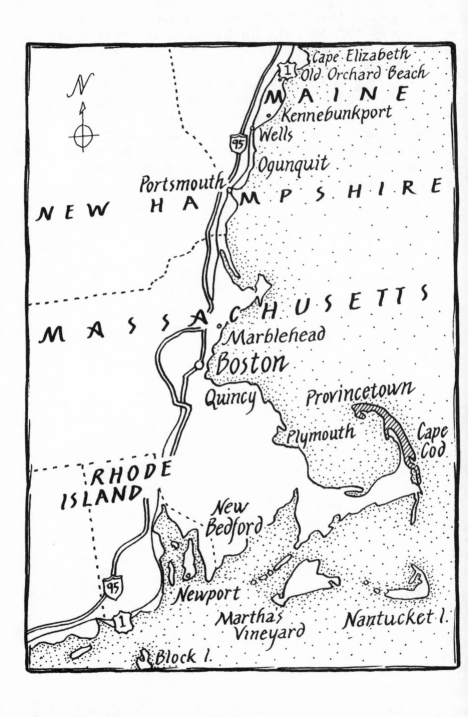

THE SANDY SHORE

HOW quaint it all looks in the old photographs. The fine long beach is sprinkled with groups of people, but many of them are in their street clothes, the men in dark suits and ties, the women in long dresses and blouses. Some are in bathing costumes, but you hardly notice the difference because the men's trunks come down to their knees and the women's skirts to their ankles. Some of the children are wading in the water and some have shovels for digging in the sand, but there are no beach balls, no Frisbees, no Boogie boards.

Behind the bathers is a boardwalk and behind that the great hotels to which families came by train to spend a week or a month. The Fitzgeralds are there with their pretty daughter Rose and the Kennedys with their handsome son Joe. At night, there were concerts and fireworks and dancing at the steel pier. That was Old Orchard Beach in 1906.

37

The next year, it all went up in flames. The big hotels were not rebuilt. After the World War I, vacationers began to come in automobiles and to stay for shorter periods, in rooming houses or small hotels or the new tourist cabins. A new pier was built, with a casino where the big bands played. Young people came for the day or the evening. By the middle twenties, Old Orchard Beach was a full-blown amusement park, noisy and jumping, with a roller coaster, a Ferris wheel, all kinds of rides and slides and penny arcades—a little sister of Revere Beach and Coney Island. That was how I remembered it from high school days.

The amusement park is still there, but hedged about now by cottages, motels, and blocks of condominiums. I arrived in the late afternoon and checked in at one of the motels. By then, the beach was emptying out and the action on the midway was picking up. But the crowds were not there. Most of the rides were whirling away, with flashing lights and blaring music, but the gaudiest of them, a contraption that spins like a pinwheel, had only four riders occupying two of its twenty-eight seats. An undulating Caterpillar slithered around its circular track with three young boys. The merry-go-round, classic of classics, had only one small rider. The bumper cars, always my favorite, had half a dozen riders, and there was something new—bumper boats that splashed and collided in a pool. There, at least, some kids really seemed to be having fun.

As afternoon waned, the families departed for their motel rooms and the midway closed. Now, for a while, the principal action shifted to the arcades—once penny arcades with peep shows and machines to test your strength or tell your fortune, now transmuted into quarter arcades with aisle upon aisle of flashing, whining electronic games. As darkness fell, Young America took over the streets, cruising the main drag in their cars and revving their Harley-Davidsons. There was a heavy police presence, on foot and in patrol cars. Just across the street from my motel, and half underground, a bar called SoHo Square—"All Day—All Night"—was jammed to its doors.

I must have been asleep for four or five hours when a Boston and Maine freight came roaring through my bed. Or so it seemed. Actually, the track was thirty feet away, but the whole building shook. My eyes still closed, I counted the sheep—I mean the cars—as they jumped over the fence—I mean the switch. There were ninety-seven of them.

Giving up on the idea of sleep, I dressed and went out. In the predawn of a new day, the SoHo Square was handing over the torch of social life to the Blue Goose Cafe, where Linda Coe, the owner, manager, and part-time cook, was brewing coffee and frying bacon. She had opened at 4:00 A.M. for late stragglers and early risers.

In the local paper, I scanned the police blotter:

- Female caller on Cedar Avenue reported that someone was possibly pulling on her back screens.

- Male caller on Saco Avenue reported two male subjects walking in the middle of the road.

- Female caller on Temple Avenue reported husband threatening to destroy her vehicle and beat up her boyfriend.

- Female caller from Saco Police Department reported males in vehicle were seen dancing in street near traffic and also mooning people.

- Female caller reported a dog doing doo on her lawn.

- Male caller said he was verbally and psychologically abused by bouncers at SoHo Square.

The sun had hardly dispelled the morning fog before the vacationers, slung about with towels and beach chairs, coolers and kites and boom boxes, were coming across the deserted streets, passing the shabby shops, and fanning out to stake their territorial claims on the beach. At three minutes of nine a shiny white and red rescue vehicle disgorged lifeguards and backed reassuringly into its station at the edge of the sand.

No one could ask for a better, cleaner, safer beach. That was the original attraction and nothing is likely to change it. But in New England, the seaside amusement park is an endangered species. In the paper, I had read that the steel pier, the centerpiece of the midway, was coming up at auction. Some of the little shops with their stuffed rabbits and ringtoss games and fried dough counters had not been making enough to pay the rent, and so the pier could not make its mortgage payments. Later, I read that the pier had been bought by the mortgage holder, but no one knew what its future would be. Time and the condos were creeping up on the whole honky-tonk resort. Already, it was looking quaint.

From here on south, the traveler follows a sandy coast, broken by points and headlands of rock and by stretches of salt marsh. Maine has only thirty-six miles of sandy beach and almost all of it is in this southern stretch, between Portland and the New Hampshire border. My friend Jane joined me at Kennebunkport, where President Bush's vacation home occupies one of the rocky points, and we drove a few miles south to Wells. Neither tacky like Old Orchard Beach nor classy like Kennebunkport, Wells is an average, middle-class summer resort. As legal chance would have it, Wells became, in the spring of 1989, the focal point of a simmering controversy between public and private rights on the coast of northern New England.

Moody Beach, a mile-long strip of sand in Wells, is lined with about a hundred cottages, built on the coastal dune and fronted by seawalls. For as long as anyone remembers, visitors have used the beach for strolling, swimming, and sunning. There was no trouble until the mid-1970s, when the number of visitors began to increase and their manners, according to the cottage owners, began to deteriorate. "They didn't leave an empty spot on my beach," I was told by Dr. Warren Jones. "And they left it littered with bottles and trash. One of them tied his dog to the railing on my steps . . . a big mean dog. I couldn't go onto my own beach. The dog's owner told me to go to hell."

Dr. Jones's comments were mild in comparison with those of other owners, who complained of "urination, defecation, and fornication" on the beach. In 1984, the property owners sued the town, asserting that under Maine law they had exclusive rights to the beach, down to the low-water mark. The suit was a threat not only to Wells, which depends heavily on its tourist trade, but to other towns in a state where public beaches are in short supply. In hopes of heading off the suit, the Maine legislature rushed through an act declaring the tidal zone, between high and low water, to be "impressed with a public trust," and affirming the right of the public to use it for recreation.

In superior court, the owners invoked the behavioral standards of the Puritan fathers who had written the ordinance of 1648 governing property rights. Judge William S. Brodrick was impressed. "The type of intense beach activity (including beach towels, umbrellas, coolers, and the slathering of bodies with various oils in search of the perfect tan) would have been repugnant to the Puritans," the judge agreed. He ruled against the town and declared the new Maine law to be unconstitutional.

After that decision, it was clear that this would be the crucial case, not only for Maine but for Massachusetts, which has the same colonial law, and very likely for some other states. In preparing its appeal, the town had the support of the state's attorney general, the Conservation Law Foundation, and scholars of property law at the University of Maine.

The history of coastal law goes back far beyond Maine's Colonial ordinance. Ancient Roman law, set forth in the Code of Justinian, declared that "by the law of nature, three things are common to mankind—the air, running water, the sea and consequently the shores of the sea." So long as Rome set the legal rules for the civilized Western world, the *ius publicum*, or public trust, prevailed. But after the Roman Empire collapsed, the right to the shore was seized, along with almost everything else in sight, by medieval barons, dukes, and kings. So it came about that King Charles I of England felt free to grant charters to companies of American colonists, giving them the right to do as they wished with the shore.

In the Massachusetts Bay Colony, as well as in four other states (New Hampshire, Pennsylvania, Delaware, and Virginia), that authority was used to grant property rights to the low-water mark. Massachusetts in particular did so to encourage seafaring entrepreneurs to build wharves and thus promote maritime trade. At the same time, it reserved the right of other citizens to cross the tidal shore for purposes of "fishing, fowling, and navigation." Had colonial legislators been gifted with foresight, they might have added the words *and recreation,* thereby obviating a lot of future controversy. But in those days, there were not many people around and hardly any of them went to the shore for a swim or a picnic, and, if they did, who cared?

When Maine was granted independence from Massachusetts, the Colonial ordinance was carried over verbatim, and since that time the supreme courts of the two states have acted as one in their strict interpretation of the coastal property laws. Over the years, only a few chinks have been opened up. Under the right of fishing, the courts have held, you may dig for clams or worms. You may gather seaweed on a private beach if it is floating in the water (but not if it has washed ashore). You can swim in front of someone else's house when the tide is up (so long as you do not let your feet touch the bottom). Still in dispute is the question of whether "fowling" extends to bird-watching.

The appeal resulting from the Wells decision was the most serious challenge to the existing law in either state. In its appeal to the Maine Supreme Court, the town argued that since the public had been using the beach "so long as the memory of man runneth not to the contrary," without objection from the property owners, the public had acquired an easement over it. Then, addressing the law head-on, the town argued that in exempting "fishing, fowling, and navigation" from the ban on trespass, the Colonial legislators had simply named the uses that seemed important at the time; that the *ius publicum* was open-ended and could be expanded to meet the changing needs of changing times.

In its decision, the court, by a four-to-three vote, brushed aside the argument for a public easement, ruling that no long-standing use had been proven, even assuming that such an easement could be acquired under Maine law. On the wording of the law, it ruled that the statute meant only what it said and could not be stretched to include recreation. Finally, it decided that the recent Maine law declaring the coast open was indeed unconstitutional, since it involved the taking of private property without compensation. Once more, the Maine court had reaffirmed what a Massachusetts court had ruled, almost gleefully, in 1814: "The owner of the adjoining land may, whenever he pleases, inclose, build, and obstruct to the low-water mark, and exclude all mankind."

Three months had passed and spring had changed to summer when Jane and I stopped at Moody Beach to see how things were going. Since we could not park at Moody Beach, we did so at the public one in Ogunquit, which adjoins Moody on the south. No fence separates the two beaches, but the town line was clear to see. On the Ogunquit side, the beach was filled, though not crowded; on the Wells side, it was virtually empty. Some of the people from the Ogunquit side were strolling along the Wells beach, with no evident complaint from the property owners, but the only people sitting down appeared to be the owners and their guests.

"So what was all the flap about?" asked my companion. "Everything seems to have worked out very well."

"Perhaps," I suggested, "that's because a lot of people who came here in other years aren't here this year. The tourist business in Wells is off. And those who did come to Wells have probably found other beaches."

"That's fine," she replied.

"But," I said, "that means that other beaches will be more crowded. Do you realize that on the whole coast of Maine only about nine miles of beach are legally open to the public? If the rest are all closed off, as this one now is, where will people go?"

"I suppose," she said, "that the towns or the state will have to buy up more beachfront, or buy rights for the public to use it. Anyway, I'm glad the people who own those houses have their beach back. Why should they have all those strangers sitting on their beach? You heard how they behaved."

I looked around at the people on the Ogunquit beach. So far as I could see, none of them were urinating, defecating, or fornicating.

"Do you think it's just a coincidence," I asked, "that according to what I hear, all four of the judges who voted to close the beach own waterfront property, and that all three who voted to open it do not?"

"Don't be such a cynic," she replied.

"Let's go on to Ogunquit," I said. "I'll show you how the coast ought to be handled."

When people talk about access to the coast, they are usually thinking of sandy beaches. But the joys of the coast are not limited to beaches. It is a fine thing to walk along a rocky shore, to look out over the ocean from a high cliff, to watch the fishing boats, the seabirds, and, in season, the harbor seals, or perhaps to sit down with a picnic lunch. All these pleasures are available on Ogunquit's Marginal Way, which begins at Perkins Cove and runs for a mile around the edge of a promontory, passing three small pocket beaches.

This coastal strip, a hundred feet wide, was given to the town a hundred years ago by the public-spirited owner of the point. Unlike the path at Prout's Neck, it does not hide itself behind the bushes but, rather, welcomes all comers. Perhaps it was our imagination, but the people we met on the Marginal Way looked uncommonly pleased to be there.

NORTH OF BOSTON

THE bridge over the Piscataqua River took us out of Maine and into New Hampshire at the fine old city of Portsmouth. Founded as a fishing village in 1624, Portsmouth rose to fortune with its shipyards in the age of sail and with its naval base, to which Theodore Roosevelt brought the Russians and the Japanese in 1905 to sign the treaty that ended the Russo-Japanese War. Portsmouth's earliest settlement can be visited in the restoration called Strawbery Banke. Its maritime heyday is recalled by the rows of mansions, including that of Governor John Langdon, who occupies a niche in American history all his own. As presiding officer of the U.S. Senate after the Constitution was ratified, he acted also as a sort of informal interim president of the new republic until George Washington could make his slow and stately progress from Mount Vernon to New York for his inauguration. Later, Washington stayed at Langdon's house in Portsmouth and pronounced it the handsomest in the town, as indeed it still is.

The coast of New Hampshire is the shortest of any state—only eighteen miles long—and, except for Portsmouth, it is a string of beach colonies. Following Route IA, you pass quickly through Rye, the Hamptons, Seabrook, and, before you know it, Salisbury Beach, which is over the line in Massachusetts. There are strips of cottages and motels, here and there a boardwalk, fried-clam shacks, a few rides, a Ferris wheel, Dodgem cars, and a theater marquee offering, halfheartedly, LIVE GIRLS 8 TO 12.

Seabrook is the site of a nuclear power plant that was completed in the 1970s but then stood idle through most of the 1980s. Even a casual observer must wonder what went on in the minds of planners who picked that site for a nuclear plant. It sits on the edge of the mainland, fronting on a marshy inlet; across the inlet is a barrier beach that is always crowded on good summer weekends. What would happen in case of a nuclear accident? How would they get the people to safety over the few narrow roads that lead from the beach to the mainland?

The rules of the Nuclear Regulatory Agency required from the governor of New Hampshire a plan to evacuate the area within twelve miles of the plant. And since Seabrook is only two miles from the Massachusetts border, it required one from the governor of that state, too. Governor John Sununu of New Hampshire, a strong backer of the plant, submitted a plan, but Governor Michael Dukakis of Massachusetts refused, advising the NRA that there was no way to get sixty or seventy thousand people off the beaches in time to avoid a disaster. So matters stood, through years of hearings, suits, and appeals, until the presidential election of 1988. Then, with Sununu ensconced in the Bush White House and Dukakis in the national doghouse, the NRA quietly revised its rule in order to allow the owners of the plant to make their own evacuation plan. By that time, the Seabrook plant was ten years behind schedule and four times over budget, and the principal owner, Public Service Company of New Hampshire, was bankrupt.

Before we left New Hampshire, we might have taken a ferry to the Isles of Shoals, which lie nine miles offshore. In the seventeenth century, the Isles were a summer base for hundreds of fishermen, a notoriously rowdy and rum-drinking lot who so enjoyed their all-male company that they banned women from the islands. The ban lasted until 1647 when a farmer named John Reynolds took up residence with his wife. The islanders petitioned a court to have her removed, along with Reynolds's goats and pigs which "doth spoile the spring of water." The judge told Reynolds to get rid of the animals but ruled that Mrs. Reynolds could stay "if no further complaint come up against her." It was an early, if qualified, victory for feminism.

The spare, windswept beauty of the Isles of Shoals has been celebrated by painters such as Childe Hassam and by writers such as Whittier, Hawthorne, and Longfellow. The Isles are still highly regarded by many visitors, but not by me. One of them, Star Island, has long been a retreat for the Unitarian Church, which is why I was taken there at the age of seven. On a Sunday morning, I was walking along the veranda of a big hotel, blowing a kazoo, when an old man with a face like granite and a beard like God stopped me and demanded, "Young man, don't you know what day this is?" Since that experience, I have never thought of the Isles of Shoals as exactly a fun place.

That, Jane informed me, was a silly, childish prejudice. She was sorry to skip the Isles of Shoals, especially after enjoying the book written in the 1890s by Celia Thaxter, the daughter of a lighthouse keeper, about her garden on Appledore. *An Island Garden*, brilliantly illustrated by Hassam's watercolors, is a classic of horticultural literature. The garden itself, planted with all the same flowers, has been recreated on the island.

We crossed the Merrimack River and came into the northeast corner of Massachusetts, a place of salt marshes, shoal waters, and expanses of sand left bare at low tide. One of its attractions is Crane's Beach in Ipswich. This curving three-mile beach, the finest north of Cape Cod, belonged to Richard Teller Crane, Jr., heir to the Chicago plumbing fortune, who built a mansion on Castle Hill, overlooking his fourteen hundred acres of beach and marshland. It is a good example of the paradox that while the rich have closed off so much of the coast, certain philanthropists among them have done more than anyone else to keep parts of it open.

The Crane family gave their estate to the Trustees of Reservations, an organization conceived by Charles Eliot, the architect son of Harvard's president, to acquire and manage "beautiful historic places and tracts of land." If that sounds like other, more widely known institutions such as the Nature Conservancy, the British National Trust, and the American National Trust for Historic Preservation, the resemblance is not accidental, for all of those admirable outfits were modeled on the Trustees of Reservations.

The policy of the proper Bostonians who compose the Trustees is not to turn anyone away. Unlike some conservation societies, which sometimes give a better break to birds than people, they provide facilities for recreational use. Sometimes they may set aside areas for the terns or the piping plovers in nesting season, but otherwise the public is welcome.

Except at Crane Beach, it is pretty hard to find a parking place and get to the water on the north shore of Massachusetts. In a geographical sense, and with lower-case initials, the north shore extends from the New Hampshire border to Boston. It includes such cities as Newburyport, Gloucester, Salem, and Lynn, some of which were important ports in the great days of ocean trade and some of which were seedbeds of the Industrial Revolution. But the upper-case North Shore, as used in the society pages of newspapers, applies to sections that remained untouched by anything more than a plow. Around the middle of the nineteenth century, rich Boston families began buying up the coast for summer estates. The farmers, whose families had owned the land for generations, thought they were stealing money from city folk so foolish as to pay them one hundred dollars an acre. But Mary Larcom Dow, who was born in Beverly and grew up to be an author of some note, wrote wistfully of the lost shore that had been hers to roam "from woods to sea."

You will not see much of that shoreline today. You will have to take the word of those who can see it from their boats that the coast is still there, just as beautiful as ever with its rocky points and small sandy beaches. Driving along the shore road, through Manchester, Beverly Farms, and Prides Crossing, you see mostly the walls, gates, and hedges of fine estates. At the few spots where you can get a glimpse of the water, you are urged to keep on moving by regiments of NO PARKING and STICKER

REQUIRED signs. The outsider has about as much chance of stopping for a swim or a picnic as she has of being invited for lunch at the Myopia Hunt Club.

All is not lost, however, so long as people like Rose McCarthy are on the alert. When I stopped off at her home in Marblehead, I found her at a table covered with designs and pieces of cloth that she uses to make nautical flags and pennants for boats, yacht clubs, and sailors' houses. While carrying on this home industry and raising six children, she has found time for a one-woman crusade to open up the shore.

Rose's effort had its start on a summer day in 1973 when she and her husband, a teacher in the local middle school, went over the causeway to Marblehead Neck, on the other side of the harbor, to watch the start of the Halifax Race. By standing on tiptoe and craning their necks, they could just catch glimpses of the boats between the walls and shrubs of the fine houses that line Ocean Drive. "I felt like a peasant," Rose says.

In fact, Rose learned, there are public lanes between some of the houses, leading from the road to the rocky shore, but no one seemed to know where they were. Rose spent the summer poring over the town records, examining the deeds to each parcel of land, and, when she found a right of way, tracking it down. The reason the lanes were hard to find, she soon discovered, was that most of them were ingeniously disguised as private property. Quietly, over the years, the abutting owners had turned them into driveways, lawns, and gardens.

One of the first public ways she identified was Fishing Point Lane. The first thirty feet had been covered with gravel to make a private parking place; beyond that was a lawn with flowers and shrubs. Once its disguise was lifted, the lane offered easy access to the massive boulders that line the coast.

Farther along the shore, Black Rock Lane had vanished just as confusingly beneath the flower beds of the adjoining house. When Rose took a reporter and photographer from the local paper to see it, the woman of the house came charging out, with fists flying, to push Rose off the property. The shoving match that ensued made a front-page picture for the paper.

Some of the disappearing public ways and the property owners bear such old-line North Shore names as Crowninshield, Peabody, and Devereux. But there were also McGees and

Lynches. "The Irish used to be servants on the Neck," says Rose. "Now they own a lot of it." Rose herself was born in an old section of town called the Shipyard, where Irish immigrants settled in the nineteenth century. "I'm still a townie," she says.

The rights of way on the Neck date from the time when it was used mainly as a pasture for cows. The selectmen of the town are required by statute to make a "perambulation" of them each year to see that they are open and unobstructed. But the law was generally ignored until Rose McCarthy went into action.

Rose had invited me to accompany her on one of her own impromptu perambulations. On the harbor side of the Neck, we came to a public way that leads down to a seawall and a stony beach. At its upper end, it looked public, all right, with a street sign and parking places. But the last thirty feet before the seawall was planted to grass. Clearly, it was used as a public way by boat owners, for their dinghies were tied up on the shore. But the stretch of grass seemed intended to intimidate strangers. On the porch of the adjoining house, Rose spotted an old lady in a rocker. "This is a public road, you know," she called out. "Oh, yes," replied the old lady. "People use it." "You planted the grass?" asked Rose. "Oh, yes," said the old lady. "It makes it nice for them." Rose was gentle but skeptical. "Well, be sure you let the people know it's public."

Another lane was no more than a footpath, so overgrown that we had to push our way through the encroaching shrubs. In the garden of the adjoining property, two women were taking their morning coffee. "It's pretty hard to get through here," Rose called out. "Nothing to stop you," one of the women replied. "These bushes ought to be cut back," Rose said. "That's not my job," the woman replied with an edge in her voice. They all know Rose, and they know the right answers.

The truculent woman with the fists no longer lives in the house on Black Rock Lane, and the new owner is more circumspect about expressing his feelings. "You're a pest," he informs Rose. For her pains, she has taken a lot of abuse over the years, but usually she has had the last word.

To show me some public ways that have always been open, Rose took me to the old part of town. Marblehead has been a fishing port since the earliest Colonial days. Although only four miles from Salem, which grew rich and worldly through its ocean trade, Marblehead remained apart, its back to the land, its eyes on the lonely fishing banks. To the residents of neighboring towns, its people seemed insular, ingrown, and sometimes downright peculiar. Visiting seamen came prepared for tavern brawls, and captains took caution from the legendary fate of Skipper Floyd Ireson, who, for his delinquencies—at least in Whittier's imaginative account—was "tarred and feathered and ridden in a cart by the women of Marblehead."

The old town has a maze of public ways, some leading to the shore but others running from one narrow street to another. In the old days, Marbleheaders used them as shortcuts to their docks or pastures or to other parts of town. Now they run between the newly restored and painted houses of affluent young outsiders who have moved in among the natives. They still serve as footpaths in one of the country's most picturesque towns.

While I was in Marblehead, Jane had been visiting the Peabody Museum in Salem, home of a unique collection begun in the eighteenth century by the East India Marine Society. The Society was limited to "shipmasters and supercargoes [owners' agents] who shall have actually navigated the Seas near or beyond the Cape of Good Hope or round Cape Horn." Members were furnished with blank journals in which to describe what they saw on their voyages, and were asked to bring back trophies. In 1799, Captain Jonathan Carnes, returning from Sumatra with a load of pepper, provided an elephant's tooth, a Batta pipe, and a goblet of rhinoceros horn. In the nearly two centuries since that first donation, the Museum has acquired not only a full record of Salem's great oceanic enterprise but a treasure of South Seas arts and artifacts unmatched in the world.

Salem's other claim to historic attention is, of course, the witchcraft trials. It has a Witch House, a variety of broomsticks and hobgoblins for sale, and even a resident witch who is always good for a story on Halloween. The actual records of the trials may be found at the Essex Institute, along with a painting entitled *The Trial of George Jacobs*. The old man is kneeling before the judges while his granddaughter and her mischievous teenage friends cry out that he is sticking pins in them. Jacobs was my ancestor, eight generations back, and was hanged on Gallows Hill in 1692.

Leaving Salem, we started up the shore to Boston. To anyone following a map, the word *up* may be puzzling. For one thing, it is up because it cannot very well be down—"down east" being the direction in which ships have always sailed, before the prevailing wind, from Boston toward Maine. But the usage of *up* on land may also have something to do with the moral and intellectual elevation on which Boston has always placed itself. No matter whether you are traveling from the south or the north, you go "up" to Boston.

Boston is a tight, congested city, totally unsuited to the automobile. One way to see it is on foot, following the Freedom Trail that winds among the sites of history. Another way to see it, in much less flattering light, is to go by boat, as George Bush did, much to his political advantage, during his presidential campaign in 1988. Since our primary interest was the coast, we chose the boat tour.

We started out in a Boston Whaler from Pier 6 of the old Charlestown Navy Yard, now in the process of conversion from a naval base to a complex of offices, shops, and condominiums. At a dock nearby lay the USS *Constitution*, still a commissioned warship, getting ready for its annual "turnaround" voyage out into Boston Harbor and back. Above us to the west rose the granite shaft of Bunker Hill Monument. A tour of Boston harbor is a tour of some of the most famous sites in American history. It is also a visit to the most polluted harbor in the United States.

Our first objective was Island End River, which empties into the upper harbor just above the Mystic River bridge. The Island End is different from most rivers. It does not have its source in a mountain spring or a lake or an upland swamp. It rises from two big sewer pipes. Unlike other badly polluted rivers, which get that way as they run down to the sea, Island End River starts out totally polluted. One of its tributary sewers carries the discharge of an old Exxon refinery, now used for the production of asphalt; the flow is heavily laden with toxic hydrocarbons. The other pipe delivers a combination of sewage and surface runoff from the city of Chelsea.

"You can tell what's coming out of the pipes by the stains around the rim," said our host, Steve Hunt. "That black stain is from oil. A light gray stain is the mark of raw sewage." Hunt is the executive director of an organization called Save the Harbor/ Save the Bay.

Aside from Island End River and other drainage canals, three respectable rivers empty into Boston harbor—the Mystic, the Neponset, and the Charles. But the flow from the sewers is approximately equal to that from all three rivers combined. Five thousand miles of pipes carry waste water to Boston harbor, not only from Boston itself but from forty-three surrounding communities, accounting for more than two-fifths of the population of Massachusetts.

The system works like this: Waste water from all sources—houses, factories, street drains, everything—flows into the same sewers, which carry it out to treatment plants on two islands in the harbor. There, the solids are allowed to settle to the bottom of holding tanks, making a sludge that is "digested" by bacteria, while the liquid is treated with chlorine. Then both effluent and sludge are released into the sea on the outgoing tide.

This is called primary treatment. When it is working properly, it removes some, though not all, of the organic contaminants. But even under normal conditions, the system is barely able to handle the load, and after a heavy rain the runoff is too great for the pipes. Then, to keep it from backing up into streets and buildings, the excess is diverted into other pipes that empty directly into the harbor.

Supposedly, the overflow pipes operate only in flood conditions but some of them, because of faulty design or poor maintenance, run all the time. The original Boston sewer system was a model installation in its day, but that day was a hundred years ago. One of its working pumps is such a classic piece of machinery that the Smithsonian Institution wants it—if the city of Boston ever takes it out of service.

Leaving Island End River, we cruised back down the harbor, passing more overflow pipes, and headed for Lewis Wharf on the downtown waterfront. The site of Lewis Wharf has figured in Boston's history since Colonial days. Here, in the years before the Revolution, stood Hancock Wharf, owned by the great ocean merchant Thomas Hancock and later by his nephew John. Here in 1768, the British seized John Hancock's sloop *Liberty* for refusing to pay the import duty on a cargo of Madeira wine, thereby provoking one of the early patriot riots.

Lewis Wharf was built on the site of Hancock Wharf in 1836, when America held the primacy in oceangoing trade and

Massachusetts had more ships than New York. As Boston's trade declined in the second half of the nineteenth century and the first half of the twentieth, the great docks fell into disrepair and decay. By the 1960s, much of the waterfront was a no-man's-land, unseen and unsafe, cut off from the rest of the city by an elevated highway.

Now, in the last part of the century, the water's edge has been rediscovered by developers as a place for affluent Bostonians to live, work, shop, and dine. In its time of transition, it looks like something out of the play *Dead End*. Slick new blocks of brick and glass rise beside the rotting timbers of wharves where clippers tied up. The windows of hotel rooms that cost two hundred dollars a night face warehouse panes that were broken before World War II.

As we approached it by water, Lewis Wharf looked like a model of waterfront reclamation. The solid gray granite building that had received the cargoes of the China trade was fitted out with balconies for the new apartments within. Twenty feet above our boat, guests were lunching on the flower-decked terrace of an expensive restaurant. Moored in front of us was a fleet of brightly painted sailboats belonging to the Boston Sailing Center. But just a few feet away was the gaping mouth of a sewer overflow, pouring its murky gray-green load into the harbor.

Leaving the downtown waterfront behind, we headed toward the islands of the outer harbor. Some of them are labeled on maps as a maritime park, and they have the makings of a fine one, but at present the label is more expressive of future intent than of actual fact. Except for Georges Island, which has a famous old fort and is reached by ferry, the islands are out of easy reach. One that attracts no visitors is Spectacle Island. Over the years, it has been a quarantine hospital for immigrants arriving with contagious diseases, then a rendering works for Boston's dead horses, and then a city dump. Its original contours, which reminded someone of a pair of glasses, have long since disappeared beneath a hundred-foot mountain of waste. "Full of toxic chemicals," Steve Hunt said. "They're all seeping into the water." Spectacle Island, I thought, is a preview, on a much smaller and less dangerous scale, of the toxic chemical and nuclear dumps we are planning for the future.

People have been shaking their heads for years about the

disgusting state of Boston harbor. But the movement to do something about it may be said to have begun with a jogger's misplaced footstep in 1982. On a summer day, a young man named William Golden was running along Wollaston Beach in Quincy when he looked down and saw that he was stepping into something fresh from someone's toilet, washed up by the last high tide.

Golden, as it happened, was the city solicitor of Quincy, and in that capacity he filed suit against the Metropolitan District Commission, which ran the sewer system, to stop the defilement of Quincy's beach. The suit came up in the court of Judge Paul Garrity, who gave the state a year to do something about the problem. When nothing was done, he issued an order that no new buildings could be connected to the sewer system, thus threatening to bring Boston's construction boom to a standstill. To underscore his determination, he went down to one of the rotting wharves in his black robes and struck an imperious pose, with the polluted waters at his feet. It was a bit of melodrama reminiscent of King Xerxes ordering the Hellespont lashed with whips for having high waves, and some thought it just as futile. But the Massachusetts legislature was finally stirred to action. A new Water Resources Administration has been created to build a new sewer system, providing both primary and secondary treatment (secondary treatment removes most of the organic pollutants from the waste water; tertiary treatment makes it drinkable). Toxic chemicals and heavy metals will be controlled, as far as possible, at their industrial sources. The job is scheduled for completion in 1999. It is likely to quadruple, at least, the cost of water and sewer service in Boston and the forty-three communities around it.

By the time the water in the harbor is clean, Boston should have an uncommonly attractive waterfront, most of it open to the public. For that prospect, it can thank in part a special circumstance of history. In Boston, as elsewhere in Massachusetts, private property runs down to the low-water mark; below that mark, the *ius publicum*, the public right, prevails. And the low-water mark that counts, the courts have ruled, is the low-water mark in 1647, the year when coastal rights were written into law. In land that was under water in 1647, the public right still holds, no matter what has been done to the land since then.

As it happens, most of Boston, and virtually all of its waterfront, is built on filled land. At the time of the Revolution, Boston was a peninsula less than half its present size, attached to the mainland by a strip of land with a single road (the road over which William Dawes, Paul Revere's fellow rider, traveled on the night of April 18, 1775). The filling in of the shore began shortly after the Revolution and continued through the nineteenth century.

This circumstance of history gives Boston the whip hand over developers. In their waterfront projects, they have been required to leave space and light between their buildings, to provide public walkways and miniature parks, to make room on the waterfront for pleasure boats, fishing boats, and ferries. The planners' eventual aim is to have a strip park running all along the shore from Charlestown to South Boston.

Perhaps the most cheerful thing to be said about a tour of Boston harbor is that if you see it today, you are seeing it at its worst. Unlike some parts of the Atlantic Coast, it should only get better from here on out.

CAPE COD WITH THOREAU

ON my way south to Cape Cod, I stopped off at Plymouth to have a second look at its various tourist attractions. The most famous of these, Plymouth Rock, is enclosed beneath an incongruous Greek-pillared canopy, safe from both the elements and the visitors. It looks as if it might indeed be the Pilgrim landing place, but that claim rests mainly on the word of one man who remembered in his old age the stories he had heard as a boy. The other main tourist attractions are reconstructions: a replica of the *Mayflower*, tied up at the town dock, and Plimoth Plantation, three miles away from the original, long-vanished colony.

56 As reconstructions go, Plimoth Plantation (which uses the name and spelling of the original colony) is one of the best. All the elements are as true to the record as research can make them—the houses, the furnishings, the thatch put up by a resi-

dent English roofer, the vegetables growing in the gardens, even the seventeenth-century Nottinghamshire accent of a guide.

In a commendable attempt at historical evenhandedness, Plimoth Plantation includes, outside the Pilgrim stockade, an encampment of the Wampanoag Indians. When I first saw it in the 1970s, however, the Indian camp must have been new, because it had not achieved the level of authenticity of the Pilgrim village. The teenage Indian girl who showed us around informed us soberly that the Indians had lived in the area for a million years. Moreover, she said, the Indians were a superior race, as evidenced by the fact that they had three lobes in the brain instead of two. I looked closely to see whether she was making sport of the gullible tourists, but she seemed quite in earnest. Fifteen years later, I was reassured to find that the Indian guides confined themselves to explaining such matters as the fire pit, the meat-drying racks, and the hollowing out of a log with burning coals to make a dugout canoe.

That process was observed and described by Champlain in 1605: "After cutting down, at a cost of much labor and time, the largest and tallest tree they can find, by means of stone hatchets . . . they remove the bark and round off the tree except on one side, where they apply the fire gradually along its entire length; and sometimes they put red-hot pebble-stones on top. When the fire is too fierce they extinguish it with a little water, not entirely, but so as the edge of the boat may not be burnt."

Twenty miles down the coast from Plymouth, Route 3 takes you to the bridge over the Cape Cod Canal. In 1849, when Henry David Thoreau made the trip described in his fine book *Cape Cod*, there was no canal to mark the beginning of the Cape and to save ships a hundred miles on the trip between Boston and New York. Thoreau traveled on the railroad to the end of the line at Sandwich, where he transferred to a stagecoach for the ride along the shore of Cape Cod Bay to Brewster at the bend of the Cape.

Thoreau knew the woods and fields and rivers of his native Concord as well as he knew his own garden. He had traveled by dory on the Concord and Merrimack rivers, by foot across the White Mountains of New Hampshire, and through the forests of Maine. But he knew almost nothing about the shore. He came to Cape Cod as to a new world.

Peering through the rain-streaked windows of the coach, Thoreau found the landscape bleak and almost bare of trees, the houses poor and weather-beaten. Even the women's faces were cheerless. "A strict regard for truth," he wrote, "obliges us to say that the few women whom we saw that day looked exceedingly pinched up. They had prominent chins and noses, having lost all their teeth, and a sharp "W" would represent their profile."

The traveler's view is much more agreeable today. While modern dentistry has taken care of the women with faces like W's, nature has been induced to line the road with fine shade trees.

On the morning after the coach trip, Thoreau and his traveling companion, William Ellery Channing, son of Boston's famous Unitarian preacher, walked across the Cape from the bay side to the ocean side, over a desolate, windswept plain, holding their umbrellas behind them to get some help from the following wind. Anyone who tries to retrace their steps today on a summer weekend will have to dodge streams of beachgoers, picnickers, campers, bicyclists, surfers, board sailors, dune drivers, surf casters, whale watchers, and other assorted holidaymakers. Thoreau, who would go off his trail to avoid disturbing a muskrat, would have been alarmed, as present-day environmentalists are, by the impact of all this human traffic on the fragile ecosystem of the Cape. But on that cold October day in 1849, he and Channing met only an occasional traveler.

Shortly after noon, they passed through a stretch of low shrubs and then a belt of sand and suddenly stood on the edge of a bluff, looking down at the ocean. They were just above the elbow of the Cape, where the great eastward-stretching arm bends at a right angle and runs north to make a clenched fist at Provincetown. The ocean side of the forearm is what Thoreau called the Great Beach, stretching unbroken for thirty miles north from Nauset harbor. Considering both its length and its quality, it may well be the finest beach on the United States coast and one of the best in the world.

I had hoped to follow Thoreau's path, as closely as possible, from the point where he first looked down on the ocean beach. But at once I had to adjust to the modern world. Thoreau and Channing slid and scrambled down the steep wall of sand to the beach below. If any visitors tried that today, they would be in line for a reprimand from the park rangers of the Cape Cod National Seashore. The dune cliffs are unstable, and sliding on them is forbidden, much to the distress of young visitors. So I tried to do my part to save the cliff from erosion by using the wooden staircase provided by the National Park Service. (To no avail, as it turned out, because during the following winter the staircase and the foot of the cliff were carried away by a storm.)

Cape Cod is a creation of the last Ice Age. As the glacier moved south over New England, it scraped off the surface of the land, picking it up and pushing it ahead like a bulldozer. When the ice finally came to a halt and melted away, it left a great curving mound of sand and gravel with deposits of clay and scattered boulders. For ten thousand years, the sea has been beating against that mound, undercutting its steep face and redistributing the sand along the shore. In the 144 years since Thoreau walked by, the cliff has retreated at an average rate of something like three feet a year. Probably it looks today just about as it looked when Thoreau was there, but the actual path where he left his footprints is now more than four hundred feet offshore.

Anything built on top of the cliff is doomed. When Thoreau was there, three small brick lighthouses stood in a row above Nauset Beach, well back from the edge of the cliff. In 1892, they fell off the edge, to be replaced by three more, and then in 1923 by a single, taller lighthouse. The only reason that not many houses have fallen from the cliff is that early settlers did not choose to live near the ocean. They built in the hollows, where they were sheltered from the wind, or along the bay side, where the water is calmer and the land lower. The men who lived in those houses were seamen and they saw enough of the wild ocean from their ships without having to look at it from the land, as well. The ocean side of the Cape was to them the back side.

On some stretches of the Cape, in recent times, vacation houses have been built close to the shore, and some of them are in trouble. As the beach in front of them washes away and the tide comes closer, the owners try different ways to do what King Canute could not. They build seawalls, which may last for decades but not forever. They put in groins or rocks or pilings to trap some of the sand that is moving along the shore. They may try sandbags or fences or nettings of wood or metal. At last, despairing, they may pick up their cottages and move them back from the shore. Sooner or later, the ocean has its way.

Why, then, do people keep on building at the very edge of the sea, not only on Cape Cod but all along the coast? One might as well ask why the farmers on the slopes of Mount Vesuvius, after an eruption that buries their land beneath volcanic ash, go right back and plant their fields. In the case of the farmers, the mountain slope is their home and, besides, the ash eventually enriches the land. The beach dwellers likewise are willing to take some risks for the joy of summers at the water's edge. And they, too, are being enriched just by staying there. Today, the extra value of a hundred front feet on a good section of the shore of Cape Cod is something like $300,000—that is, $300,000 added to the price that the property would bring if it was not on the shore.

The National Park Service, which runs the National Seashore, has learned the folly of fighting the forces of nature. There used to be a parking lot on a stretch of low-lying beachfront by the old Coast Guard station in Eastham, not far from the spit of land where Henry Beston wrote his Cape Cod classic, *The Outermost House*. The parking lot was torn to pieces by the great storm of 1978, which also carried away the Outermost House. It has not been rebuilt.

Nautical charts show another spit running ten miles south from Nauset harbor, past Pleasant Bay and Chatham to the elbow of the Cape. But since the second day of January 1987, it has been three miles shorter. On that day of fierce storm and high tide, the ocean broke through the spit, making an island of the southern section. The break, which was measured at first in yards, has since widened to a mile and a half.

No one should have been surprised. The swirling currents and shifting sands of this coast have posed a threat to mariners at least since 1620, when Capt. Christopher Jones of the *Mayflower* almost ran aground in Pollock Rip and prudently sailed back into Cape Cod Bay. At intervals over the years, the sandy barrier has lengthened and shortened, broken apart and reunited. The only thing new in the picture is that the Cape itself has been developed. Opposite the break, the mainland shore has now eroded and half a dozen houses have fallen into the water. For

Chatham's commercial fishermen, the break has been a mixed blessing. While it has cut three hours off their daily voyages to the open ocean, it has begun filling up with sand the shallow harbor where they moor their boats.

As they progressed along the Cape, Thoreau and Channing would walk for a stretch on the sand and then climb the cliff to walk on the plateau above. Here the law-abiding modern hiker often cannot follow them. In order to control erosion, the National Seashore has put many sections of the land behind the dunes off limits. The dunes are held in place by the long, twisting roots of the beach grass; if the grass is trampled, it dies and the dunes become a moving desert.

Thoreau, who hated all restrictions, would not have liked being told where he could or could not walk. But if he were around today, he would probably admit that the National Seashore has been the saving of Cape Cod. The park was established in 1961, in the nick of time, largely through the influence of President Kennedy. If it had not been saved then, much of the Outer Cape might look like parts of the Jersey shore, where cottages are lined up ten deep along the water.

The Seashore is unique among national parks in that it was superimposed on established towns that had been there since the time of the Pilgrims. More than 65 percent of Wellfleet is in the park and 70 percent of Truro. The taking of so much settled territory by the federal government was not accomplished without concessions to the towns and their residents. The towns retain control of their established beaches, including the right to close them to outsiders. Owners of houses within the park may keep them or sell them freely, although they are discouraged from making large additions. The Seashore administration has been diligent about protecting the captive property owners from trespassers, but at the same time it brooks no violation of its rules. The owner of one beach cottage, which was being threatened by the sea, moved it to higher ground without permission; while he was absent, a park crew demolished it.

Not all offending cottages are so easy to get rid of. Among the dunes at the tip of the Cape is a scattering of wooden shacks that range in structural condition from spare to dilapidated. In the eyes of of the Seashore administration, the shacks are blots on the natural landscape and, because that part of the land has always been public, the occupants are squatters. A few years ago the superintendent announced that when the occupants' temporary permits expired, the shacks would be removed. But hold! The Provincetown shacks are not just anybody's seaside camps. Over the last half century or so, they have given shelter and perhaps inspiration to the playwright Eugene O'Neill, the critic Edmund Wilson, the writers Jack Kerouac and Norman Mailer, the poets e. e cummings and Mary Oliver, the dancer Paul Taylor. To tear them down, said their champions, would be like bulldozing Thoreau's cabin at Walden Pond. The Seashore, bowing to the indignation of the preservationists, backed off and agreed that for now at least, the shacks could stay. Their admirers are trying to have them declared a national historic site.

One of the park superintendent's tasks is to balance the conflicting interests of different groups that use the National Seashore. Recently, the sore point has been the use of ORVs— off-road vehicles such as jeeps and dune buggies. Before the Seashore was established, ORVs had the run of the beach, from Provincetown to Chatham. Heeding the protests of sunbathers, who did not like to have sand thrown up in their faces, and environmentalists, who deplored the damage to the beach grass, the administration has gradually closed in on the ORVs. The ORV drivers are not, for the most part, joyriding teenagers but, rather, local fishermen who use their vehicles for transport. I heard both sides at a hearing held at the Seashore headquarters. The spokesman for the jeep drivers was belligerent in defense of what he evidently considered to be an ancient right. The environmentalists, on the other hand, were represented by determined ladies in sensible skirts and sandals who looked as though they came from Beacon Hill. The drivers were badly outnumbered and seemed likely to lose most of the beach.

Almost as long-running as the ORV controversy has been the nudist controversy. Skinny-dipping was an accepted practice at the end of the Cape long before the National Seashore was established. It became an issue only in the late 1960s when word of the free beach at Truro began to attract large numbers of off-Cape nudists, along with nonnudists carrying binoculars. Nudists are now officially banned, but they are still seen on remote stretches of the beach, where a truce has been reached. Several times in the course of a day, a guardian of the law comes putt-putting along on a little sand cycle. His leisurely approach gives the sunbathers plenty of time to pull on their bathing suits before he arrives.

Another endangered species is the overnight camper who drives his traveling home onto the beach for a vacation. At Race Point in Provincetown, the motor homes huddle together beneath the disapproving gaze of scenery lovers, who find them unsightly and inappropriate. Still, the car campers are better off than the tent campers, who are not allowed anywhere on Seashore land.

Year by year and season by season, the beach is always changing. High tide in summer may leave a broad expanse of sand; in winter the sea may run up to the cliff, trapping unwary walkers. During one summer, at Wellfleet or Truro, the ebbing tide may leave an offshore playground of bars, spits, and lagoons, where small children wade and older ones build a sand city of castles, forts, pyramids, and Mont-Saint-Michels. The following summer the bars and spits may all be under water.

Thoreau chose October for his visit to the Cape because he liked the clear, crisp air of sunny fall days in place of the "thick" atmosphere and frequent fogs of summer. He also liked the storms that stirred up the sea and sent it crashing against the land. "An outward cold and dreariness," he thought, "lend a spirit of adventure to the walk." Those reasons hold good today, and another may be added. The summer crowds, which spread out like occupying armies from every access point, are gone.

The only human beings Thoreau and Channing met were "wreckers" who combed the tide line for flotsam washed ashore. They were silent, expressionless men, loners like Thoreau himself. He described one wrinkled face: "It was like an old sail endowed with life—a hanging cliff of weather-beaten flesh."

Thoreau heard tales of an earlier time when "moon-cussers" set out false lights to lure ships onto the shoals. At least it was true that when a ship was wrecked, the men would line up on the shore and use poles to pull in whatever floated by. In one town, it is told, they kept the competition fair by limiting themselves to ten-foot poles, but they allowed the minister a twenty-foot one.

When Thoreau left the beach and climbed the sand cliff, he found himself on a tableland stretching all the way across the

Cape. Modern visitors may be puzzled by his description of this "bare and flat plateau . . . a virtual desert . . . hardly a tree in sight." That description does not coincide with what you see today and neither does it square with what the early explorers reported. In the seventeenth century, by all accounts, there were hardwood forests, made up of trees that were stunted but all the better fitted to withstand the wind and salt spray of the Outer Cape. Those primeval woods were almost entirely destroyed by the axes of the European settlers. The lumber went to build and heat their houses and make their ships. By the time Thoreau saw the tableland, it was one great barren heath supporting only shrubs such as bayberry, bearberry, and wild plum. At Truro, however, he saw the pattern of the future—a stand of little pines planted in rows. The pitch pine was planted to make good the loss of the hardwood, and after Thoreau's time it spread, through cultivation and natural seeding, until it became the prevailing tree growth of the whole Cape. Only now is it giving way to a second growth of oak.

The tableland is broken by small valleys, known on the Cape as "hollows." They were formed by rivers running down from the face of the retreating glacier. These partial breaks in the sandy cliffs were used by wreckers and stranded seamen, as they are used by beachgoers today. At dusk on the second day of their walk, Thoreau and Channing turned into Newcomb Hollow and knocked on a door to ask for lodging. Had he been traveling alone, Thoreau might have chosen to sleep under the sky, but Channing liked a roof over his head. At the house, they were welcomed by a garrulous old man who kept them up until late at night, telling them about his youth (he had heard the guns of Bunker Hill across Massachusetts Bay) and about his life as a Wellfleet oysterman. The next morning, while waiting for breakfast, the old man resumed his stories, pausing to aim streams of tobacco juice at the fireplace, where cakes, doughnuts, applesauce, and eels were warming. In describing the scene, Thoreau told how he and Channing tried to pick out the dishes farthest removed from the oysterman's line of fire.

That day, Thoreau and Channing crossed the Cape to have a look at the bay side. Instead of a wild beach, they found a settled shore with fishermen's houses and fields. Though the water is often warmer in the bay, its fish include northern species brought down by the Labrador Current, while the waters on the ocean side have southern species swept up by the Gulf Stream. On the bay side, as on the ocean side, the shoals are full of surprises. Old maps show Billingsgate Island, then an apparently solid piece of land outside Wellfleet harbor, with houses, a church, a school, and a lighthouse. Early in this century, the island disappeared beneath the sea. At low tide, you can still see the tumbled foundation blocks of this small Atlantis in Cape Cod Bay.

On the bay, Thoreau was outside the boundaries of what is now the National Seashore. And everywhere outside those boundaries, the Cape is greatly changed. A modern visitor finds that the shore is lined with summer cottages, that many of the beaches require local parking stickers, and that some of them are marked PRIVATE. If perchance one drives across the causeway to Oyster Harbors on the Nantucket Sound shore, one will be stopped by a guard who steps out of his gatehouse to ask which of the Mellons or du Ponts or the other residents one wishes to see. Still, the barriers are not generally as daunting as they are on other parts of the New England coast. Indeed, on the bay around Brewster, the tide goes out so far that any pretense of private property disappears. It is not practical to claim ownership of the tidal zone when it extends a mile from shore.

Just before sunset, Thoreau and Channing walked back across the Cape, which is only two miles wide at Truro, to spend the night with the keeper of Highland Light. This famous lighthouse stands on the highest and wildest stretch of the shore. Here, the coastal cliff takes the brunt of gales so fierce that Thoreau, who knew both places, compared them to the famous winds on the top of Mount Washington. The storms that blow against the Cape combined with the shoals around it to make these waters a death trap for ships—more than three thousand of them by some counts.

From Highland Light, Thoreau saw the mackerel fleet come round the tip of the Cape "in countless numbers, schooner after schooner, until they made a city on the water." Treacherous though the shoals might be, they afforded one of the world's great fishing grounds. Cape Cod was a place where a boy went to sea so young that, as Thoreau remarked, he "leaped from his leading strings into the shrouds."

Beyond High Head, the land drops off sharply to a low sandy

plain that stretches ten miles to land's end at Race Point. High Head marks the end of the glacier-made Cape. The low land beyond—the clenched fist on a map—was dropped there by the sea, which builds up one part of the shore while it eats away another.

The end of the Cape is a true desert, covered by dunes that shift and move at the urging of the wind. Travelers before Thoreau thought that the sand would surely engulf the crescent of wooden houses at Provincetown. But in fact, the Cape Codders had already learned to tame the dunes by planting clumps of beach grass on them. The battle is never wholly won. In places, the moving sand still buries the gnarled and stunted oaks, almost to the tops of their trunks, and would bury Route 6, the main highway, if bulldozers did not regularly plow it off. This rolling Sahara is a playground for dune buggies. Only the beach grass, now managed by the park rangers, keeps the desert within bounds.

From the surface, a clump of beach grass looks like a fragile thing to hold a dune, a wisp of vegetation with blades that bow before the wind and draw little circles in the sand, perfect, as if they were made with a compass. But when Thoreau tried to pull out some of the beach grass, he discovered the depth and toughness of its root system. "Thus," he wrote, "Cape Cod is anchored to the heavens, as it were, by a myriad little cables of beach grass, and if they should fail, would become a total wreck and ere long go to the bottom."

A greater fear today may be that the Cape will sink beneath the weight of the people who are crowding onto it and the houses that are being built on it. On a hot summer weekend, a visitor may wait for an hour to get over the Cape Cod Canal and then drive almost the length of the Cape before finding a National Seashore beach with space in the parking lot. But in the autumn, he or she can still follow Thoreau's footsteps, beyond the staked domain of man, onto the natural shore.

During his days on the Cape, Thoreau the countryman, the panegyrist of hills and rivers and freshwater ponds, had been won by a new world of sand and sea. The sparseness and emptiness made a special appeal to one who, by his nature, had a limited taste for human company. "A man," he wrote in his valedictory to Cape Cod, "may stand there and put all America behind him."

OFFSHORE

THE glacier that formed Cape Cod left other mounds of sand and rocky debris on the plain that stretched south from what is now the southern coast of New England. The seas, raised by the melting ice cap of the northern hemisphere, flowed back among those clumps of higher land, making them into islands. Since the end of that early formative period, the sea has worked away on the islands, like a never-satisfied landscape gardener, shifting sand from one place to another, sculpting bays and barrier beaches to shape the islands as they are today.

The little string of Elizabeth Islands, stretching out from Woods Hole, is little changed in appearance since Bartholomew Gosnold, the first explorer of this coast, saw them in 1602. The largest of them, Naushon, is the private preserve of the Forbes family of Boston. The farthest out, and the only one with ferry connection to the mainland, is Cuttyhunk, where Gosnold tried to establish the first English colony in the New World. The colonists stayed just long enough to build a makeshift fort and gather a payload of sassafras but then gave up and returned to England. Cuttyhunk was finally settled, but only sparsely. By a recent count, its year-round population was twenty-five, and only two children were left in the village school. In summer, it has several hundred vacation residents and a transient population of yachtsmen.

By contrast, the neighboring islands of Nantucket and Martha's Vineyard have had some of the fastest growth and dizzying price rises of any real estate on the Atlantic Coast. Nobody except the developers likes the runaway boom that occurred in the eighties. Many of the year-round residents feel that they are losing their islands to the summer people. The summer people fear that the islands will lose the quiet charm that brought them there in the first place. But people keep coming, for the season, the month, the week, the day.

One of the charms of an island is that getting to it is something of an adventure. Certainly that is so in the case of Nantucket. The visitor who shows up at the dock in Hyannis on a summer day without a reservation for his car will be told by the regulars that he should have made one in January. As it is, he may have to wait in the standby line through several ferry departures or even leave his car to be sent over on the night boat.

There may be unexpected diversions on the voyage. On my last trip, I found myself in a boatload of high school and college vacationers, all headed for the annual Madaquecham Jam. This midsummer beach party, which started up spontaneously a few years ago and has grown each year, is a small and comparatively decorous sister of the mammoth, rowdy Florida spring break, but enough of an intrusion to upset Nantucketers, who prize quiet. The local police, taking no chances, had called for reinforcements to control beer drinking on the beach. Aboard our ferry was a contingent of Massachusetts State Police with a cruiser and a van of four horses.

Most of the teenagers on the ferry were quiet enough, but a few, I judged, were victims of a hearing impairment peculiar to their generation. Having listened too long to superloud music, they were unable to converse with one another except in shouts.

"It's Cisco," one cried.

"No, it's Nobadeer," another screamed.

In fact, none of them knew on which beach the Jam would be held, since it is never planned in advance. When they reached the island, the jamgoers scattered, probably to camp out at the houses and yards of friends' parents. Not until the next morning, when they were milling around the dock, did the word spread— "It's Cisco"—and off they went by car, bike, and moped. Alas, the sky was cloudy and shortly after noon it began to rain. The party ended early, leaving the rented mounties in control of an empty beach. Better luck next year.

Jam or no jam, anyone who brings a car to Nantucket is likely to wish that it was half its size. The streets in the old part of town were designed for horses and carts, some of them so narrow that two cars cannot pass. The houses stand side by side and close to the streets, seemingly huddled against the chills and fogs of long winters. The town does not gladly accommodate the needs of twentieth-century life as perceived by mainlanders.

Ever since the great days of its whaling past, Nantucket has had a sense of its own apartness. Nowadays, it divides the population of the world into "islanders" and "off-islanders." In earlier periods, especially during the American Revolution and the War of 1812, it sometimes drew a distinction between "Nantucket" and "America." At such times, it seemed that the islanders were not entirely settled about the indissolubility of their ties to the United States.

Many of Nantucket's whaling merchants were Quakers, morally opposed to war. All of them were free traders dependent on safe sea-lanes to their best market in England. When war loomed, their first instinct, on both counts, was to stay out of it. Even before the Revolution began, however, they were caught up in the struggle between Britain and the colonies. Of the three ships that arrived at Boston in November 1774, carrying tea on their return voyages from London, one was chartered to William Rotch, Nantucket's leading merchant, and another belonged to his brother Francis of New Bedford. After the tea was dumped by the patriots into Boston harbor, Nantucketers found that they had few friends on either side. At one point, they petitioned the Continental Congress for a declaration of neutrality; it was scorned. During the war years, the whaling fleet still put to sea, but it was fair game for warships and privateers on both sides. By the end of the war, Nantucket had lost three-quarters of its fleet, and among the island's five hundred families, it is said, there were 202 widows. No wonder that the little platforms on top of houses, where wives kept lookout for their husbands, are known as widow's walks.

The whaling fleet was rebuilt with more and larger ships, devastated again in the War of 1812, and rebuilt again. In those later years, the ships were often gone for two or three years on voyages around Cape Horn and into the rich whaling grounds of the Pacific. The industry brought the stench of oil to the waterfront, wealth to the counting houses, and some mansions with brick fronts and Greek columns to Main Street.

Then quite swiftly in the 1840s, the boom ended. The bigger ships, heavily loaded, could not get across a sandbar that was building up at the entrance to the harbor. The whaling enterprise moved its chief base to New Bedford and for almost a century time on Nantucket stood still. That long pause ensured for Nantucket the quality of quaintness that has done much to bring about a new kind of boom, this time as a summer resort.

Faced with a surge of development after World War II, Nantucket acted more swiftly than many other communities to keep it under control. For the most part, it used the governmental tools available to planners everywhere, but it also invented some of its own.

An early decision, which had general approval, was to keep the old part of Nantucket town and the village of Siasconset (called Sconset) on the other side of the island unchanged. Both historic districts are protected by a building and design code that some say is the most rigid and minutely detailed in the country. The basic principle is not to allow anything that would not have looked appropriate in the year 1846, the whaling-era pinnacle. That means that with the exception of the mansions on Main Street, the houses must be of gray shingle, with the trim in one of several specified shades of white or light gray. Any change in the design of a doorway, the height of a fence, or the pitch of a roof must have the approval of the Historic District Commission. Stores must have approval for any sign larger than two feet in length or six inches in width. Proceeding on the general principle that signs are meant to identify the premises, not to sell wares, the proper shape, color, lettering, and placement are spelled out in twenty-eight pages of specifications.

The attempt to keep things as they have always been, however, stopped short of the waterfront. For better or worse, the harborside as it exists today is the work of one man, Walter Beinecke, Jr., a longtime summer resident and heir to the Green Stamps fortune. In the 1960s, Beinecke bought up most of the decaying dock area as well as blocks in the center of town. Along the waterfront, he built a complex of small shops, galleries, studios, and apartments, shingled in gray and standing on the piers of a full-service marina. It was Beinecke's purpose to attract well-to-do sailors with their own boats rather than day-trippers who, as they say on the island, "come with one shirt and one ten-dollar bill and don't change either." Beinecke's power in island affairs was resented by some of the old residents, including fishermen, who felt they were crowded out of the waterfront, and other islanders, who sold out to Beinecke for a song, only to see their former property skyrocket in value. Others, mindful of the way in which many old waterfronts have been desecrated by fast-buck developers, are inclined to respond, "Think what the place would look like if Beinecke hadn't bought it."

During the summer, Nantucket harbor is filled with more than a thousand boats, doubtless worth many times what the whaling fleet was in its glory days. For an overnight stay at the marina, a forty-foot boat pays $90, for a full season $10,000. On only one occasion has a yachtsman found the harbor inadequate. That was when Donald Trump learned that the channel, now dredged to seventeen feet, was too shallow for his *Princess*. Trump sailed away, I was told, promising to return the next summer with his own dredge. Before that could happen, however, Trump himself ran aground on financial shoals and the *Princess* was put up for sale.

Outside of town limits, the greatest force for preservation of the island has been the Nantucket Conservation Foundation, founded in 1963 by local conservationists, including most notably my old boss, Roy Larsen, then president of Time, Inc. By gift and purchase, the Foundation has acquired large tracts of open land, especially on the flat plains and rolling moors that cover a great part of Nantucket. Its holdings, together with those of the Massachusetts Audubon Society, the Trustees of

Reservations, and smaller nature trusts have grown to comprise more than one-third of the entire island.

None too soon. In the 1960s, the first wave of a boom in real estate sent land prices soaring. As usual, the pressure came from a combination of outside developers and the local establishment of real estate brokers, lawyers, bankers, and businessmen. In the 1970s, friends of the island were jolted by the sight of a new shopping development and a spread of condominiums, both recognized at once as "not Nantucket." The planning board quickly tightened the rules on new construction.

The effort to preserve the landscape has been less successful than the one to preserve the old town. A stated objective of the island plan is to maintain the "village concept"—that is, small waterfront communities with vistas of open space between them. But in fact, new houses have been built mostly in strips along the shore or else scattered across the interior, each on the highest point to be had. On the largely treeless interior, they stand up like pieces on a Monopoly board.

On an island where one out of every seventeen residents is a real estate broker, it was hard to slow down the building boom. At its peak, because living on the island is so expensive, construction crews were being flown in every morning from the mainland and flown back at night. Between 1980 and 1986, the average price of a house more than doubled, to $354,000.

In 1984, the town meeting voted to impose a 2 percent tax on property transfers and to use the proceeds to establish a land bank. It is believed to have been the first such tax in the country with that exclusive purpose. So far, the land bank has bought up about one thousand acres, including almost a mile of shorefront.

The recession has given Nantucket a breather, but, with one-third of its space already developed and one-third under conservation protection, the future of the last third is uncertain. "We have to wonder," says Carl Borchert, the head of the Nantucket Land Bank, "what Nantucket will be like in twenty years. Will we want to live with twice as many people, twice as many houses, twice as many cars?"

The alternative to runaway growth, some think, may be runaway values. If there are few new houses for sale, the price of existing properties keeps on rising. Little old houses in town, so gray and modest on the outside, have been gutted and redone inside by the most expensive decorators. On Main Street, the five-and-ten and the town's only department store have given way to upscale shops and boutiques that sell $3 ice cream cones and $1,000 lightship baskets. There is danger that Nantucket may end up as just another enclave of the rich.

For now, at least, Nantucket extends a welcome to all comers, so long as they are well-behaved. In town, the close-packed houses, almost without exception, are bright with flowers in the window boxes and side yards. Main Street is paved with cobblestones, just as it was in the old days when the stones were brought back in ballast by whaling ships; now they are deliberately left uneven to slow down the cars to bicycle speed. Every arrival of the ferry is a small festival in itself and even the day-trippers add to the holiday feeling, keeping the shops open and the town alive until the evening ferry leaves.

Perhaps the most important element in Nantucket's feeling of openness is that the beaches, which rim the whole island, are open and available to all. This has always been the custom, and most of the natives as well as the visitors take it for granted. But in legal fact, only two and a half miles of the sixty-nine-mile shorefront are publicly owned. The rest is private property, down to the low-water mark, and the roads that lead to the shore in many places run over private land. Actually, the beaches are open because there is a long tradition and strong public feeling against closing them.

Not all summer residents share that feeling, especially new people from off island who have paid $3,000 a front foot for their shore and think they should have exclusive use of it. Beach owners object to cars parked on private property, to litter left on the beach, and, most of all, to dune buggies charging up and down the sand.

"It's not the people who live here that cause the problem," says Borchert. "The local people use their ORVs to get to fishing spots or picnic places. It's the visitors who rent jeeps and race along the beach for the fun of it. One of them told me, 'It's so great because we can't do it anywhere else.' "

Indeed, Nantucket has been more tolerant of ORVs than most other places on the coast. Limits and licenses are probably coming in the near future. Nantucket knows that it had better keep its beaches clean and quiet. Otherwise, as Brian Wiese, the town planner, told me, "One of these days, one of the landowners will get so mad, he will say, 'I've had enough. I'm closing it off.' And that might start a rush to enclose the shore." That is what has happened in many other places, including Martha's Vineyard. It would be a sad day for Nantucket.

Martha's Vineyard is often referred to as Nantucket's sister island, but the relationship is that of sisters who are quite content to see little or nothing of each other. Natives of either island, asked about the other, are likely to respond, "Don't know. Never been there."

The Vineyard is twice as big as Nantucket, with six separate townships, and hence does not seem all of a piece, as Nantucket does. Moreover, it it closer to the mainland and looks more like it, with some rolling hills and fields. Russell Baker in *The New York Times* spoke for Nantucketers some years ago when he described the Vineyard as "a nice place to visit—if you like the Pennsylvania countryside." To which the late Henry Beetle Hough, editor of the *Vineyard Gazette,* responded: "Those who have affection for Martha's Vineyard also like the sea, but tend to believe that a vista is best that has something green and solid in it, such as a beech tree in full leaf. . . . Moors and ocean will stand only so much looking at."

"Down-island" on the Vineyard is the eastern end, where the ferry comes in from Woods Hole. It has fine old houses in Edgartown, a legacy of the time when the Vineyard had a lucrative whaling industry. Down-island also, in the town of Oak Bluffs, is a village of little Victorian houses built to surround a Methodist campground. With gingerbread fronts, hand-cut with scrolls and curlicues, and brightly painted, they look like an outsize reproduction of a little girl's old-fashioned Christmas plaything—especially so each summer on the night of the Grand Illumination, when the whole village is hung with Chinese lanterns.

The "up-island" towns of Chilmark and West Tisbury are still rural in appearance, with stretches of woods and meadows. All the way up-island is Gay Head, a three-hundred-foot cliff of multicolored sand and clay, the one geographical feature of the island that antedates the glacier. Its layers of red, blue, brown, and yellow record the history of millions of years when Gay Head was sometimes under the water and sometimes above it.

This high western tip of the island is still home to the Gay Head Indians. After a long battle with the federal government, they were finally recognized as a tribe and awarded compensation for their lost lands, including a stretch of the coast adjoining that of Mrs. Jacqueline Onassis.

Martha's Vineyard has a winter population of 11,000 and a summer one of 94,000, including perhaps a smaller proportion of corporate CEO's than Nantucket but a greater proportion of celebrities from the New York worlds of arts, letters, and entertainment. In coping with the pressures of growth, it has followed Nantucket's lead, but a step behind. It now has a property transfer tax and a land bank and tightened regulations on building. Thanks in large part to conservation outfits, some sizable areas have been saved from development, both on the Vineyard itself and, across a narrow channel, on its famous little neighbor, Chappaquiddick. But most of its best beaches are closed to nonresidents, with one notable exception: the mile-long stretch of South Beach in Edgartown.

A few years ago, Vineyarders discovered to their alarm that a speculative investor had bought about a third of South Beach, which was privately owned, though traditionally open. What he meant to do with it was not to develop it in any way but simply to close it off and sell beach rights to a few hundred families at $25,000 apiece. All that a shareholder would get for his money, apparently, was the right to keep other people out.

After a round of hearings and legal battles, with financial help from the state, Edgartown was able to buy out the new owner. South Beach was saved from closure, if not from the ocean. As luck would have it, a storm in 1991 leveled the dunes and greatly narrowed the beach. At least it was still open.

FISHING GROUNDS

THE whales that come to spend the summer off the coast of Massachusetts these days are treated as visiting celebrities. Boatloads of whale watchers go out to greet them, with binoculars, cameras, and offerings of hot dogs and buns. Marine biologists study them when they rise to the surface, identifying them individually by the markings on their tails, scrutinizing them for new scars caused by boat propellers, recording and naming newborn calves. At the Center for Coastal Studies at Provincetown, they are logged in by Charles ("Stormy") Mayo and his staff. Mayo is the coast's leading expert on whales, and their best friend in time of need. If a whale is in trouble anywhere on the coast, Mayo is the man who goes out in his rubber Zodiac boat to free it from a fisherman's net or to administer first aid.

That is whaling today. To see what it was like in the old

76

days, you may drive off the Cape and along the shore of Buzzard's Bay to the old, shabby, hard-luck city of New Bedford. There, in the Whaling Museum on Johnny Cake Hill, you will find an impressive collection of the arts, tools, and trophies of the whaling era, including a half-size model of a ship. (To see the last real New England whaling ship, you must go farther along the coast to Mystic Seaport in Connecticut.) Across from the museum is the Seamen's Bethel, made famous by Herman Melville in *Moby Dick*. As in Melville's time, the walls of the chapel bear memorial plaques with the names of crews lost at sea and sometimes an inscription:

> Oh, God, the Sea is so great
> And my boat is so small.

On the streets and docks of New Bedford, Melville's narrator, Ishmael, found, among the country boys from Vermont and the runaway slaves or freedmen from the South, an assortment of "wild specimens" from Fiji, Tonga, and such exotic ports of call. The memorial tablets in the Seamen's Bethel bring the ethnic record up through the transition from whaling to commercial fishing. They show that in the early part of this century Norwegian names were common on New Bedford vessels. The predominant element for many years, however, has been Portuguese. Some of the families have been resident for generations, while other Portuguese seamen still come and go between New Bedford and the old country or their native islands, the Azores and the Cape Verdes.

In the whaling enterprise, New Bedford had its first cycle of boom and bust. The second was the rise of the cotton-textile industry in the nineteenth century and its loss to the South in the twentieth. One thing that kept the city going through rough times was commercial fishing. And now that is in crisis.

When I went down from the historic district of Johnny Cake Hill to the working waterfront, I found Rodney Avila in the wheel house of his trawler, the *Trident*. Ranged along two adjoining docks were six other sword-fishing boats, all but one of them owned by members of the extended Avila family and all of them idle. Avila, a burly, middle-aged man in a red shirt, was steaming with indignation.

"Just this week," he said, "we were two days out at sea, one hundred and fifty miles off Nantucket, ready to begin our sword-fishing season. Then we got a radio message from the Fisheries Service in Washington, telling us that we had new quotas. The limit for gill-net fishermen on the whole northeast coast was sixty thousand pounds—that is, thirty thousand for the half year. And of that thirty thousand, the message said, twenty thousand had already been caught by another boat. Well, they were wrong, the other boat had caught only eight thousand. But never mind. With that kind of quota for the whole fleet, it wasn't worth putting our nets out. We turned around and headed back empty. So here we are with our crews idle and our ice melting in the holds."

The basic reason for Avila's plight is that in the shallow seas of the continental shelf, off the New England coast, the sword-fish stock is in a precipitous decline. Since 1978, according to scientists, it has been reduced by at least 60 percent.

To make matters worse, United States fishermen have lost part of their most productive ground to the Canadians. In 1976, when countries extended their territorial waters to the two-hundred-mile limit, the United States and Canada found them-selves with overlapping claims to Georges Bank, east of Cape Cod. In 1985, the dispute was resolved at the Hague by the World Court, which awarded the larger part of the bank to the United States but the northern section to Canada. That "northern peak," as it hap-pens, is of special importance to sword fishermen, who used to count on a season lasting from June through October. The big fish, in their annual circuit of the Atlantic, arrive on Georges Bank in June and by the end of July most of them have crossed the "Hague line," bringing an end to the American season.

Rodney Avila began fishing in his father's boat when he was nine years old. For more than thirty years, he has run his own boat, trawling for groundfish most of the time but going after swordfish in the summer. During most of that time, he caught swordfish the old-fashioned way, with a harpoon. He was one of the best harpooners on the coast, standing in the pulpit at the bow of the boat and hurling the harpoon by hand, just as the whalers used to do.

"That's the way I would still do it if I could," Avila says. "But there aren't enough swordfish left to make that economic."

In the 1980s, most of the sword fishermen changed over to "long lines," a method in which a line carrying hundreds of hooks is set out between floats, left overnight, and pulled in the next morning. That is how most swordfish are caught today in Atlantic waters. Avila tried it for a few years but then began using a gill net, which is dragged behind the boat and then pulled in by winches. Both methods are indiscriminate and wasteful. The long lines bring in fish that are undersize and fish of unwanted species; some of the swordfish die on the line, with some loss of market quality. Gill nets allow undersize fish to escape through the mesh but bring in everything else, sometimes including porpoises. By whatever method caught, undersize fish of regulated species are thrown back, but few of them survive.

Gill nets have a very bad name among conservationists, mainly because of the way they have been used in the Pacific by large trawlers from Taiwan, Japan, and other Asian countries. In setting quotas, the National Marine Fisheries Service allotted 6 million pounds to the long-liners and only sixty thousand pounds to the gill-netters. Many thought it was a step toward a total ban on the use of gill nets for sword fishing.

Avila thinks it is unfair. "In the Pacific," he says, "they use drift nets thirty or forty miles long, with a small mesh that leaves nothing behind. Our nets are only about a mile long and have a large mesh. The entire catch of the New Bedford fleet doesn't equal that of one Taiwanese boat. And our nets are less destructive of the fish stock, especially of the young fish that haven't spawned yet, than long lines are."

Avila insists that he is a conservationist himself. "I'm fourth generation in this country," he says. "Our fathers taught us that you must preserve the fish. Don't take too many, and especially don't take the young ones. You have to let them spawn or there won't be any fish left."

Few would quarrel with such obvious common sense, but it is hard for fishermen to accept the corollary—that conservation means regulation. In the memory of man, the oceans have been free and open to all. Anyone could build or buy his own boat, fashion his own gear, and by his own efforts gain a living from the sea. That is what has drawn many present-day fishermen to their arduous livelihood. "I couldn't stand working in an office or a factory," they say. "I want to be my own boss."

The collapse of the fishery has come so suddenly that some fishermen try to deny it. In the past, they have seen one species virtually disappear from the fishing grounds and a few years later come back in full strength. But never before have stocks of all the desirable species fallen off so far or so fast. According to biologists at the Northeast Fisheries Center at Woods Hole, Massachusetts, efforts to restore the stocks in New England waters have yet to produce a single success story.

The richness of the waters of the continental shelf, off the coasts of New England and Canada's Maritime Provinces, is legendary. John Cabot, returning from his voyage of exploration in 1497, reported that fish were so thick in the water that they almost stopped his ship. In Colonial times, as in the first half of this century, cod, haddock, and flounder were mainstays of the fishery. Since the time of the Revolution, a carved image of the "sacred codfish," a symbol of New England's first commercial enterprise, has hung in the legislative chamber of the Massachusetts State House in Boston.

To find and hook his fish, until quite recent times, the fisherman relied on his knowledge of the water, the currents, the ocean bottom, and the habits of the particular species he was after. In *Captains Courageous,* Kipling described a Gloucester captain at the rail of his schooner:

> Disko Troop thought of recent weather, and gales, currents, food supplies, and other domestic arrangements, from the point of view of a twenty-pound cod; was, in fact, for an hour a cod himself, and looked remarkably like one.

When Captain Troop had found his spot, he dispatched his crew in two-man dories to row out from the schooner and catch fish, one by one, on hand lines.

That was pretty much how fish were caught until the middle of the twentieth century. Engines replaced sails and heavy rope nets replaced hand lines, but the captain still had to rely on his years of experience and his understanding of fish behavior. The hunt was a fairly even contest between man and fish.

Then, in the mid-1960s, something new arrived on the banks—the European factory ship, equipped with powerful engines and electronic fish-finding instruments. Instead of a small, heavy net, the factory ship put out a huge net of lightweight synthetic fiber and pulled it through the water at high speed. Then it was pulled in over the stern by powerful winches and emptied out on the deck. No fish were thrown back. Food fish were processed and frozen on board; the rest went for pet food or fertilizer. The factory ship, built to stay at sea for months and looking more like an ocean liner than a trawler, had comfortable bunks, freezers full of food, television sets, and, in the case of Russian ships, women crew members.

In *Captains Courageous*, Harvey, the boy who was washed overboard from a liner and picked up by a Gloucester vessel, marveled at the sight of the nineteenth-century fishing fleet— nearly a hundred ships anchored on the Grand Banks, often so close together that the men could shout jokes and insults at one another.

"It's a town," said Harvey. "Disko was right. It *is* a town."

Eighty years later, William Warner, who sailed with the factory ships for his book *Distant Waters,* heard a seaman evoke the same image but in grimmer terms. Of the towering German, Russian, and Polish factory ships, working all night and ablaze with lights, he said, "It looked like the city of Chicago."

American fishermen, appalled by the devastation of their historic fishing grounds, appealed to Washington for help. In 1976, the United States and other nations extended their territorial waters from twelve miles to two hundred miles offshore. Congress promptly passed the Magnuson Act, effectively barring the factory ships and giving the National Marine Fisheries Service power to impose controls on the American fleet.

And so, it seemed, the crisis was over. The American fleet, encouraged by federal-loan guarantees and tax breaks, was revived and expanded. World food experts predicted that the oceans would provide food for millions who could not live off the produce of the land. "Inexhaustible" was still the popular word for the resources of the sea.

For a few years, things looked good. Fish stocks appeared to be recovering. Catches were definitely up. But then the statistics leveled off and began to decline. By 1989, the number of fishing vessels increased by more than 60 percent. The new fleet of stern trawlers had more powerful engines, big lightweight nets, and all the electronic fish-finding gear of the foreign ships. A cod, traveling to his spawning ground, would no longer have to elude just the calculating mind of a New England fishing captain. He and his mates would be picked up on a sonar screen until a net was lowered to catch the whole school.

The cod is a plentiful and a rugged fish. It has survived the electronic fleet better than the other most-valued species. According to the Fisheries Center at Woods Hole, which keeps count of the fish population, the stock of haddock on Georges Bank has fallen 94 percent since 1965.

One of the first casualties of the new, deeper crisis was the word "inexhaustible" as applied to the supply of fish in the oceans. Virtually all of the fish on the Atlantic Coast live in the shallow waters of the continental shelf, where they find food in plenty. Few fish live in the deep ocean, and those that are there do not look like the sort of thing a cook would want in her kitchen. Moreover, the cold waters of the northern coast are far richer in plankton, the microscopic basis of the oceanic food chain, than the southern seas. Georges Bank, where a circular current, or gyre, provides abundant nutrients, can scarcely be matched, acre for acre, anywhere in the world as a rich fishing ground. Yet its population of desirable species is only about a quarter of what it was thirty years ago. What are left are "trash" fish—skate, squid, scup or porgie, and, in greatest numbers, the despised dogfish. Some of these species have a market, in Asia and in ethnic districts of this country, but most Americans will not eat them. Yet they are what the fleet brings up in ever-increasing proportion.

Responsibility for conserving the fishery rests initially with eight regional councils—one for New England, one for the Middle Atlantic states, and so on. The New England council has at its disposal a variety of controls: limits on the length of the season for different species and on the number of days a boat can be at sea, temporary closure of spawning areas, limits on the size and mesh of nets, on the size of fish that can be kept, on the horse power of engines and the capacity of holds, on the total catch by one boat or the whole fleet. Some of these controls have been tried with varying success on various species. But the fishermen and their representatives, who dominate the council, have been reluctant to crack down in ways that might in the short run bring hard times and, to some, financial ruin.

There is one control that fishermen, almost to a man, have resisted: a limit on the number of fishing boats or fishermen. Such a limit would mean that no one could enter the commercial fishery unless someone else got out. "Limited entry" is the established system in Canada, where a few big companies dominate the industry and receive quotas from the government. The method has had some use in this country. The Mid-Atlantic council has stabilized the surf clam harvest by allotting it to a limited number of boats. Florida confines the fishery for Spanish mackerel, mullet, and several other species to established operators. Off Alaska, where the halibut season is open to all comers but only for a few days of frenzied fishing, the North Pacific council may put a lid on the size of the fleet.

There is more at stake here than the practical matter of managing the fishery. The idea of closing the door to new people goes against the grain of the fiercely independent fishermen of the Atlantic Coast. "How would my sons be able to get into the business as I did?" I was asked by fishermen from Maine to Florida.

The idea of the ocean as a last frontier of freedom dies hard, as the idea of the western frontier died on land. Yet the land got fenced and at length the farmers learned to live with government controls, called in their case subsidies.

The West offers another lesson for the maritime East. The great herds of buffalo supplied the Indians with food and clothing as long as they were hunted by bow and arrow. But they were wiped out in a few years by the Sharp's Big Fifty rifle. The buffalo rifle had nothing on the sonar fish-finder.

For some light on the future of the fishery, I sought out Robert D. Smith, whose boat, the *Trudy S.*, is part of the fleet at Point Judith in Rhode Island. Smith has been a fisherman since he was a boy and now, in what he thinks of as semiretirement, sets out eight hundred lobster pots. As a member of the New England Fisheries Management Council for the last ten years, he has played a part in all the frustrating attempts to arrest the decline in the fish stocks and the catch.

Bob Smith's judgment is that the right combination of controls, if strictly enforced, could bring back the fishery, but not without pain. In the short run, there would be a shakeout of the less efficient producers, including outsiders who got into the business for what looked for a while like easy money.

The specter of total collapse of the fish population, he thinks, is exaggerated. "We're never going to catch the last fish," he says, no matter what the environmentalists say. "There comes a point for any species at which it doesn't pay to go after them. Then the pressure is off and the fish have a chance to come back."

"That, however," he continues, "would mean a cycle of ups and downs, as other industries have. And that is not what the scientists or the government people want. They would like to bring back the steady fishery of years past."

The way they mean to do it, Smith believes, is by limiting entry into commercial fishing. The system often proposed would be to issue transferable quotas, which the individual fishermen could exercise or sell to others. The end result, as in Canada, might be a concentration of the industry in a limited number of large operations.

Bob Smith regrets the closing of the unregulated fishery, but he is philosophical about it. Thirty years from now, he says, a new generation won't even remember that the ocean used to be a free frontier.

THE SOUND

RHODE Island has good reason to call itself the Ocean State, since a seagoing ship can sail two-thirds of the way through the state in the deep waters of Narragansett Bay. Providence, at the head of the bay, and Newport, on an island at its mouth, became in Colonial times the centers of a thriving maritime trade. Their cargoes included fish, lumber, rum, ponies, and other New England products, but the big money was in slaves, bought with rum on the coast of Africa, transported to the Indies, and sold for molasses to make more rum. Whereas Salem turned a stern face to the slave trade and Boston was forever ridden with guilt about it, the Rhode Island cities seem to have kept their consciences under control. When you see an imposing Colonial or Federal mansion on the shores of Narragansett Bay, you have to wonder whether its original owner was a slave trader.

85

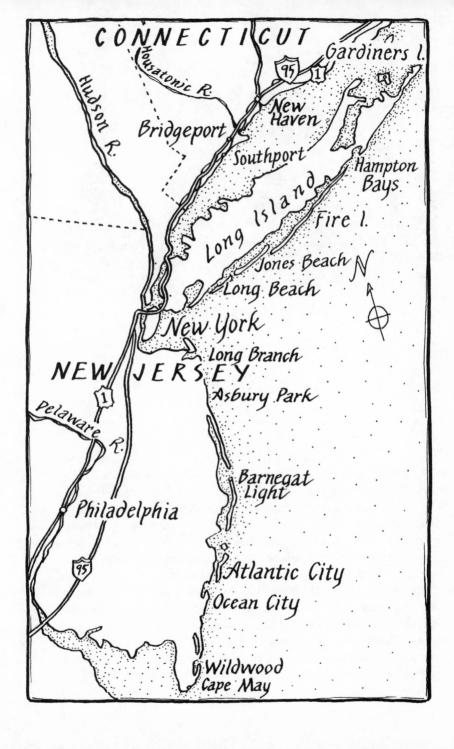

In the nineteenth century, the two ports took opposite directions. Providence became a major manufacturing center, while Newport blossomed into the most elegant of seaside resorts. Wealthy southern families, who found Newport a cool relief from the heat and fevers of the Carolina low country, were Newport's first summer people, but after the Civil War they gave way to the new-rich families of the North.

Arriving at Newport, Jane and I found our way to the Cliff Walk, which runs for three miles along the eastern shore of the island, between the great mansions and the ocean. For all their money, the owners of the mansions were not able to buy exclusive rights to their own ocean views. The path along the cliff has been a public way since earliest times, used mainly by fishermen making their way from cove to cove. In the time of mansion building, one of the owners tried to block it off, but a court told him to open it up, affirming "the vested right of the humblest citizen of Newport in the Atlantic Ocean."

The ocean we saw, on a sparkling day in early spring, did not have the familiar slate blue aspect of the wintry North Atlantic. At one particular cove, where the waves were breaking from two directions, it looked almost tropical. The rocky points, the pocket cove, the high surf—all might have been in Maine. But the color of the water was more like the sunlit aquamarine of the Caribbean.

From the Cliff Walk, in places where the hedges are not too high, you can see the gardens and the ocean-facing sides of the mansions. Builders of waterfront houses nowadays may think of the water side as the front, but these "cottages" were built for show, with imposing columned fronts on the street side.

It is hard to imagine how even an Astor or a Vanderbilt could have enjoyed living in them. Of course, they were not designed so much for everyday living as for splendid balls and dinners, but even those were not always joyous occasions. I once talked to a man who had dined with Mrs. Vanderbilt in the great, cold dining room of The Breakers, where each bronze chair is so heavy that it had its own footman to move it. My friend noticed that the dinner guests spent much of their time slapping mosquitoes. The windows of The Breakers had no screens because, as Mrs. Vanderbilt explained, "They don't bite me."

The most unusual of the great houses is Belcourt, built by

the renowned whip Oliver Hazard Perry Belmont to accommodate his horses on the ground floor and his family above. I don't
know where the present owners get their guides. The sweet
young thing who took us on a tour of the impressive collections
of armor and paintings identified one small picture as a Michelan-
gelo. "Mr. Angelo was here himself a few months ago," she
informed us.

Newport's architectural distinction does not depend on the
marble mansions—"white elephants" to Henry James—which
are copied in part from such various foreign structures as the
Château de Blois and the Temple of the Sun at Baalbek. More
significantly, Newport was the birthplace of the Shingle Style
in great seaside houses, a style that Vincent Scully, the noted
architectural scholar of our own day, calls one of the purely
American contributions to architecture.

Until the closing decades of the nineteenth century, there
was no real demand for a distinctive coastal architecture. In
earlier times, wealthy families built their houses on the main
streets, leaving the shore to fishermen's cottages. Even when
summer houses began to be built on the seacoast, most of them
looked much like those inland, bearing no special relationship to
their sites. The great Shingle Style houses, on the other hand,
seem to belong naturally on the New England coast.

The structure that pointed the way, known as the Watts
Sherman house, was designed by Henry Hobson Richardson and
built in 1874. It drew inspiration in part from the Queen Anne
wood-and-stone houses of England and in part from the simple
shingled houses of Colonial America. Soon afterward, the prodigious Richardson turned to other designs and the Shingle Style
was given its classical form in Newport by the firm of McKim,
Mead & White.

Such a summer house, facing the sea, typically presents a
long, low profile, often with gables and dormers set into a sloping
roof. Across the front, there are likely to be porches or a long,
wide veranda, the outdoor social center of the house. The down-
stairs rooms are apt to be dark, because of the wood paneling
and the shading veranda roof. Shrubs hug the walls and lawns
slope down to the water.

Unfortunately, Newport is not the best place to see Shingle

Style houses today. Many have been altered or destroyed or let go to decay. The finest one left, called Southside, is carefully screened from public view. We got a peek at it through the bushes, which had not yet leafed out, but the only way to get a real view is from the Cliff Walk, over a high wall. It helps to have a small ladder or a periscope or a lift from a strong companion. Newport may not be the social citadel that it used to be, but it still mans the barricades against the hoi polloi. When I asked the name of the mansion's owner (it's Goelet) at the local historical society, I was told, "We couldn't possibly tell you. He's one of our members."

The best place in Newport to get a look at the Shingle Style is at the Newport Casino, designed by Stanford White. The Casino, which now houses the National Tennis Hall of Fame, is not a house and is not on the shore, but it has all the elements of the style, such as the intricate joining of walls and the elaborately varied courses of shingles—hell to keep up, I was told by the curator.

The big shingle houses were built wherever there was money on the New England coast. They could be seen in quantity at Bar Harbor, Maine, until the fire of 1947, and some survive. Others stand on the north shore of Massachusetts, at Manchester and Beverly Farms. They are not being built anymore, partly because they are expensive and require fine craftsmanship, but their lines can still be seen, with or without shingles, in the best beach architecture of our own day.

Leaving Newport, I drove west along a part of the Rhode Island shore that most travelers skip. Between Point Judith and the Connecticut border, the coast is lined with sandy beaches, barrier spits and islands, and, behind them, salt ponds and marshes. In Colonial times, the southernmost of the post roads that ran between New York and Boston crossed this southwest corner of Rhode Island, but the modern corridors of traffic pass it by. Hence, it has been spared, at least until recently, the worst pressures of development. Even Route 1, where it runs through miles of conservation land, following roughly the path of the old post road, is a true born-again parkway.

The land is sprinkled with Indian names: Ninigret, Matunuck, Quonochontaug, Weekapaug, Misquamicut. The Indians liked this part of the coast because of its relatively mild climate and the abundance of shellfish. It was here in the Great Swamp that the Narragansetts met their bloody end as a nation.

I found my way down a rutted road to a rise of ground in the middle of the swamp. At Wakefield, I had asked directions from Louise Wedlock at the Bureau of Indian Health. A Wampanoag Indian herself, she told me that I would find a monument there but added, rather reproachfully I thought, "It's a monument to the settlers, not to the Indians."

The monument is a rough-cut granite column and a stone block with a plaque that reads:

ATTACKED WITHIN THEIR FORT UPON THIS ISLAND THE NAR-RAGANSETT INDIANS MADE THEIR LAST STAND IN KING PHILIP'S WAR AND WERE DEFEATED BY THE UNITED FORCES OF THE MASSACHUSETTS, CONNECTICUT, AND PLYMOUTH COLONIES IN THE GREAT SWAMP FIGHT SUNDAY 19 DECEMBER 1675.

King Philip, as the English called him, was Metacom, the son of Massasoit, the Wampanoag chief who had befriended the Pilgrims at Plymouth. The inscription says nothing of the half century of sporadic conflict, with atrocities on both sides, that led up to the war. Nor does it give the gruesome details of the swamp fight.

Three or four thousand Narragansetts, allies of Philip, were crowded within a log palisade. A Colonial force of a thousand men broke through the fort, defeated a small defending force of warriors, and massacred the rest, mostly old men, women, and children. The site, with its bare-bones inscription, and the dark surrounding swamp is a gloomy place still. I can well believe that neither the descendants of the colonists nor the Indians of today have any heart to commemorate what happened there.

It did not take long to reach the western tip of Rhode Island, where Watch Hill juts into the sea. From there, it is only a hop, skip, and a jump over Fishers Island, shallow water, and Plum Island to Orient Point on the north fork of Long Island. From time to time, ambitious highway builders such as Robert Moses have proposed building a bridge along this line of shoals and islands, making a short route from New Jersey to New England, bypassing the traffic jams of New York City. The towns at either end of such a crossing, however, do not fancy their future as truck stops on a coastal throughway. Orient Point remains the end of the line on Long Island. Watch Hill rocks away on its shingled verandas, an exclusive old summer resort protected from outsiders by street signs that proclaim it one big Tow Zone.

The line on which the bridge did not get built is the eastern entrance to Long Island Sound, a body of water unique on the Atlantic Coast. Unlike the bays and sounds that lie behind barrier islands farther south, it is a legacy of the Ice Age. When the glacier rolled down over the Connecticut coast and out across the coastal plain, it dropped its heavy load of sand, gravel, and rocks to form what is now Long Island. Between the new island and the mainland, it left a basin which, as the ice melted and the seas rose, flooded and became Long Island Sound.

Almost enclosed by land, the Sound has much in common with the Mediterranean. Its eastern entrance is cluttered with islands and shoals, making a tricky passage for boats of all sizes, while its western entrance, or exit, is a narrow sluice, only partly cleared of dangerous rocks. The names of the entrances refer to the swift rush of tides—the Race at the eastern end and Hellgate at the western.

Following the Connecticut shore from east to west, the traveler passes through scenes of maritime history. Stonington, just over the Rhode Island border, was once an important fishing and whaling port, and still has a small fleet of fishing boats, mostly scallopers. Thanks to its early prosperity, Stonington is famous for fine houses and trees—too famous to suit some of the older residents, who bemoan the influx of tourists and the cute shops that cater to them.

Mystic, the next port, makes no such complaint about tourists. It is a reconstructed seaport of the early nineteenth century, sort of a maritime Williamsburg, with docks, sail loft, ropewalk, countinghouse, and taverns. Mystic's showpiece is the *Charles W. Morgan*, last of the whaling ships, restored to its original condition.

Beyond Mystic is Groton, where submarines are built. To bring the maritime record up-to-date, Groton has its own historic exhibit, the USS *Nautilus*, the world's first nuclear submarine. A young visitor, who learned at Mystic how to hurl a harpoon at a whale, can see at Groton how a Polaris missile might have been launched at Moscow.

Since the days of mail riders and stagecoaches, the Connecticut shore has been the most heavily traveled section of the Atlantic Coast. It was early settled and early industrialized. Remarkably, one place, that has escaped the pressures of development is the mouth of the Connecticut River. In its 380-mile course from northern New Hampshire to Long Island Sound, New England's greatest river flows past a dozen industrial towns and cities. In earlier times, before the age of trucks, it was a major artery of commerce. But marshy banks and a sandbar at the river's mouth kept factory builders away from the lower basin. Therefore, the Connecticut, uniquely among the major navigable rivers of the U.S. East Coast, has no city at its mouth. Instead, it has miles of wooded banks and the pretty, expensive little towns of Essex and Old Lyme.

The best way to see the waters and shores of the river basin is to take the excursion train of the Valley Railroad, a line whose guiding spirit is my old friend Oliver Jensen, the former editor of *American Heritage* magazine. The train carries passengers in old-fashioned cars behind a steam locomotive along the western shore from Essex to a landing at Deep River, where passengers may transfer to a riverboat for a cruise around the basin.

In the century between the peak of the whaling enterprise and the coming of the nuclear age, the most splendid ships to ply the Sound were the paddle steamers that ran between New York and the major ports along the southern coast of New England. Passengers found them much more comfortable than the jouncing stagecoaches or even the rattling railroad cars. The moguls of the time, from Commodore Vanderbilt to Jim Fisk to J. P. Morgan, invested money to make their staterooms and dining saloons ever more luxurious. In those days before the Cape Cod Canal was dug, they ended their runs at Providence or Fall River. Passengers could board the steamer at New York, enjoy a fine dinner and a good night's sleep, and then, the next morning, transfer to the railroad for the short run to Boston. Older residents of the Connecticut shore remember the great steamers ablaze with light passing quietly through the night, sweeping the water and the shore with searchlights.

The last survivor among the lines was the Eastern Steamship Company, whose ships made the full run from New York to Boston through the Cape Cod Canal. As late as the 1930s, an uncle of mine would not make the trip from Boston by any other mode of transportation. By then, the splendid public rooms were gray and dim. The table settings were pieced out with plates and knives from the Fall River Line, the Old Colony Line, and other lines already gone. Beset by rising costs, government regulation, and labor troubles, the last Sound steamers made their final runs in 1941.

The Sound is a friendly inland sea for boats of all sorts and sizes. Except for a few commercial fishing vessels, tankers, freighters, barges, and ferries, the owners of the boats are afloat for the fun of it. Seen from the air on a summer weekend, especially at the western end, the surface is sprinkled with sails— and sailboats are only a small proportion of all the boats afloat. It is not hard to believe that there are more boats on Long Island Sound than on any other body of water of comparable size anywhere in the world.

There is hardly room to moor them on the shore. Fortunately, the Connecticut coast is broken by many inlets, bays, and mouths of rivers. And almost every one of these safe harbors is chockablock with watercraft. In the old days you might moor a boat to a buoy and let it swing free. Now most of the boats are crowded side by side at finger piers.

At some places, you can buy, for $50,000 or so, a "dockominium," in which you can keep your boat forever or at least for ninety-nine years. What you get is a rectangle of water beside a dock, with services such as gasoline and ice (which, of course, you pay for). The old definition of a boat as a hole in the water into which you pour money becomes no longer a wry joke but a statement of fact.

I stopped at Westbrook to find out why that small community, many miles removed from any large city, had more boats than any other Connecticut harbor except Stamford. "I would even challenge that," said Len Mierzejewski, the harbormaster. "I think we have more." The reason is that Westbrook, situated at the confluence of two small rivers, has plenty of mooring space. Basins dredged out of the marshes accommodate twelve hundred boats, more of them sailboats than motorboats. Besides that, hundreds of visiting boats drop anchor offshore in Duck Island Roads.

Mierzejewski has only kind words for the boaters at Westbrook, possibly because so many of them are sailors. "They're much more careful about the environment than they used to be," he says. "You don't see so much plastic junk floating ashore these days."

At other harbors, farther down the Sound, where motorboaters may outnumber sailors ten to one, harbormasters and marine police officers are not so complimentary. Some of their thoughts:

"A lot of those birds don't know the difference between a red buoy and a black one."

"The only chart they have is one they picked up in a seafood restaurant."

"Some of those cowboys think they're on the Connecticut Turnpike."

"They don't think there are laws against drunk driving in boats."

The seagoing cowboys in their overpowered speedboats have spoiled things for responsible skippers, young and old, who like the traditional freedom of boating as an escape from rule-bound life ashore. The prospect is that Connecticut will be the first state to require examinations and licenses for motorboaters.

The farther west one goes on the Connecticut shore, the harder it is to find a mooring. Beyond Bridgeport, in the New York City commuting country, moorings become family treasures. A boat owner guards a mooring as he would his aisle seats at Lincoln Center or his place on the fifty-yard line at the Yale Bowl. Moorings are handed down from father to son or allocated in divorce settlements, along with the house and the children.

At the outer edge of the commuting area is Southport, a village of fine old houses, old trees, and old money. When I got there, I found that the residents were being unamused by Don Imus, the obnoxious talk-show host of New York's station WFAN. Imus, having bought a house on the water, was demanding admission to the well-bred Pequot Yacht Club. When that proposal was met with stiff silence, he announced to his radio audience that he was going to stand on his terrace and shoot one sailboater a day until he was admitted. For the moment, there seemed to be a standoff. Imus had not opened fire and the yacht club skippers had not armed their Thistles.

Imus was going about it the wrong way. His wife, if any, should put in a few years of volunteer work for the right local charities, say the Women's Exchange and the Near and Far Aid Society. Their children, if any, should be sent to the right schools, say Fairfield Country Day and St. Paul's. Then, if they showed real interest and some proficiency in sailing, they might make it into the yacht club. Meanwhile, Imus could apply for a town mooring in the little harbor. But that, too, would take time. According to the president of the Sasquanaug Association for Southport Improvement, the wait is about twenty years.

The Connecticut shore has no great sandy beaches to compare with those on Cape Cod or Long Island. In many places, when the tide goes out, it leaves only flats of gray, muddy sand. In the life of those who live on the shore, the tide is a major factor. As it flows back over the flats, it raises boats, docks, and people's spirits. High tide is the time for swimming, diving from docks or floats, waterskiing, and inshore boating. It is the time for picnics, parties, and clambakes. At high tide, the shore comes to life.

The ocean waters that pour through the Race twice a day are constricted as they pass down the Sound, causing the normal rise of tide, which is three and a half feet at Stonington, to be seven feet at Stamford. Great storms increase the surge dramatically, as I found out one August day years ago when a hurricane was coming up the Atlantic Coast. Having heard that the eye would pass far to the east of our house on the shore at Westport, I was about to leave for work when I noticed that the water was three or four feet above its normal high mark. Then I realized that high tide was still three hours off. I stayed home and we moved whatever we could to the second floor. In an uncanny calm, under bright sun, the sea rose over the seawall, over the lawn and terrace, and stopped just short of the first floor. My sons dived off the seawall and canoed down the road.

The greatest threats to the well-being of those who live on that shore, I found, come not from nature but from the schemes of men. Our house stood on a spit of land between the Sound and a salt marsh. Adjoining it was a promontory with a beach on the far side. Some years before I lived there, a developer had bought the point and was all set to cut it up into tiny house lots. The town stopped him, however, and the point became a public park with a beach and boat basin.

Another threat came from the Army Corps of Engineers. After one of the hurricanes, Congress appropriated money to protect the coastal sections from future damage. One of the criteria, sensibly enough, was that the value of the area to be protected should be greater than the cost of protection. Not too many places on the East Coast met that test, but one that did was the Compo Beach area through which we drove to reach our road. The Engineers proposed to build a twelve-foot-high wall around that area. A gate in the wall would allow access to our road, but on the approach of a storm the gate would be closed, leaving us on the outside. Fortunately, the residents of Compo Beach had no more enthusiasm for living behind a twelve-foot wall than we did for being left outside it. Although the town would have had to pay only 10 percent of the cost, the plan was turned down. Twice more, the Engineers came back with revised plans, and twice more they were turned down.

Meanwhile, someone in the state government at Hartford floated a scheme to tear down all the houses on our road and add our land to the public park. The suggestion was that this could be accomplished at reasonable cost after the next hurricane had inflicted severe damage on the houses. As it happened, no such hurricane struck.

The next threat came from the United Illuminating Company, which proposed to build a nuclear power plant on Cockenoe Island, directly offshore from us. It would, they said, be a "low-rise" installation. Under questioning, *low-rise* turned out to mean eighteen stories tall. The town rose up to defeat it.

Our spit of land was saved from all those threats, but the marsh behind it was not. Suddenly and quietly the town itself filled in half of the marsh to extend two fairways of the municipal golf course. The town fathers were working against a deadline. Soon after the taking of the marsh, a stringent new state law prohibiting the destruction of any wetland was passed.

Connecticut's wetlands have suffered severely from the

heavy development of the shore. When the New Haven Railroad was built in the 1880s, the builders drove straight across miles of salt marsh, sometimes filling them, sometimes shutting them off by embankments, with or without channels to the Sound. Other stretches of marshy "wasteland" were filled in to make dry land for factories or for other commercial use. Not until the second half of this century did lawmakers get the message from marine biologists that salt marshes are the nursery of marine life, a basic resource of the fishery, and a vital support to the health of the Sound. Now it is illegal to pull up so much as a clump of sea grass, but half the possible damage has been done. A landform map of the Connecticut shore shows more miles of "artificial fill" than it does of marshes.

The loss of the wetlands is only one of the insults inflicted on the Sound and its tributary rivers during the last two centuries. The rivers were turned into drainage ditches for the sewage of growing cities and the waste of industrial plants, including toxic chemicals and metals. In the age of intense industrialization, most people would probably have agreed with the senator who, in opposing the Clean Water Act, assured Congress, "That's what God made rivers for."

In recent times, I have been told that "the Sound is dead" (this from a former Connecticut sailor now retired to Florida). On the other hand, I know that salmon are back in the Connecticut River and that squeamish bathers still shrink from creepy, crawly things in the eelgrass.

For the truth about the subject, I sought out Terry Backer, who bears the title of Soundkeeper. The terminology derives from England, where the royal Swankeeper is an officer of the Crown, charged with looking after the Queen's swans on the river Thames, but Backer owes his appointment to the Connecticut Council of Fishermen. A third-generation fisherman himself, Backer was president of that organization when it sued the city of Norwalk for failing to control the discharges of sewage into the Sound. The fishermen won an award of $170,000, which they used to establish the institution of the Soundkeeper.

Backer runs his patrol from his office on the second floor of an old oyster house on the East Norwalk waterfront. Using three boats and mostly volunteer help, he polices the entire Sound, looking for signs of pollution from sewers, dumps, factories, marinas, and ships at sea. With his bushy red beard and boundless energy, he is a figure to be reckoned with at town hearings and legislative meetings.

"I fight them all the time," he says, speaking of industrial polluters and especially developers. "They accuse me of corruption and political ambition, but I don't let them escape. You've just got to grab them."

The threat to the Sound is hypoxia—the lack of enough oxygen to support animal life. The influx of sewage stimulates riotous growth of algae that exhaust the oxygen supply in the water and make it a desert for fish. Hypoxia is an especially serious threat in the western end of the Sound where the north and south shores close in.

To show me that the Sound is not dead, and, in fact, is clean enough for the cultivation of shellfish, Backer took me next door to the Tallmadge Brothers oyster plant. Baby oysters are started on the banks of tidal rivers or in marshes, where the water is less salty. Ten months later, when they are about the size of a dime, they are transferred to beds in the open Sound, where they grow for three more years before they are harvested. The waters where they grow and the oysters themselves have to pass the purity tests of state inspectors before they are shipped to markets all over the country.

Norman Tallmadge likes to point out that while aquaculture may be a new thing in the fin fishery, it has been practiced in the oyster business since the seventeenth century. Oystermen have long known that there are certain areas on the bottom of the Sound where, for whatever mysterious reasons, oysters acquire the maximum succulence. The bottom is owned by the state and is franchised in sections to oyster growers. Tallmadge showed me a map of the leases, which looked for all the world like a diagram of mining claims in the old West.

Back in his office, Terry Backer gave me a balance sheet on the Sound: The rivers are a lot cleaner than they used to be; cities and towns are not dumping raw sewage into the water anymore. That's the good news. But other sources of pollution are harder to control. There is leakage from dumps and old factory sites. There is runoff from streets and parking lots, and pesticides from farms and lawns. There is leakage from cesspools and failed septic systems along the shore. There is acid rain from motor cars and smokestacks. There are discharges from boats and occasionally from oil tankers.

"We're working on all those things," he said, "but it's a constant fight. Don't forget, one out of every ten Americans lives in the watershed of the Sound."

His final word: "We are just about holding our own."

LONG ISLAND

ONE of the ironies of history is that cultures build their greatest monuments when they have already passed their peaks. New York's monuments are its skyscrapers, and the tallest of them are the twin towers of the World Trade Center in lower Manhattan.

During the years when I worked in New York, I never got around to visiting the twin towers. When I did so, for the purposes of this book, I found myself in a room-sized elevator, surrounded by numbers of American tourists and larger numbers of foreigners, both Asian and European. On the observation deck of the east tower, they moved from telescope to telescope, picking out the sights of the hemisphere's greatest harbor. Within our range of vision, I counted twenty-five vessels in motion: three or four freighters, a couple of barges with tugs, several sailboats, the Staten Island ferry, and a little commuter ferry from New Jersey, and others not so easy to identify. The harbor looked beautiful, exciting, and, from the height of 107 floors, clean. One thing it did not look was busy.

On the south-facing side of the deck, I noticed a dumpy little man sitting on a bench by himself, transfixed by the view. Perhaps, I thought, another Gibbon, brooding upon the history of the great port as the historian, sitting amid the ruins of the Capitol in Rome, brooded upon the decline and fall of the Roman Empire.

I followed his gaze down the Upper Bay to The Narrows, the channel between Brooklyn and Staten Island. That is where, almost five centuries ago, the first European explorer laid eyes on New York harbor. Giovanni da Verrazano, an Italian captain in the service of France, having come into shoal water, dropped anchor and went on for a ways by small boat, with an escort of Indians in canoes. The Indians were friendly and the harbor, he reported to François I, was "commodious and delightful." If he were anchored in the same place today, he would be able to look up and see above him the graceful span of the Verrazano Bridge.

Manhattan was still a green, forested island, almost another century later, when Henry Hudson, an Englishman serving the Dutch East India Company, got safely through The Narrows and sailed on up the river that bears his name. He was sorry to report to the States General that he had not found a passage to the Orient, but he suggested that the tip of Manhattan Island would be a good place to found a colony.

New Amsterdam was built just east of the spot where the twin towers now stand. When a British fleet arrived fifty years later to take it away from the Dutch, it found a snug little city of seven thousand occupying the tip of the island between the Battery and a wall built to keep out the Indians, at what is now Wall Street. Renamed New York, the city grew to three or four times that size, but on the eve of the Revolution it had still not caught up with Philadelphia. An artist's view of Brooklyn in 1776 shows grassy fields in the foreground and, across the East River, a skyline dominated by church steeples.

During the Revolution, the British fleet occupied New York harbor, but it did not quite go unchallenged. From the top of the east tower I was looking down—or so I fancied—at the spot where, on a summer night in 1776, a curious contraption called the American Turtle, elliptical in shape and built of oak stave with iron bands, was submerged in the bay. The plan of its inventor, David Bushnell, was to fasten an explosive charge to the hull of Admiral Howe's flagship, the *Eagle*, and blow it up. A volunteer sergeant named Ezra Lee, using a system of paddles and rudder, maneuvered the Turtle into position under the ship but then could not bore through iron plates to fasten the mine. With dawn approaching, he jettisoned the charge, which exploded harmlessly in the bay. Though the British did not even know what had happened, a small milestone in naval history had been passed. It was the beginning of the age of submarine warfare.

In the half century that followed the Revolution, New York came into its own as the premier port of the New World. Lithographs of the city—admittedly sometimes embellished—show a continuous fringe of piers along both sides of Manhattan and the facing shore of Long Island, with hundreds of vessels at dock and scores more at sea. A handful of those sailing ships can still be seen at the South Street Seaport restoration on the East River.

From the west side of the east tower, one can trace the route of Robert Fulton's *Clermont* as it moved from New Jersey up the Hudson River in 1807 to open the age of steam. The south side of the tower looks out over the Statue of Liberty and Ellis Island, where in later years the transatlantic steamers, growing ever larger as the century passed, delivered their millions of immigrants.

Through most of its history, Manhattan remained a city of relatively low-rise buildings. It was late in the nineteenth century when Finance, the child of Trade, erected on the tip of the island one of the world's great sights, the New York skyline. From the tower you can look down and see all those skyscrapers below you. Then you can look north and see, halfway up the island, a second cluster of towers. Those midtown skyscrapers betoken a change in the orientation of the city. The industries they serve were not drawn to New York because it was a great port but because it had become, in Walt Whitman's words, "the great place of the western continent, the heart, the brain, the focus, the mainspring, the pinnacle, the extremity, the no-more-beyond of the New World." The waterfront was no longer the focus of the city's life.

The port's time of glory lasted through the first third of this century. That was the heyday of the transatlantic liners and especially the classic Cunarders—the *Berengaria*, the *Lusitania*, the *Mauretania*. For the leaders of American society, it was almost as important to sit at the captain's table on the way over as it was to have their daughters presented at court when they got to London.

The largest of the liners were yet to come off the ways—the *Queen Elizabeth*, the *Queen Mary*, the *Normandie*—seaborne palaces so grand and seemingly so independent of their natural element that Beatrice Lillie was moved to inquire, "Captain, when does this place get there?" But a cloud had appeared in the sky above the harbor—a cloud no bigger than Charles Lindbergh's plane—and the days of the liners were numbered. By the middle of the century, the celebrities and the immigrants alike were coming by air and looking down, not up, at the Statue of Liberty. From the western side of the east tower, you can see the long, empty docks on the North (Hudson) River where the liners used to tie up side by side.

Looking farther west, across the Hudson, you can see what happened to most of the commercial traffic that used to arrive at docks on the waterfronts of Manhattan and Brooklyn. Those broad, flat areas on the Jersey side of the harbor reflect the revolution in shipping that took place after World War II. Before that, ships arrived with mixed cargoes in all shapes and sizes, to be unloaded on the docks by gangs of stevedores. Now, most goods come in huge containers of uniform size. The system is much more efficient and much less labor-intensive, but the container ships require big staging areas. Because the crowded shores of Manhattan and Brooklyn afforded no such space, the Port Authority built the terminal of Port Newark on the Jersey shore. On the New York shore, most of the docks are torn down or derelict, and the once mighty Longshoremen's Union is reduced to a tenth its former size.

Before I left the World Trade Center, I called at the offices of the Port Authority to ask what moved in and out of New York by sea these days. The Port Authority divides its statistics into two categories: bulk cargo (things such as oil, ores, and grain) and general cargo (all the rest). In the category of bulk cargo, the largest item, measured by tons, is scrap metal, being shipped to steel mills in Japan and Europe. In that of general cargo, the largest item is wastepaper, to be recycled in Taiwan and other Asian countries. The reason these low-value exports lead the list is that New York imports twice as much, measured by value, as it exports. If it was not for scrap metal and wastepaper, many of the freighters would go out half-empty. Weep for the American balance of trade.

On the following day, as I drove up along the East River, headed for Long Island, I wondered what was under that turbulent waterway. Probably an archaeologist's treasure trove of artifacts dating from American, English, Dutch, even Indian times— times when people routinely threw their junk in the rivers. Certainly there are many sunken ships on the bottom. An acquaintance of mine was part of a diving party that attempted to salvage one of them. Before the divers went down into the murky water, a police inspector asked them to report any bodies they found. They did not find any, perhaps because they were not in the right spot. The gangland service business known as Murder, Inc., used to dump its victims in the river near the end of Atlantic Avenue. Most of the skeletons have probably been carried away by the currents or buried deep in muck, but there might be a chance of finding one of those celebrated mobsters whose feet were encased in cement to keep them down. Divers might also keep an eye out for the boatloads of slot machines that Mayor La Guardia dumped in the river during his crusade against "one-armed bandits."

"Fish-tailed Paumanok" is what Whitman, using its Indian name, called Long Island. When you cross the East River to Brooklyn or Queens, you are in the head of the fish. One hundred and twenty miles east, the two flukes of its tail end at Montauk and Orient Point. Whether you follow the northern shore, along Long Island Sound, or the southern shore, along the ocean, you will be traveling on routes put in place by New York's great builder of parks and parkways, Robert Moses.

When Moses began his work in the 1920s, New York met Samuel Johnson's description of a much smaller London as "the Great Wen." The huddled masses—poor and middle-income alike—needed someplace to get away from the crowded city, especially in the summer. The best they had was Coney Island, which was just as crowded, at the end of the subway line. Eastward of the city limits, Long Island had plenty of open space for parks and beaches, but no good roads led to them. When Moses was appointed Long Island State Park Commissioner by Governor Al Smith, he decided that his first job was to build new parkways, no matter what stood in the way.

What stood in the way of Moses's proposed route for a Northern State Parkway was *Gatsby* country. A list of the landowners in its path read like a directory of America's Greatest Fortunes: Vanderbilt, Phipps, Grace, Harkness, Ryan, Whitney, Otto Kahn, and so on. In defense of their estates, the owners mustered the best lawyers and legislators that money could buy. With ruthless energy and with guile bordering on deceit, Moses fought them in the courts and the legislature. In the end, he got his road, though with twists and turns and one long dip to skirt some of the estates.

On the south shore, as well, Moses had to contend with wealthy landowners. In his biography of Moses, *The Power Broker*, Robert Caro describes a meeting at which some of them appealed to the governor. Al Smith seemed to be giving them a sympathetic ear until one of them explained that he did not want "rabble" overrunning his town. "Rabble?" said Smith. "That's me," and he renewed his support for the parkways.

Moses's efforts were crowned with success in 1929 when he was able to open Jones Beach, on the ocean just forty miles from Times Square. It was everything that Coney Island was not— easy to reach by car, handsomely designed and landscaped, free of carnival rides, scrupulously clean, with acres of parking and miles of beach. City planners acclaimed it as the best beach development in the world.

Long Island is so big that it has its own barrier islands and spits, extending all the way from New York City to the Hamptons and enclosing a string of bays. Even before he had established Jones Beach on one of those islands, Moses had set his sights on the next coastal strip, Fire Island. Forty miles long and nowhere more than half a mile wide, Fire Island had a string of small summer colonies, reached by several separate ferries that ran from the mainland across Great South Bay. Moses's idea was to build a four-lane highway along the island from end to end, connecting by causeways to the mainland. From most of the residents, the answer was a swift No. They did not want to be overrun by outsiders and, for that matter, they did not particularly want to see any more of each other. Some of the colonies were family resorts, some of them catered to swinging singles who rented group houses, and some had acquired a reputation as gay beaches. They liked their differences.

In those years, the prodigious Moses was taking on other challenges—upstate dams and parks, city housing, and two World Fairs. He backed off from the island highway, and presently another player entered the game. In 1954, the National Park Service singled out Fire Island as one of the last available sites on the Atlantic Coast for a National Seashore. The summer colonies, happy to be delivered from Moses, struck a deal whereby the Park Service promised that it would not build a highway and would not interfere with the colonies' chosen lifestyles.

For visitors, the National Seashore is a string of separate segments, connected only by the ocean beach. At the western end, they can drive across a causeway through Robert Moses State Park to the Fire Island Lighthouse. At the eastern end, they can cross another causeway to a seven-mile wilderness area. For any of the beaches in between, they must park on the mainland and make a day's outing by ferry.

To Park Superintendent Jack Hauptman, the public and private parts of the Seashore are a single island with common problems. Like other barrier islands, it is slowly retreating landward, rolling over on itself. Also, there is a longshore current that moves sand steadily westward, building up the western end of the island but narrowing the eastern. Over the years, cottages built on the dunes have been undermined and washed away. A few months before I talked to Hauptman, a one-two punch by northeast storms had demolished half a dozen cottages and damaged others.

Such storms give the Seashore an opportunity to get rid of houses that should never have been built so close to the water. Superintendent Hauptman may then approach the owner of a damaged house with an offer to buy the land and remove the building. Usually, the owner is reluctant to sell. "But sooner or later," says Hauptman, "if he sees other houses destroyed or left standing in the water, he will give up the idea of rebuilding. It's a game of chicken we play with them. If they don't accept a buy-out, they may lose the chance."

Often, there is room for argument about the extent of the damage or the likelihood of destruction by future storms. "One owner," Hauptman says, "called me after his house was hit, hoping to get my support for rebuilding. He told me how many years he had been there, what a big, wide beach he used to have, what beautiful roses used to grow in front of the house. Everything he told me was a reason why he should not rebuild."

In the long run, Hauptman would like to see all houses removed from the open beach. His idea is that residents should give up the idea of individual ownership and swap it for what he calls "development rights." That means that they would rebuild in clusters on the back side of the island and leave the dunes to nature.

East of Fire Island, just across Moriches Inlet, the ocean barrier is continued by the narrow spit of Westhampton Beach. There, I found, when I drove back west along Dune Road, the recent storms had done their worst. The road ended abruptly at a barrier flanked by signs warning that parked cars would be towed and trespassers prosecuted. Walking on, I saw that beyond that point the sand had been washed out from under the cottages, leaving them standing or teetering on stilts, with sewer pipes dangling and at least one septic tank open to the air. The constable who presently drove up to arrest me (but relented when he satisfied himself that I was not a looter) said that the storms had washed out Dune Road from there to the inlet. After storms in other years, the road had been rebuilt three times, with federal, state, and local funds. Enough was enough. Even if some of the cottages could be restored, they would be reachable only over the sand.

The eastern end of Long Island, beyond the town of Riverhead, is split into two forks, enclosing Peconic Bay. To this day, the North Fork is a rural landscape with broad fields that still grow potatoes, while many on the South Fork now bear a permanent crop of houses. On the South Fork, history began long before the coming of the Long Island Railroad and the state highways. In the eighteenth century, Sag Harbor was a whaling port that held its own with Nantucket. Southampton and East

Hampton got their starts as fashionable summer resorts at a time when the quality came by steamer. Sag Harbor still looks like a small town, although many of the fishermen's houses have been bought, at steadily escalating prices, by writers, artists, and other part-time or full-time refugees from the city. East Hampton's handsome village center still breasts the torrent of summer traffic, protected and cherished—"ferociously," I was told—by the Ladies Village Improvement Society.

From the Hamptons east to Montauk, the mainland faces the open ocean. It is too late to regret that the superb beach, unmatched on the northeast shore except on Cape Cod, was not saved to become a National Seashore. Instead, it has become a display case for modern coastal architecture, the best as well as the worst. Some of the showiest houses, all concrete and glass, look more like industrial laboratories than inviting summer retreats. The best of them, notably including those designed by Robert A. M. Stern, are modern counterparts of the great shore-hugging, ocean-facing Shingle Style houses of the last century.

The affluent towns of the South Fork have shown a tendency in recent years to close their beaches to all but residents. As something of an offset, the fork is well endowed with state parks, including all of Montauk Point, and with tracts protected by nature conservancies or land trusts. Constant vigilance is the price of conservation. During my visit, I found that local environmentalists were alarmed by a report that the U.S. Fish and Wildlife Service was thinking of selling its Morton National Wildlife Refuge. Given by a private owner in 1954, the refuge consists of a sliver of wooded land, a connecting tombolo of sand, and a neck that stretches two miles into Peconic Bay. Now, it seemed, some auditors in the Department of the Interior, parent of the Wildlife Service, had decided that the refuge was "underutilized" and recommended that it be, as they say in the art world, deaccessioned.

A young friend of mine who visits it regularly assured me that the refuge was utilized not only by great flocks of migratory birds, including such threatened species as terns and piping plovers, but by hikers, birders, swimmers, and boaters. Another friend insisted on taking me there to see how the chickadees would perch on our hands to take seeds. By the time I left the South Fork, some of the environmentalists were hoping that the idea of selling the Morton refuge was only a trial balloon, possibly launched by number-crunchers left over from the James Watt regime in the Interior Department. At a time of steadily increasing pressures on the coast, it seemed pretty late in the game to surrender any of the wild areas that remain, whether they be used by birds or people or both.

In Whitman's image of Long Island as a great fish, the head of the fish nuzzles Manhattan, the most heavily populated island on the coast. The flukes of its tail embrace Gardiners Island, the most lightly populated island of any size on the coast. Indeed, during the winter, except for a caretaker, Gardiners Island is not populated at all.

The island gets its name from Lion Gardiner, an English military engineer who was sent to America in 1635 to build a fort at the mouth of the Connecticut River. As a reward for good work, he got a royal grant to the island, which at that time was a summering place for the Montauk Indians. Prudently, he had nailed down his title by also buying the island from Wyandance, the Montauk chief, paying "ten coats of trading cloath," one large black dog, a gun and ammunition, and some rum. The two became lifelong friends.

After Lion Gardiner died, the "Lordshipp and Mannoir" passed to his son, David, who left it to "John, my son, and his eldest heir, male, to the end of time." Like the Dutch patroons on the Hudson River, the Gardiners were feudal lords. Unlike them, they managed to hold on to their domain.

Following the example that the family founder had set with the Indians, the later Gardiners kept good relations with whatever powers there were on land or sea. In the years before the Revolution, that sometimes meant the pirates who found haven on the island. In 1699, Capt. William Kidd buried several chestfuls of treasure there. (It is the only treasure of his that has ever been found, despite searches all along the Atlantic Coast.) After Kidd was taken into custody, the third lord surrendered the treasure to the British Colonial governor in Boston—most of it, anyway. According to family legend, one diamond rolled across the floor and Mrs. Gardiner grabbed it, saying that it was no more than her due after all the trouble the treasure had given them. During the Revolution, the family kept a foot in both camps, Abraham Gardiner dining as a guest on the British warship *Royal Oak,* which anchored off the island, while his son Nathaniel joined the Continental army.

The sixteenth "lord of the manor," as he likes to call himself, is Robert David Lion Gardiner. The laws of entail having long since been breached, he shares ownership of the island with his niece, Alexandra Goëlet, but does not share it gladly. He accuses his niece of plotting to build development houses, and her husband of trying to run him down with a truck. The feud became so bitter that a judge ordered them to use the manor house at different times. Most recently, Bobby Gardiner, hale but childless at eighty-two, has talked of adopting a distant cousin as his son and heir to keep his niece from inheriting all of the manor.

Meanwhile, the ospreys make their own claim. Flying in each spring from winter ranges in Florida, the Caribbean, and Brazil, they reclaim or rebuild their huge stick nests in the tallest trees. On a summer day, while smaller birds scatter, they hover over the bay, then plunge, feet first, to fasten their talons into passing fish. Twenty years ago, the ospreys were almost wiped out because the fish they ate had been poisoned by DDT. Now they are back, in greater numbers here than anywhere else on the coast. No one doubts that the ospreys are the natural lords of Gardiners Island.

THE JERSEY SHORE

THE reason so many people have such a bad image of New Jersey, I suspect, is that the part they remember is the part they see from the northern stretch of the New Jersey Turnpike. It is a seemingly endless, lifeless nether world of oil tanks and refineries, the terminus of the sea-lanes that stretch from foreign oil fields to New York harbor. It does not smell as bad as it used to, but it mocks the license plates that proclaim THE GARDEN STATE.

Travelers from the north can get a much better impression of New Jersey by crossing the Hudson on the Tappan Zee Bridge and taking the Garden State Parkway. That was the route I took after I returned from Long Island and started south again. At Perth Amboy, I turned onto the coast road, which curves around to Sandy Hook, at the northern end of the Jersey shore.

Sandy Hook is a thumb of land thrusting up into New

111

York's Lower Bay. Sometimes it has been an island and it might be an island now if sand was not regularly dumped at its base to keep it tied to the mainland. Near the tip of the Hook is a lighthouse familiar to mariners approaching New York from the sea, and Fort Hancock, built long ago to protect the harbor from enemy warships. The warships never came, and the Hook is now a National Recreation Area with a fine six-mile beach, convenient to great centers of population and therefore crowded on good summer weekends. Because it is close to the floating waste of New York harbor, some people think twice about going into the water. I was reassured, however, by the park ranger that while the beach may be littered with plastic junk, it hardly ever has to be closed because of the water quality.

Before starting south from Sandy Hook, the traveler should take a good look at the ocean, because she will not see it again for several miles. Between the road and the ocean, in the town of Sea Bright, there rises a solid wall of rock and concrete. Behind it are rows of houses that have no view of the water, no easy way to get to it, and no beach if you do get there.

The first seawalls and groins on this stretch of the coast were built early in this century to stabilize the shore and protect the road and houses from being overrun by the sea during storms. The remains of those early structures can still be seen in places at low tide, well seaward of the present wall. Over the years, the wall has been rebuilt higher and wider until Sea Bright and its neighbor, Monmouth Beach, must be the most thoroughly fortified towns on the Atlantic Coast. At Monmouth Beach, I walked along one massive section that rose about ten feet high on the land side and dropped about eighteen feet on the ocean side, with enough room on top for a small marching band. Extending for eight hundred feet or so, it protects just seven houses. Their backyards, abutting the wall, do not look as if anyone would want to spend time in them.

Once committed to such a program to hold back the ocean, can you ever stop? At Sandy Hook, I put that question to Dery Bennett, executive director of the American Littoral Society, which is devoted to the well-being of the coast. "It will go on forever," he said, "and get more expensive all the time."

And where does the money come from? Certainly not in any great amount from the little towns on the shore. Some of it comes from the state of New Jersey but most from the federal government. For many years, the north Jersey shore had a powerful patron in Congress: James Howard, chairman of the House Committee on Public Works. The latest bill for rebuilding the seawall was $60 million.

For marine geologists, the Jersey wall is a prize example of the folly of trying to stabilize a naturally unstable beach. Left to itself, a barrier beach will slowly retreat toward the mainland, maintaining its shape but not its position. If you block the ocean with a wall, the waves will sweep the sand aside and attack the wall itself, gradually undermining it and breaking it apart.

The U.S. Army Corps of Engineers, which built many of the walls along the coast, has come to recognize the facts of nature and now seeks to maintain beaches by periodically pumping sand onto them. That makes more ecological sense, but it costs a lot of money. For one thing, there is not much use in replenishing a small section of beach, because the new sand washes away at both ends, as well as out to sea.

"They've gotten a little smarter now," Bennett says of the Engineers. "They understand that you can't just treat Sea Bright. You've got to treat the whole system. So they're going to do everything north of the Shark River Inlet, fifteen miles or so. They're going to spend a quarter of a billion dollars."

And what will happen to all that sand? "The beaches will go away in an awful hurry," Bennett predicts, "and we'll be back to a bare wall."

The most impressive wall I had ever seen before this one was the one that the Emperor Hadrian built across the North of England in the second century to keep out the wild Scottish tribesmen. The Great Wall of Jersey, while not as long, is just about as high and massive. The Scots never did attack Hadrian's Wall, but when the Romans withdrew from their British province the tribesmen came on through. In some distant time, when Americans tire of fighting nature, perhaps the sea will do the same thing in New Jersey.

The problems of the Jersey shore arise in large measure from the fact that it was built up so early. Long before much was understood about the effects of waves and storms on a sandy coast, Sea Bright and Monmouth Beach were laid out by developers who moved in right after the Civil War, dividing the land into lots and giving buyers deeds that now carry private-property lines up and over the seawall. At that time, Long Branch, just to the south, was already a well-established resort. The first boardinghouse was opened there in 1788, catering to Philadelphians who came by horse and carriage. During the Gilded Age, a railroad brought Society—Astors and Goulds from New York, Drexels and Biddles from Philadelphia. High rollers such as Diamond Jim Brady and Lillian Russell dazzled the gambling casinos. Long Branch seems to have been especially attractive to Presidents, beginning with Grant, who summered there during his White House years. He was followed by Garfield, Arthur, Hayes, Harrison, McKinley, and, finally, Wilson.

St. James Episcopal Church, which most of them attended, is now a museum known as The Church of the Presidents. Its paint is peeling, its shingles falling off in great patches, some of its windows broken. I had arranged to meet Edgar N. Dinkelspiel, president of the local historical association, who has had the thankless job of trying to keep it up. He was looking extremely crestfallen, and with good reason. "This is the second time the burglars have been in," he said, pointing to broken display cases. "This time, they got our portrait of President Grant."

I asked him why the church was in such bad shape.

"The old people have died off," he said. "Their children have moved away or don't care."

The fate of the church is a fair sample of what has happened to Long Branch. With the coming of the automobile, the resort's closeness to New York was no longer an asset. The prosperity that the railroad had brought, the Garden State Parkway took away. Vacationers passed it by, in favor of resorts farther south, and the town began its long, slow decline.

From the center of Long Branch, the coast road runs through the Elberon section, with its marble mansions once owned by Guggenheims, and through Deal, with substantial, well-kept houses that have a turn-of-the-century look. But then it runs into Asbury Park. If Long Branch represents the decline of the north Jersey shore, Asbury Park represents its fall.

Asbury Park was founded as a Methodist camp-meeting site but soon turned into an amusement center with a boardwalk, rides, and a convention pier. In the 1930s, it was famous for the big band concerts of Glenn Miller and Harry James; in the 1970s, it was celebrated in the rock-and-roll lyrics of its favorite son, Bruce Springsteen. But decay was already setting in when crime and race riots speeded it up.

On a beautiful June morning, I found the boardwalk all but deserted. Most of the shops were closed, the rides were stopped, the beach almost empty. The great Casino was derelict, the Convention Hall closed. In its vast forecourt, a sign read NO BICYCLE RIDING—NO SKATEBOARDS—NO ROLLER SKATES—NO ALCOHOLIC BEVERAGES. There were also no people. On the shopping side of the boardwalk, a young woman in a booth was selling beach badges for $2.50 apiece, while across the boardwalk a senior citizen was waiting to collect them. I thought it strange that the city should be charging a fee for going off the boardwalk onto the sand when almost no one, so far as I could see, wanted to go there. I asked a waitress in a restaurant what she thought of the policy. "It's dumb," she said succinctly.

Later, as I went along the coast, I discovered that almost all the towns that invite tourists charge a fee to go onto the beach. I could understand a fee for parking a car, but to exact an entrance fee to the sand seemed like charging a fee to walk on a sidewalk— worse, in fact, since the town paid for the sidewalk but nature made the beach.

Cross the town line, going south from Asbury Park, and you are back in another century. Ocean Grove, too, was founded as a site for a Methodist camp meeting and, unlike Asbury Park, that is exactly what it is today. The entire community, with its clean streets and Victorian houses, is owned by the Camp Meeting Association. Residents hold their houses on ninety-nine-year leases that may be renewed, as some of them have already been. The leases may also be sold, but, while the buyers need not be Methodists, they must be approved by the Association. Around the auditorium and village green, standing on permanent wooden platforms, are square canvas tents that are occupied by the same families each year and handed down from generation to generation.

Until 1979, Ocean Grove put up a chain on Sunday mornings to keep visitors out. It is down now because the New Jersey Supreme Court ruled it unconstitutional, but the beach and the boardwalk are still closed until after the church service.

Ocean Grovers, like *Mayflower* descendants, identify

themselves by generation. Jenny Balinsky, the pretty and helpful girl at the reception desk of the Camp Meeting office, told me that she was fifth generation. I asked her how Ocean Grove managed to stem the tide of liquor, drugs, crime, and general schlock on the north Jersey shore. It was getting harder, she said, especially since the state began releasing mental patients to roam the streets. I could understand why some of them would wander over from the boardwalk at Asbury Park to the neat parks and clean sidewalks of Ocean Grove.

From Bay Head, a string of barrier islands and spits runs along the coast, all the way to Cape May, enclosing Barnegat Bay and other bays and sounds. It is on these narrow barriers that the rush of development since World War II has hit hardest. Developers seemed bent on finding out how many houses they could fit onto a strip of land between the ocean and the bay. Ocean Beach, for one, is a huge checkerboard of cottages, each fronting a sandy street and each with just enough room for a parking space and a narrow strip of flowers or small shrubs.

Don Bean, who was sitting at the bar in the local restaurant, said that he had come down to the Barnegat peninsula after World War II to visit his wife's family and had fallen in love with the place, especially because of the great swordfishing. He was taken aback by the speed of development. "There was just a little stretch of sand and then you looked out and it was full of little houses. They'd put them up in a week."

These are not the dream cottages that you see in travel folders, but if you want to vacation on the crowded mid-Atlantic coast, within yards of a fine, wide beach, this is what you can get for a reasonable price. Better, some would say, than a condominium.

Fifty years ago, there were long stretches of open coast between the towns on the barrier islands. Now, they are mostly filled up, and visitors who want to spend a day at a beach instead of a boardwalk increasingly find themselves unwelcome. Many of the towns try to keep their beaches for residents only, discouraging outsiders by NO TRESPASSING signs, beach tags, and parking restrictions.

In New Jersey, as in most other coastal states, private property extends only to the mean high-water mark, and the state supreme court takes a wider view of the public-trust doctrine than do the high courts of Maine and Massachusetts. The court has ruled that the public must be provided with reasonable access to the shore in front of private property for the purposes of swimming, sunbathing, and general recreation. It has also recognized, without actually ruling, that the people's right to the foreshore is not effective, when the tide is up, unless they can move up onto the dry private beach. Furthermore, the towns cannot charge nonresidents excessive fees for parking or beach tags.

Just what those decisions mean in actual practice is still not entirely clear. Certainly the towns must open their beaches to all comers and must provide access to the foreshore in front of private houses. Whether they must also provide parking space, and in what quantity, is still a matter of local dispute.

One of the less accommodating towns is Mantoloking, which found its picture in *The New York Times* a few years ago because of a sign that read MANTOLOKING BEACH ASSOCIATION. MEMBERS ONLY. M.B.A. BADGE REQUIRED. The sign is gone now and the town issues badges at $2.50 per person. There are access paths over the dunes, but the shorefront they lead to is public only below the high-tide line. Parking spaces are exceedingly few and the parking limit is two hours. According to the borough clerk, who issues the badges, this is to make it possible for more cars to use the same space, but it hardly suits the convenience of a family that wants to spend a day at the beach.

A leaflet given to beachgoers, along with the badge, offers this curious advice: "The Mean High Water line is closer to the ocean than is generally realized. It is about where the swash of a *low tide* wave reaches." I asked Ross Pilling, the town Dune Inspector, for an explanation of this geographic phenomenon. He said, "It's like a bathtub. The water level is not where it is when you stir up the water. It's where it is when the water is absolutely still." I pondered that for a while but decided it did not matter much. Mantoloking's real protection from the summer hordes is that they cannot find a parking space.

At the end of the Barnegat peninsula is a ten-mile stretch of coast that has neither boardwalks nor NO TRESPASSING signs. This is Island Beach State Park, formerly known as the Phipps estate. Henry Phipps, who was Andrew Carnegie's partner in the steel business, built a mansion for himself and planned to sell off tracts of land to his wealthy friends. The stock-market crash of 1929 ended that dream, and eventually the property was bought by the state. It is now an unspoiled refuge for both birds and beachgoers. The park naturalist thinks everything turned out just right: "Thank God, I say, for the multimillionaires who saved the land, and thank God for the crash that made them sell it."

Birds flying south from there will pass over Long Beach Island, another barrier strip with half a dozen summer colonies, and very likely spend some time at the Brigantine wildlife refuge. This is the site of a program to bring back the peregrine falcon, one of the most endangered birds on the coast and also one of the deadliest attackers of small birds. There are still only a few of the falcons, but tasty little terns and plovers would do well to keep an eye out for them.

In passing Atlantic City, the birds have an advantage over people. They can keep their distance from the gaudy oceanfront and the shabby areas that lie behind it. For migrating birds, the boardwalk is unfriendly territory, staked out by year-round gulls that perch among the domes and minarets of Donald Trump's Taj Mahal casino and zoom down to grab scraps of food left by patrons of a hundred food stands. In its nineteenth-century heyday Atlantic City originated the boardwalk, the wheel since called Ferris, saltwater taffy, and, later on, the Miss America Pageant. Sixteen years ago, the city was rescued from apparently terminal decline by the legalization of gambling casinos.

The most splendid of them, the Taj Mahal, bears no discernible resemblance to the lovely marble mausoleum of that name in India. According to its architect, Frank Dumont, the structure derives from Rajput Indian palaces, Indo-Chinese temples, St. Basil's Cathedral on Red Square, and, most of all, from King George IV's Royal Pavilion at Brighton. On the morning when I was there, the bus people from New York were just arriving to fill up the vast floor of three thousand slot machines. I looked in vain for Telly Savalas, my image of a high roller. He may have been somewhere in back or upstairs among the roulette wheels and the baccarat tables, but I did not see him at the slots. I contributed five dollars' worth of quarters to the financial rehabilitation of Donald Trump and made my escape.

After lunch at the New Delhi Deli and an afternoon on the six-mile boardwalk, I checked in at a hotel even more garish than the Taj. On that Saturday evening, when the casino was thronged, the expanses of red carpet, the golden panels and crystal chandeliers looked merely tawdry. On Sunday morning, when the crowd was reduced to a hollow-eyed, grim-faced remnant, they were chilling.

Just south of Atlantic City, a sight not to be missed by any connoisseur of roadside Americana is Lucy, the Margate elephant. Standing six stories tall, with a wooden frame and a tin hide, Lucy was built in 1881 as a real estate promotion. By way of steps in one of her hind legs, visitors can climb up into Lucy and look out through her eyes at the ocean.

On the south coast of New Jersey, one can judge a resort by its boardwalk. The one at Ocean City is scrupulously clean, with some nice-looking shops (including, of all things, a bookstore) and, running down the middle of the boardwalk, a close-order file of trash cans calculated to intimidate the most hardened litterer. There are lots of young families and no bars, for Ocean City is dry.

Wildwood's two-mile boardwalk, on the other hand, is all that its brochure promises: "Glittery lights . . . fresh salt air . . . one hundred dazzling rides . . . bumper cars . . . wet slides . . . non-stop fun." Wildwood is for teenagers and immediate post-teenagers.

Wildwood lies at the southern end of New Jersey's string of barrier islands. The summer people who came to these coastal barriers, long before the First World War and in far greater numbers since the second, generally had one thing in mind: to get as close to the water as possible. They built their cottages on the open shore. If there was a dune in the way, they sometimes pushed it down; if there was grass, they sometimes dug it up. When storm waves threatened their houses, one response was to block the ocean with seawalls or boulders. Another was to build groins of concrete rocks, or wood pilings, extending out from the shore in hopes of trapping sand. Where there is a longshore current, a groin will usually collect sand on its up-current side, but only by starving the down-current side. If every owner builds his own groin, the shore may come to look from the air like a wide-toothed comb. But the chances are there will be no net gain of sand.

The dynamics of the beach are now well known, thanks in

particular to Professor Orrin H. Pilkey, Jr., of Duke University. But by the time his book *The Beaches Are Moving* was published in 1979, most of the available Jersey shore had already been developed. In older resorts such as Long Branch and Ocean City, whole rows of waterfront cottages had been washed away by the sea. "We like to think in New Jersey," Dery Bennett told me, "that we've had the ultimate experience in how not to build on the beach."

Just south of Wildwood, at the southern tip of New Jersey, is the old Victorian resort of Cape May. Between the two, in 1911, the Army Corps of Engineers built long jetties to keep Cape May Inlet clear of sand. The jetties worked just like beach groins, on a larger scale, trapping the sand that was being carried south by the current. Half a century later, Wildwood had the widest beach on the Jersey shore, while Cape May had none.

Faced with a sharp decline in its tourist trade, Cape May saved itself by restoring its Victorian buildings and getting itself declared a National Historic Landmark. Americana buffs began to come in place of beachgoers. Now, after a multimillion-dollar replenishment project, Cape May has a new beach and, for the time being at least, the best of all tourist worlds.

Cape May attracts birders, too, for this is an autumn staging area for migrants on the Atlantic flyway. Here they pause to rest, fatten up on the bounty of the marshlands, and, if necessary, wait for good weather to make the flight across Delaware Bay. When I was there in October, most of the birds had passed through (as had clouds of monarch butterflies on their way to Florida and points south), but a Halloween treat was promised. Had I stayed, I might have seen the nocturnal flight of owls as they passed through the beam of the Cape May lighthouse. Instead, I took the ferry across the mouth of the Delaware to Cape Henlopen and headed for the eastern shore of Maryland.

CHAPTER TWELVE

THE BAY

IN reading up on the condition of Chesapeake Bay, I was struck by one statistic: For every hundred oysters that used to be in the bay, only one is there today.

What makes that news so shocking is that, historically, Chesapeake Bay has been, acre for acre, the most productive source of seafood in the United States and possibly the world. Its vast bounty of fish and shellfish, as well as waterfowl, was first reported by Capt. John Smith, who explored and charted the bay in a shallop in 1608. The fish, he declared, were so plentiful that he could catch them with a frying pan. The doughty little captain took the bad with the good: clouds of mosquitoes in the air, shoals of nettles (jellyfish) in the water, and a stingray that nearly killed him. Still, he declared, "Heaven and earth never agreed better to frame a place for man's habitation."

What Smith said of the bay, as regards both its charms and

121

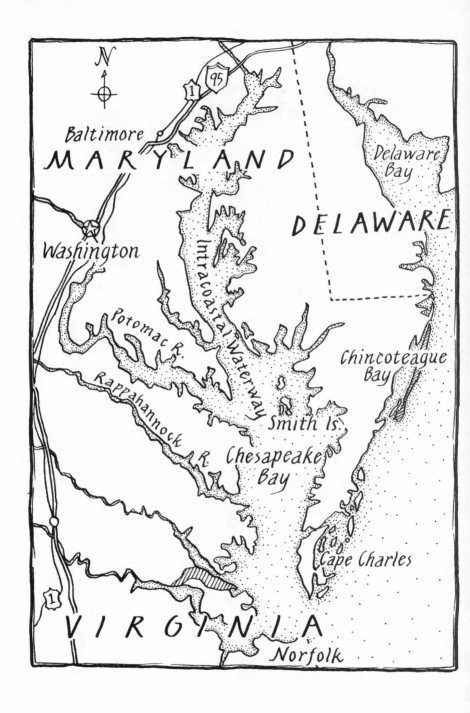

its productivity, could have been said with little qualification up until the middle of this century. To those who sail the bay in boats and do not see below the surface, it is still a place of surpassing beauty. Its shores are fringed with so many inlets, harbors, river mouths, and half-hidden gunkholes that a yachtsman can sail all summer and find a different mooring every night. At sunset, the bordering marshes glow with silver and gold as they did in the Indians' day.

The change occurred beneath the surface of the bay, and it was catastrophic. By the 1960s, the annual catches of shad, herring, and rockfish (known everywhere else as striped bass) were in sharp decline. Sturgeon, which used to produce tons of caviar, had almost disappeared. The decline in the harvest, moreover, was occurring in the face of an increased fishing effort, as measured by the number of boats, the power of motors, and the efficiency of gear. If the harvest was dropping while the fishing effort was increasing, biologists knew that the stock of fish in the bay was falling even faster.

The clearest indicator of biological loss was the disappearance of underwater grasses from great areas of the bottom. In the bay's ecosystem, the underwater grasses play much the same role in the open water that marshes do on the surrounding shores. They are nurseries for the young of both finfish and shellfish, as well as feeding grounds for waterfowl. As the grass disappeared, so did the the creatures that depended on it.

The reason the grass was disappearing, biologists determined, was that it was not getting enough sunlight to grow. The reason it was not getting enough sunlight was an explosive growth of floating algae that obscure the sun and make the water murky. And the reason for the explosion of algae was an excess of nutrients, mainly nitrogen and phosphorus. Quantities of those nutrients, along with toxic chemicals, were coming from city sewers and industrial-waste pipes on the shores of the bay and the banks of its tributary rivers.

What makes the Chesapeake Bay so difficult to keep clean is not only that it is enclosed on three sides, it is also very shallow. Running down the middle is a deep channel, cut by the Susquehanna River when all the rest of the bay area was a coastal plain. That channel makes it possible for large seagoing ships to reach Baltimore, at the upper end of the bay. The average depth of the bay, however, is only twenty-one feet, and much of it is barely deep enough to accommodate small sailboats. Into this shallow basin flows all the runoff from a watershed that extends four hundred miles north to upstate New York and covers twenty times the area of the bay itself. In earlier times, the tides had been sufficient to flush out the burden of pollution. But as the load increased, the tides could not handle it, and by the 1960s the life of the bay was ebbing away.

In its time of crisis, the Chesapeake has inspired more good writing than any other place on the Atlantic Coast. Two outstanding books of description are Tom Horton's *Bay Country* and William W. Warner's *Beautiful Swimmers,* the latter devoted to the lore of the blue crab and the watermen who hunt it. James Michener and John Barth have woven both history and description into their novels. Theirs is a literature of celebration but also of lament.

At the same time, the crisis of the bay inspired one of the most effective cleanup campaigns in this country or, for that matter, the world. To find out how it was going, I went to Annapolis, the headquarters of the Chesapeake Bay Foundation, which has been the moving force behind the campaign.

"We're getting there," said Rodney Coggin, the Foundation's spokesman. "We aren't there yet, but we're getting there." The turning point came in 1983 when the states of Maryland, Virginia, and Pennsylvania and the District of Columbia, as well as the federal Environmental Protection Agency, agreed on a joint effort to reverse the downward slide.

Sewers were the first target. Largely with federal funds provided under the Clean Water Act, sewage-treatment plants were put in place in cities around the bay and along the major tributaries. The most monumental of these installations, designed to clean up the Potomac, is the Blue Plains plant. Known to some as the Craphouse Taj Mahal, it has done its job so well that shad have been seen in the Potomac for the first time in years.

Industrial wastes, including metals and chemicals, are more intractable. They do not flush out but settle to the bottom in a deep layer of sludge. The worst hot spot is the James River, where quantities of Kepone, an ant and roach poison, were dumped by the Allied Chemical Company. It is there to stay, for decades if not centuries. Since many metals and chemicals flow right through sewage treatment plants, the effort since 1983 has been to stop them at their sources.

Environmentalists had hoped that when the flow of sewage and industrial waste had been stemmed, the water quality would rebound. So it did, but not as much or as fast as they had expected. Looking around for other culprits, the experts focused more of their attention on the runoff from agricultural land, especially around Lancaster County, Pennsylvania. The farmers of that region, including the plain-living Amish, are famous for their careful stewardship of the land, but their livestock produce more manure than their fields can use, and some of it seeps into the Susquehanna. Will there have to be sewage-treatment plants for cows? No one has figured out the final answer, but the Foundation is putting out a *Manure Management Manual*.

A widely noticed barometer of water quality is Bernie Fowler's view of his own feet. In the 1950s, Bernie used to wade out into the Potomac River, look down until he saw a crab near his feet, and catch it with a dip net. Over the years, the water grew ever cloudier until the crabs and his own feet disappeared from view. As a state senator and an environmentalist, he has continued to take periodic sightings in the river. It is a little clearer, he says, but he still can't see his feet.

Rodney Coggin looks at the bright side. "Twenty years ago," he says, "we used to tell our children, 'Don't touch anything that comes out of the bay near Baltimore harbor.' Now people are swimming in the Potomac." Not many swim in the bay itself, but that is because during the summer months it is full of nettles—small, stinging jellyfish that Tom Horton describes as "a test of character" but most bathers regard as a reason for heading to the Atlantic side of the Eastern Shore.

The next morning I myself crossed the Chesapeake Bay Bridge to what is always capitalized as the Eastern Shore of Maryland. Until the bridge was opened in 1952, the Eastern Shore was a very low, very flat, very quiet place with a few historic towns, some fine old Colonial houses, truck gardens and cornfields, and landed estates where gentlefolk rode to hounds and shot ducks from blinds. All those are still there but crowded about by weekenders, tourists, retired people, and all the service businesses that grow up among them. On summer weekends, Route 50 carries an endless stream of cars from the Washington-

Baltimore area to Ocean City, Maryland, and other resorts on the Atlantic shore. Now, in the off-season, bulldozers were crawling all over some sections of the highway. SIX LANES COMING NEXT YEAR, flashed a sign. Was that good news?

Twenty miles south of the bridge, I turned off to St. Michaels, an old-time shipbuilding center. St. Michaels's most memorable moment came just before dawn on a summer day during the War of 1812, when a British fleet arrived offshore to attack the shipyards. The canny townspeople, counting on a morning fog, had extinguished their house lights and hung lanterns in the tallest trees. All the British cannonballs except one soared over the town. That one crashed through a roof and rolled down the stairs.

St. Michaels is a yachtsman's town and the home of the Chesapeake Bay Maritime Museum. Gathered there, afloat and ashore, are specimens of the many and various watercraft that have plied the bay, ranging from the sharpie, the bugeye and the skipjack to the log canoe and the sneak-box, a duck blind with a sail. All have one thing in common: a very shallow draft. There is not a deep keel in the fleet.

While the number of working boats on the bay has been dwindling, the number of recreational ones has been multiplying. On a scale of elegance, they range from yachts that might have led even J. P. Morgan to inquire the cost, to beat-up rowboats that Rat of *The Wind in the Willows* might have loved to mess around in.

At a rickety pier in one of the fishing ports, a young man was loading a box of bait and a cooler of beer onto a boat that looked like a square raft with a square box on top of it. With three friends and a dog, he was out for rockfish. "It's unfair," he said. "We can only take two fish apiece in the whole season. If we were on a party boat, everyone on board would be allowed to take two fish a day. The trouble is, the sport fishermen don't have enough friends in the legislature."

The story of rockfish, or striped bass, is one of the saddest in the Chesapeake fishery but one that may have a happy ending. For years, the stripers were the prime sport fish of the northern Atlantic Coast, and 90 percent of them were hatched in the rivers emptying into Chesapeake Bay. Every spring, they would come up the bay from the open ocean, each heading unerringly for the headwaters of the river in which it had begun its life. For the rockfish, as for the shad, the predictability of their behavior was their undoing. Fishermen could stretch nets far out into the channel and trap them on their way to spawn. George Washington did it on the Potomac and fishermen were still doing it two centuries later.

Rockfish have always gone through cycles of ups and downs in their annual spawns, but in the 1970s the population count headed sharply downward and by the early 1980s, as the biologists say, it crashed. Maryland had already banned gillnetting and in 1984 it imposed a total ban on taking rockfish. Under pressure from the federal government, most of the Atlantic states adopted either total bans or limits so strict that the rockfish was treated as an endangered species. It was the first time that any species of fish had received such protection.

According to the Department of Commerce, the closing of the bass fishery cost 7,500 jobs on the East Coast and $220 million in lost economic activity, but the drastic effort was successful. In 1989, there was a sharp jump in the rockfish count and cautiously the Maryland restrictions were eased. Commercial fishermen and sport fishermen were assigned equal quotas, but the sportsmen turned out in such numbers—an estimated eighty thousand the first weekend—that their quota was exhausted in ten days. Now there is hope that the rockfish will not only bring back a steady fishery but will set the pattern for the management of other species in the bay and indeed in the country.

Deal Island, just offshore and reached by a bridge, is the site of a different and altogether unique conservation effort. In Maryland waters, the only boats that are allowed to harvest oysters by dredging are sailboats. That is the reason for the continued use of skipjacks, which might otherwise have rotted away or disappeared into museums, along with the whaling ship and the down-easter. As it is, there are some two dozen left, more of them at Deal than anywhere else, and when they sail out together they afford one of the great sights of the bay.

Oysters once carpeted the bottom of the bay so thickly in places that they built up "reefs" like coral. They were relished by the Indians and then by the settlers, but it was not until the coming of railroads in the latter part of the nineteenth century that they were shipped out by the carload to satisfy appetites such as that of Jim Fisk, the robber baron, who liked to start a meal with six dozen of them. Looking back, biologists compare the harvests of those years to strip-mining. The yield began to fall and by the 1930s Maryland watermen were exchanging rifle fire with Virginia watermen over their respective rights to the oyster beds.

At a dock on Deal Island, Capt. Art Daniel was getting his skipjack, the *City of Crisfield*, ready for the opening of the season. With its wooden hull and deck, its tall single mast and long boom, a skipjack takes a lot of work. I had wondered whether perhaps the historic craft were being kept in operation as a hobby or as a tourist attraction, like the wild ponies of Assateague Island, but Captain Daniel assured me otherwise. He started his working life on a skipjack when he was seventeen, and fifty-three years later he has no intention of easing off. "You have to love it," he said, "because it's hard work, but you can make a living at it."

Tongers, who scoop up the oysters with rakes that resemble giant fireplace tongs, are given a head start in September, even though they use power, while the dredgers have to wait until the first of December. "We have to go out in the coldest weather," Daniel said. "They ought to let us start when the tongers do. But we don't have the influence at Annapolis."

The oyster harvest has been dragging on bottom at about a million bushels a year, down from 12 million a century ago. Overharvesting is not the only cause. Pollution has wiped out some of the beds and two parasitic diseases, called MSX and Dermo, have devastated others. The people at the Chesapeake Bay Foundation would like to see the best remaining beds set aside as sanctuaries until the stock recovers. "We could still catch the last oyster," they warn.

About the only species that still flourish in Chesapeake Bay are those that do not reproduce in the bay but in the open ocean, notably the bluefish, which has become almost by default the premier game fish of the East Coast, and the menhaden, which are caught in great quantity, only to be ground up, gruesomely, for chicken feed and fertilizer at a plant in Reedville, Virginia.

The most important survivor is the blue crab, which is hatched in deep water near the mouth of the bay. The crab owes its abundance in part to its tremendous fecundity—about a million eggs for every crab that reaches maturity—and in part to its skill in adapting to an ever-changing environment. Like most marine creatures, the crab thrives in a rather narrow range of salinity, whereas the bay has a very wide range. Fresh water from the Susquehanna and other rivers constantly mixes with salt water flowing from the mouth at every tide. The two streams do not simply meet and mix, however. The salt water, being heavier, normally sinks to the bottom and flows in, while the fresh water flows out over it. Strong winds add to the confusion of currents, carrying crab larvae every which way and sometimes out to sea. Luckily, the crab larvae are programmed by nature to rise and drop in the water and thus ride currents that will take them to shallow, grassy feeding grounds. That is where the crabbers catch them, either in "pots," which are really rectangular traps not unlike lobster pots, or by the rakelike dredges.

Crisfield, which calls itself with good reason "the crab capital of the world," is the takeoff point for two famous watermen's islands, Smith Island on the Maryland side of the state border that runs across the bay, and Tangier Island on the Virginia side. Both were settled in the seventeenth century by English colonists whose descendants still live there. Pirates gave them trouble in the eighteenth century, using the islands as bases. In the nineteenth century, an evangelist known as "the log-canoe preacher" converted them to strict Methodism. Otherwise, they were left alone, as isolated as any communities in the country. The mark of their isolation is a peculiar accent that some linguistic scholars say derives from the Cornish speech of Elizabethan England. Others say it is a local dialect, evolved by a people living almost wholly by themselves.

A few tourists who took the ferry to Smith Island with me and landed at the town of Ewell seemed at a bit of a loss for what to do. It took about fifteen minutes to walk up Front Street and then down Back Street, past rows of neat white houses. There were few people to be seen but kindles of kittens and sords of mallards, wandering together in a peaceable kingdom. All roads lead to the church and its adjoining graveyard, filled with headstones bearing the same, repeated names that are found on the island today—Tyler, Evans, and half a dozen others. It was easy to believe that Smith Island has never had need of a local government, a policeman, or a jail. Whatever disputes arise are settled within the walls of the church; whatever decisions are required about town policy are made there.

Down by the shore are the watermen's shanties, where the work of the island is done. When a waterman returns with a load of crabs, they are dumped onto big trays to be sorted. Some will be packed and shipped as hard crabs for restaurants. Others will be broken apart and their flesh plucked out by women pickers, to be sold as crabmeat. Others will go to market as soft-shell crabs, the supreme delicacy of the trade and a Smith Island specialty.

The term *soft-shell* does not refer to a special kind of crab but to a stage—a very brief stage—in a crab's life. The sorters look for crabs that are just about to shed their shells in the periodic molting. Those are removed to separate trays and carefully watched, every few hours, day and night. Within a day's time after the crab molts, a new shell will begin to harden. Before that can happen, the crab is taken up, packed in sea grass, refrigerated to keep it from growing a new shell, and shipped live to market. It is exacting work, requiring the waterman or his wife to get up at least once during the night. For years, it was the only exception allowed by the church to the rule of no work on Sundays.

On the ferry going back, I asked a Smith Island lady how it happened that most of the soft-shell crabs came from Smith Island. I am not quite sure what she replied in her island accent, but I think it was, "Nobody else wants to do it."

The visitor is left with some questions about Smith Island's future. One is whether the crab fishery will hold out. The harvest of the bay still comes to as many as a quarter of a billion crabs a year, but the watermen find themselves in much the same situation as Maine lobstermen. With better boats and better gear, they are working longer and longer to get the same catch. How long can that go on?

Another question is how long the separate island culture will endure, now that its isolation is ended. Island children nowadays commute to the mainland for high school, and some go off to college. The watermen, one notices, are mostly of middle age or older. There are easier livings to be made elsewhere.

And finally, how long will Smith Island be there? Its average elevation is two feet above sea level, and during storms the water sometimes flows down the streets. Over the years, the waves have eaten into sections of the shore, forcing residents to move their homes to higher ground (the highest ground being five feet). Just down the bay is what remains of Watts Island, which once had its own community of watermen. It is all but inundated now. Smith Island has time left, but, if the sea level keeps on rising, that time may not be forever.

Before I went back to the Chesapeake Bay Foundation at Annapolis, I knew what their scientists would say about the prospects for the crab fishery. Yes, it could be preserved and put on a sustainable yield basis, but only if sensible controls are in place. That may mean stopping dredgers from digging up the females in winter after they have burrowed into the sand at the mouth of the bay, and imposing whatever limits may be needed from season to season.

The striped bass have been brought back from the verge of extinction by much more drastic measures. The shad would come back if dams were removed from the rivers where they used to spawn. Even the oyster population can be restored if some way can be found to control the diseases. As for the watermen, they traditionally hate regulation, but most of them now admit that the days of the wide-open fishing frontier are gone.

Does that mean that, with pollution from sewers and industrial plants now under fairly good control, and fishing regulations increasingly accepted, the bay has been "saved"? No, say the scientists. Having gotten a lock on the widely recognized problems of pollution and overfishing, they come up against environmental threats that are more pervasive and harder to meet. Those threats come from no specific source but from the growth and development of the whole bay area. Every time a stand of trees is cut down, the earth loses some of its resistance to erosion and its capacity to absorb pollutants. Every time a plot is cleared for a house, some of the earth runs into the nearest stream. Every time a parking lot is paved, it accumulates wastes that have to drain off. Every time a lawn is fertilized, some of the chemicals seep into the watershed. Every time a car runs along a highway, it discharges toxic particles that may eventually fall into the bay. "It's acid rain," says Rodney Coggin. "Not just acid rain from Midwest power plants but our own homemade acid rain."

Since World War II, the population of the bay area has

nearly doubled, and there is no end in sight. The bay is only an hour's drive from the seat of the federal government, which, as is often remarked, keeps on growing in good times and bad. Currently, the highway engineers are promoting a plan to relieve the chronic congestion on the Washington Beltway by building a bypass—a beltway around the Beltway—which will bring more intensive development to the bay area. Stopping that highway is now high on the agenda of the Foundation and other environmental groups.

If that seems like a long stretch for an organization founded to clean up a bay, it is only the beginning of a new environmental agenda. Looking ahead to the next century, the Foundation is calling for some fundamental changes in the way people live. The pattern of residential building that has prevailed in the last half century—single houses with single lawns in sprawling developments—is seen now as wasteful of land. (Better, the planners say, to have cluster housing, with common greens—presumably fertilized by processed sewage rather than chemicals.) The automobile is an extravagant way of getting to work or to the shopping center. (Better to have cheap, attractive public transportation, ideally powered by nonpolluting fuels.) People fleeing the blighted cities only blight the countryside. (Better to fix up the cities.)

All that may be a hard sell. To wean the American people from their Jeffersonian love affair with single houses and their devotion to automobiles may be more of a job than selling industry on toxic cleanup or selling watermen on fishing limits. Still, the planners say, it may come to that or else to holding down the growth of population. And that could be an even harder sell.

CHAPTER THIRTEEN

PAST THE CAPES

DELAWARE (named for Baron De la Warr, a governor of the Jamestown colony), Maryland (named for the queen consort of Charles I), and Virginia (named for the chaste Elizabeth) are all names that call up memories of America's Colonial past. Scrunch them together and you get Delmarva, which sounds like a modern industrial conglomerate. That, however, is the best that anyone has been able to come up with for the peninsula, lying between the Delaware and Chesapeake bays, that includes the coasts of all three states.

Returning to the Atlantic seaboard from Chesapeake Bay, I reached the Delaware shore at Indian River Inlet. Here, as at other inlets, the jetties that were built to keep the channel open have interrupted the flow of sand in the longshore current, building up the beach on the up-current side and eroding it on the down-current side. In other places, the solution has been to

133

replenish the down-current beach by periodic dredging. Here, however, the Army Corps of Engineers has installed a novel pumping system that sucks up sand on one side of the inlet and sends it through a pipe, suspended under the highway bridge, to the other side. It was the first such system installed on the Atlantic Coast and one of only three in existence, the others being in Australia and California. According to the park ranger at the office of the Delaware Seashore, which owns the beach, the system is working well.

The Delaware Seashore has preserved most of that state's ocean-facing barrier coast from development—which is not to say that nothing has changed. At the ranger's office, a woman who had not seen the place for a quarter century was dismayed by what she now found. "When my father used to bring us here," she said, "we were all alone. We would build a camp fire and sleep in a tent and never see anyone else." Now, she had just learned, she and her husband would have to get there early on a summer day to find a place for their trailer in the huge parking lot. Nevertheless, for those who come for a day at the beach, there are miles of unspoiled dunes.

Just to the south, across the state border, Maryland's Ocean City caters to a different taste in seaside pleasure. Ever since the Chesapeake Bay Bridge was built, this stretch of coast has been a magnet for beach lovers from the great population centers of Washington and Baltimore. Ocean City has a boardwalk, rides, games, and mile upon mile of hotels, motels, cottages, and condominiums. Unfortunately, many of the cottages and condos were built on shifting sands at the water's edge. Some of them have already toppled into the sea, while engineers keep pushing up sand to save others.

If the Delmarva peninsula had been easier to get to, in the years before the bridge was opened, the whole coast south of Ocean City might have been built up on that model. Instead, it has almost all been preserved in its natural state, thanks in part to the federal government and in part to the Nature Conservancy.

As early as the 1930s, the National Park Service had its eye on Assateague Island, the barrier that runs along twenty-two miles of Maryland's coast and fifteen miles of Virginia's. Bills had been introduced in Congress to make it a National Seashore but then had died in committee. By the 1950s, developers had bought up miles of beachfront, put in a road, and begun to sell lots. In 1952, just in time, nature conspired with the Park Service by sending a severe storm that tore up the road and discouraged the developers. Three years later, the National Seashore was established, making federal parkland of Assateague and most of Chincoteague Island, which nestles inside its southern end. No road runs the length of Assateague, but the National Seashore can be reached at its northern end near Ocean City or at its southern end through Chincoteague. Hoping to see some of the island's wild ponies, I chose the southern approach.

People now grown who had the good fortune to read Marguerite Henry's book *Misty of Chincoteague* when they were young and who formed a mental picture of a little old-fashioned fishing village where a wild silvery pony found a happy home are in for some measure of disillusionment. The marshes that separate the town from the mainland are just as beautiful as the book says, but the causeway that runs across them is lined now with billboards that provide a regrettably faithful preview of the town itself.

There seems to be some natural law that commercial sleaze shall look its worst just outside the gates of national parks. The reason, I realize, is that those places supply all the goods and services that the parks do not. But a modest amount of planning and zoning might make the contrast between civilization and nature less jarring. Unless you are in urgent need of sandwiches, Cokes, sunscreen, or rock-and-roll tapes, the best thing is to drive through Chincoteague without stopping and get across the bridge to Assateague.

Legend has it that the ancestors of the shaggy island ponies swam ashore from a sinking Spanish galleon in the seventeenth century. Whether that is true or whether they were pastured there by early farmers and then abandoned, wild ponies have ever since been the emblem of Assateague. Once every summer, on Pony Penning Day, the foals are rounded up and herded down to the shore. Cheered on by crowds of tourists, they swim across the hundred-foot channel to Chincoteague, where they are sold at auction for the benefit of the town fire department. During the rest of the year, the ponies run free in certain areas where, with luck, tourists may catch a distant sight of them.

Below Assateague Island, the coastal barrier is not a long,

narrow strip but a string of smaller islands stretching along the Virginia shore to Cape Charles. Theirs, too, is a story of just-in-time preservation, but in their case the saving force has been the Nature Conservancy. In 1969, developers were all set to turn three of the islands into a resort with thousands of house lots, a shopping mall, and a convention center, all connected to the mainland by a causeway across the marshes. Through a combination of environmental arm-twisting and generous financial offers, the Nature Conservancy induced the developers to sell out, and proceeded to acquire most of the other islands, creating the Virginia Coastal Reserve.

The Nature Conservancy is a single-minded organization whose mission is to "preserve biotic diversity"—in other words, to safeguard habitat for threatened flora and fauna. That may mean bald eagles in Iowa or ocelots in Texas, but in the Virginia islands it means primarily the water birds.

In the spectrum of environmental groups, the Nature Conservancy stands at the farthest remove from organizations such as Greenpeace that slash tuna nets and board atomic warships. Its officers own neckties and speak the language of corporate directors and wealthy widows. When an opportunity presents itself, the Conservancy usually has the money at hand or knows how to raise it. In the case of the Virginia Coastal Reserve, much of the money came from a trust created by a granddaughter of Henry M. Flagler, the Standard Oil partner.

The Nature Conservancy can not only act much faster than a government agency, it can also wheel and deal with a free hand. The Virginia acquisition is a case in point. It would not be enough, the conservancy decided, to preserve the islands themselves. They were part of a biosphere that included the facing mainland and the bays and marshes between. David E. Morine, who was in charge of acquisitions, tells in his lively book *Good Dirt* how the Conservancy quietly bought up mainland parcels with deepwater frontage that might have attracted developers. At the same time, it has encouraged local enterprises that did not imperil the environment, sometimes selling them land or lending them money in return for conservation easements.

Tree-huggers sometimes call such flexibility "dealing with the Devil," but it has enabled the conservancy to undertake projects that might otherwise be beyond the scope of a private organization. When a habitat has been saved, as often as not, the Conservancy sells it to some state or federal agency such as the Fish and Wildlife Service, thus replenishing its treasury for other projects.

While the Conservancy is trying to save the species of the planet for the long-run good of mankind, it feels much less obligation to the present generation of vacationers. It does not have, as the National Park Service has by law, and some other environmental outfits such as the Sierra Club and Audubon clubs have by choice, a purpose to provide recreation to the public. Visitors are permitted on many of its properties for such activities as hiking and bird-watching but much less often for swimming, camping, or picnicking. As for the Virginia islands, about the only way to see them is to have your own boat or to sign up for an occasional organized and shepherded nature walk.

I viewed the islands from afar and continued on down the peninsula to Cape Charles. From there, a remarkable motorway, combining bridges and tunnels, runs for seventeen miles across the mouth of Chesapeake Bay to Cape Henry. In earlier times, some famous vessels passed between those capes. In 1607, a little fleet composed of the *Susan Comstock,* the *Godspeed,* and the *Discovery* brought English settlers to found the settlement they named Jamestown on a river they named the James. In the American Revolution, Admiral de Grasse deployed his French fleet between the capes to prevent Cornwallis from escaping from Yorktown. In the Civil War, the Union ironclad *Monitor* steamed by to engage the Confederate *Merrimack* in the battle at Hampton Roads.

The protected waters inside the Virginia capes are home now to modern vessels of every kind: warships (for Norfolk is the base of the Atlantic fleet), fishing trawlers, oceangoing freighters (for Norfolk is gaining on New York as the largest shipping port on the East Coast), and recreational boats with sails or motors. The guardian angel of all the commercial and pleasure boats, now as in the days of lighthouse keepers and surfboats, is the United States Coast Guard. On the waterfront at Portsmouth, I found the headquarters of its Fifth District, which includes the mid-Atlantic coast from New Jersey to South Carolina.

In the Operations Room, Lt. Andy Blomme stood before a wall map showing all the stations from which boats, planes, and helicopters can be summoned to answer calls of distress. "Search and rescue" is still the Coast Guard's first responsibility. Thanks to radio beacons and direction finders, including LORAN and OMEGA, not many merchant ships run aground these days. Skippers who put to sea for pleasure, on the other hand, seem to have an infinite capacity for getting into trouble.

"Just last week," said Lieutenant Blomme, "a young fellow came out of the little Pasquotank River into Albemarle Sound on a jet ski, and just disappeared. We got a call from his family and sent a boat to the place where he ought to have been. No sight of him. That day and the next, we had helicopters searching all the waters he could possibly have reached. Still no luck. And where do you suppose we finally found him? Wading through a marsh, pushing his jet ski in front of him. He said he was looking for a gas station."

I asked how much the search had cost.

"Maybe a hundred thousand dollars," he said.

Some months earlier, at the headquarters of the First District in Boston, I had asked Lt. Jim Donovan what was the most frequent call they received from boaters.

"Where am I?" he said

And the next most frequent?

"I'm out of gas."

Lieutenant Blomme added another: "I'm broken down."

Except in emergencies, calls for repairs or gas are passed on to private service suppliers, who generally charge fees high enough to make a boater more careful about his preparations the next time.

More time-consuming are calls from worried wives: "My husband said he would be back for dinner and I haven't heard from him." For such purposes, Coast Guard stations often keep a list of marinas and nearby bars where, in some cases, the missing mariners are found and advised to call home.

The Coast Guard grew out of earlier, separate services. One of them, the Revenue Cutter Service, used fast sailboats to chase down smugglers at a time when the tariff was the nation's chief source of revenue. By the 1920s, that branch of the service was chasing rumrunners; now, with boats, planes, and helicopters, it goes after drug smugglers.

The Life-Saving Service was manned by crews that pushed surfboats through breaking waves to rescue seamen from stranded ships. ("You must go out," crewmen were told. "You don't have to come back.") Nowadays, the rescue may sometimes be made, with no less risk, by crewmen dangling from helicopters.

The old Lighthouse Service has evolved into a complex electronic system designed to keep boats out of trouble. Among its acronymic aids to navigation, the latest is EPIRB (for Emergency Position-Indicating Radio Beacon), whose special virtue is that it operates automatically. Even if a vessel is suddenly capsized or its skipper disabled, the distress call will be heard.

The only problem with EPIRB is that if it is accidentally upset, it sends out its signal, causing the same kind of embarrassment that a householder suffers when he accidentally triggers his home alarm system and the police show up at his door.

"Some of the false alarms come from the Navy," Lieutenant Blomme told me. "We get a call and zero in on the transmitter, and find it's on a Navy ship. Probably some seaman was painting and set if off by mistake."

An EPIRB might have saved the Coast Guard one of the most expensive searches in recent times when a yacht vanished at sea during Hurricane Bob. Only after a ten-day search were four of the survivors located on a rubber raft, a fifth crew member having died at sea. That is why Lieutenant Blomme would like to see all oceangoing private boats, as well as commercial vessels, equipped with an EPIRB.

Opposite the Coast Guard headquarters, huge freighters line the Norfolk bank of the Elizabeth River. But they are not alone. You don't have to wait very long to see some expensive-looking yacht pass by on the Intracoastal Waterway. As marked on the charts, that inside waterway begins far north of here, at Cape Ann in Massachusetts. Boats that follow it all the way pass through the Cape Cod Canal and Long Island Sound, inside the barrier islands of New Jersey, up Delaware Bay, through the Chesapeake and Delaware Canal, and down Chesapeake Bay. Norfolk is the most important gathering place because, from here on south, it offers a protected passage behind the Carolina capes that used to present such a peril to coastal mariners.

Since there is no through road along the coast from Virginia Beach south to North Carolina, I decided instead to follow the waterway. In that way, I could see something of the inner passage through the sounds and then double back on the Outer Banks.

Soon after leaving Norfolk, the southbound yachtsman has to make a choice between two canals. He can take the Chesapeake and Albemarle Canal, the wider and deeper of the two, which is clearly the route for commercial vessels. Or he can take the Dismal Swamp Canal, which is smaller and shallower and meant for pleasure boats that do not draw more than six feet of water. If they were parts of a coastal highway system, the Chesapeake and Albemarle would be busy, commercial Route 1, while the Dismal Swamp route would be Scenic 1A. It runs along the edge of one of the last and most haunting wilderness areas of the coastal plain.

The Great Dismal Swamp was given its name by Col. William Byrd II, the Virginia grandee who led an expedition through it in 1728 to mark the boundary between Virginia and North Carolina. After wading and slashing his way through the barely penetrable bog, he reported it to be "a vast body of dirt and nastiness." Later on, however, some other Virginia gentlemen, including George Washington and Patrick Henry, looked upon the swamp as a source of lumber and conceived the idea of building a canal to get it out. Washington was one of six investors who owned forty thousand acres of the swamp and who dug a small waterway that is still there and is known as "Washington's Ditch." The enterprise did not flourish, however, and Washington withdrew from it. The present canal, dug by slave labor, was opened to traffic in 1803. It, too, was a financial disappointment to investors, largely because the competing Chesapeake and Albemarle Canal was built a short time later. Both of them were eventually taken over by the federal government and put under the control of the Army Corps of Engineers.

At a lock in the town of Deep Creek, Virginia, boats are raised twenty feet to the level of the canal. When I got there, I found C. L. ("Connie") Thomas, the lockmaster, hard at work grooming the grassy terraces beside the lock. He had locked several boats through at 8:30 A.M. in the first of four daily openings, and was holding others for the next opening at noon.

"Once in a while," he said, "a skipper gets impatient, like one I had the other day who was carrying a Rolls-Royce and a helicopter on his boat—from New York or New Jersey, I think." But most of the skippers do not mind waiting, probably because they are taking this route for the fun of it.

I drove south on Route 17, which runs beside the canal along what used to be the towpath for horses. To the east, the swamp has been drained and cleared for farmland, but the canal itself is a ribbon of tranquil water, shaded by cypress, black gum, juniper, wild cherry, and loblolly pine trees. The real reason it is still maintained is that it provides drainage for Lake Drummond at the heart of the swamp, now a federal wildlife refuge. In time of scant rainfall, the Army Corps of Engineers must apportion water between the needs of the refuge and the needs of the canal.

An obliging member of the Corps of Engineers took me by motorboat up the feeder ditch that connects the canal with the lake. The enfolding swamp, a dark tangle of trees and shrubs, is home to a few bear and bobcats, enough deer to permit a hunting season, and great numbers of small mammals and birds. It is a wilderness covering more than 100,000 acres, accessible to visitors only by canoe or other small boat or by dirt bike or by foot.

A boat traveling down the canal at six miles an hour reaches the southern lock at Elizabeth City in three and a half hours. From there, the Intracoastal Waterway runs through rivers, sounds, and connecting canals, inside the barrier islands of North Carolina and on down the coast to Florida.

Any sailor who thinks he might get bored during the weeks that he spends on the waterway would do well to take along a copy of the classic account of that voyage, entitled *The Boy, Me, and the Cat.* The author, Henry M. Plummer, was a retired Massachusetts insurance man who made the trip in 1912 with his son Henry Junior and a small fuzzy cat that was given to fits. Setting out from New Bedford in the late fall, they sailed down Long Island Sound and through the boiling tides of Hellgate into New York's East River, where the wind failed and swirling currents sent them crashing into a barge. With the help of their three-and-a-half-horsepower motor, they escaped without serious damage. Except for that mishap and the cat's periodic fits

("I never saw a little cabin so full of one cat before") they had a safe, though very cold, passage past Norfolk and into Albemarle Sound.

Of the marshy North Carolina shore that they passed at night, without a light in sight, Plummer wrote in his log, "Gosh! but it is an awful long ways to anywhere in these parts." Even today, that stretch of the mainland is one of the least developed sections of the Atlantic shore.

In port towns such as Edenton, Bath, and New Bern, some fine old houses and churches recall a time before the Civil War when slave plantations and waterborne trade brought prosperity to a small land-owning class. In the years that followed, indifferent farming and good fishing were the mainstays of a sparse population. Things changed—and not for the better—in the 1970s, when big farming enterprises bought up a great part of the swampy forestland on the shore of Pamlico Sound, drained it, cleared it, and planted it to corn and soybeans. Many of the little farmers gave up and the fishermen fared no better. The fast runoff of rainwater from the cleared land upset the saline balance of the estuary, on which many shellfish depend, while pesticides from the farmlands degraded the water.

The Intracoastal Waterway threads through this low, flat country, avoiding the sometimes storm-tossed waters of Pamlico Sound, and comes out to the coast at Morehead City, just inside Bogue Banks. In 1965, this spot was the scene of a curious confrontation that made its mark on coastal law. A man named Larry Capone was paddling down the coast from Coney Island to Florida in a homemade craft, using his arms to turn paddles and his feet to steer. At Morehead City, he came to a pier that stuck out a thousand feet from the shore. When he paddled up to the pier, intending to go under it, the pier's owner ordered him off and began throwing soft-drink bottles at him. One of the bottles hit him on the head, opening a cut that required twenty-four stitches to sew up. The court case that followed raised a constitutional issue: Did a shorefront owner have the right to build a pier and keep people away from it? In a decision that was noted in all the coastal states, the court ruled that the owner did have the right to build the pier but that the public had the right to pass under it.

Half a century earlier, when the Plummers came this way,

the Intracoastal Waterway had just been given its impressive name, but it still lacked many of the channel markers that it has today, and some of its links were yet to be completed. When he got to Cape Fear, Plummer faced the choice of running through the dangerous "slews" outside the Cape or getting through a badly marked inlet. With night falling and a storm coming up, he tried to find the channel through the inlet and ran hard onto a shoal. As water flooded the cockpit, a wave sent their trailing dinghy flying toward the hull. His log: "Crunch-o, the nose of the launch went through our bilge for a 6 in. hole. Up she went again and bang-o, there was another hole. My eye! we would soon be a pepperbox at that rate."

The Plummers got a patch on the hull, the dinghy went under, and high tide left the boat afloat but stranded. Plummer's aplomb, if nothing else, was intact. He wrote:

> About eight o'clock a man turned up in a skiff and came on board. . . . He said he thought our launch was sunk. He was a very truthful man. I gave him eggs on toast and coffee at once. While he was eating, tide turned ebb and along came our ground tackle and we for the bar once more. "My man," says I, "cut out the egg and coffee habit, jump right into your skiff, underrun that anchor and carry it up stream." He was a sailor all right, and with no back talk, he was away on the job. First one anchor and then the other. I kept him at it and soon had her kedged all snug and comfy out of harm's way.

After a week of repair work, the Plummers got off again and sailed without further incident to Miami, where the cat succumbed but father and son spent the rest of the winter before sailing back in the spring. I wondered how many present-day travelers on the Intracoastal Waterway would have the skills to get out of such a fix as the Plummers got into. Fortunately, modern yachtsmen have the Coast Guard to call on for help.

In following the inside route down the mainland of North Carolina, I had already bypassed the Outer Banks, and was looking for a place to stop. The Plummers had given high marks to Beaufort, and I saw no reason to consult another travel guide. In December of 1912, they had found the harbor crowded with fishing boats and the gardens blooming with roses. I, too, found it a pleasant old city with a museum of maritime history and with more yachts now than fishing boats on the handsome waterfront. In order to see the Outer Banks, I would now have to turn back north again. At Cedar Island, the next day I met my friend Jane for a ferry trip to Ocracoke.

THE OUTER BANKS

THERE is something to be said for approaching the Outer Banks from the south. Instead of driving across a bridge, as you can do farther north, you must take a two-and-a-half-hour ferry ride from the mainland to the southern tip of Ocracoke Island. Nothing beats a ferry trip for making you feel that you are coming to another world, far out at sea.

Anyone who looks at a map can see that the Outer Banks of North Carolina are unlike any other geographic feature on the Atlantic Coast. They form a far-flung arc, running more than half the length of the North Carolina coast, enclosing Pamlico and Albemarle sounds. They are some of the lowest, narrowest, windiest, and most unstable of barrier islands, constantly being rearranged by blowing sand and overwashing seas.

The ferry put us ashore in that part of the Outer Banks that has been least changed by the influx of summer visitors in recent

145

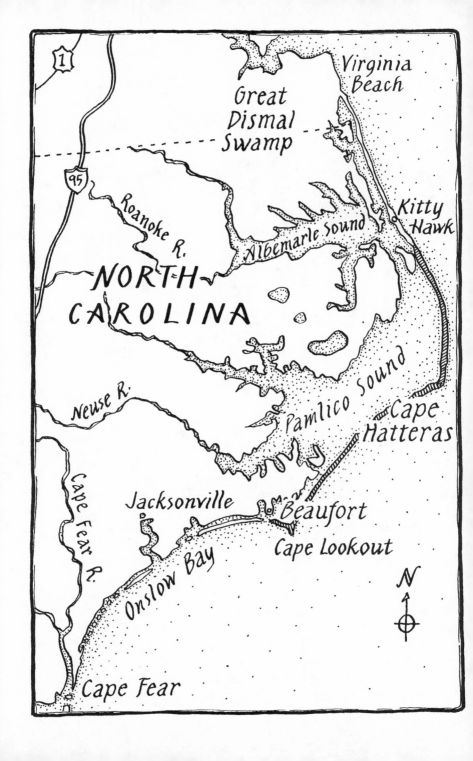

times. From the dock, we drove through the old fishing port of Ocracoke and in less than a mile entered the Cape Hatteras National Seashore. The National Seashore runs north for ninety miles, forever wild and forever desolate, except for a few settlements that were there long before the National Seashore was established in 1937.

Charles F. Johnson, a young soldier in the Union army, which occupied the Outer Banks during the Civil War, wrote of these villages: "The houses are dismal enough. . . . Everything on the island seems to be devoid of paint—dwellings, barns, and windmills, of which there are a greater number than I supposed were in existence in the whole country."

Aside from the windmills, which are gone, the scene is much the same today. Or it would be if a creeping plague of motels, shops, and restaurants had not added pockmarks to the bleak but self-reliant faces of the old towns.

Some of the native fishermen are Bankers of the sixth and seventh generations, often with the same few family names: O'Neal, Midgett, Howard, Garrish, Gaskill, Ballance. In the old days, Bankers found a source of extra income in the wrecks of ships that ran aground on the shoals, and some scoundrels among them may have lured ships onto the shoals by setting false lights. A local legend is that Nags Head, the chief town of the Outer Banks, owes its name to a Banker who hung a lantern around his horse's neck and drove the horse along the beach, so that the light would look to captains at sea like a bobbing buoy. In historical fact, Bankers manned the federal Lifesaving Service, often risking and sometimes losing their lives to rescue the crews of wrecked ships.

Still, it is true that the Outer Banks have had more than their fair share of rascals, runaways, pirates, smugglers, wanderers, and other refugees from the legal and social constraints of mainland life. In 1681, the royal governor of Virginia complained that North Carolina was "the sink of America, the refuge of our renegades." Thirty years later, the harbor of Ocracoke became notorious as the nest of pirates, including Edward Teach, known as Blackbeard, who liked to enhance his fearsome aspect by sticking lighted cannon fuses into his beard. Blackbeard, it was generally understood, bought the protection of North Carolina's Governor Eden by cutting him in on the spoils. A later governor of Virginia sent Lt. Robert Maynard with two sloops to chase the villain down. In a fierce engagement at Ocracoke Inlet, Maynard captured the pirate ship, cut off Blackbeard's head, and sailed back to Virginia with the head mounted on his bowsprit.

There are no pirates on the Outer Banks today (except, loosely speaking, for developers who sell lots without any protection from a surge of salt water and without any supply of drinkable fresh water), but the islands still attract adventurers, drifters, free spirits, and pilgrims testing the outer limits of the continent or the soul.

After crossing by another ferry from Ocracoke to Hatteras Island, we arrived at Cape Hatteras, famed among mariners as the most dangerous place on the Atlantic Coast. Somewhat to our disappointment, the sea was calm, the waves just big enough to satisfy the surfers hanging offshore. The sharp angle of the Cape, sticking so far out to sea, seems to act as a magnet for all the bad weather of the western Atlantic. The northeast storms of winter and the hurricanes of summer and fall use it as a staging area for attacks on the coast. Beneath the surface of the ocean, the warm waters of the Gulf Stream collide with the colder waters of the Virginia Coastal Drift. Off the Cape, where all these natural forces meet, are the Diamond Shoals, long ago dubbed "The Graveyard of the Atlantic." On these shoals and along the coast, more than six hundred wrecks have been located, including that of the Civil War ironclad *Monitor*, and scuba divers are finding more of them all the time.

Cape Hatteras Light, the tallest (at 208 feet) and most famous of all the Atlantic lighthouses, is something of a problem now. When it was built, brick by brick, in 1870, it stood fifteen hundred feet (the length of five football fields) from the water's edge, but now it would be in the ocean if sand had not been dumped around its base. As a navigational aid, it could easily be replaced by a simple steel tower with an automated light on top, but it is such a historic landmark that no one wants to let it go. The latest plan is to move it inland.

I asked an engineer who happened to be standing nearby whether that could be done.

"If they ever get enough money," he replied. "And if it doesn't fall apart."

It does not take long for the weather to change at Cape

Hatteras. A short time later, when we looked out over Diamond Shoals, separate systems of waves were rolling in at different angles and crashing against one another, throwing up geysers of surf and spray. It looked as if some of those sea monsters imagined by medieval cartographers were thrashing about beneath the surface.

Driving up Route 12 through the National Seashore, you have Pamlico Sound on your left and the ocean, unseen behind a high dune, on your right. The dune is not entirely natural. About the time the Seashore was established, the Civilian Conservation Corps erected fences and planted beach grass along the existing dunes in order to trap more sand, prevent overwashes, and protect the road. In time, the dune rose to a height of fifteen feet or so, but the change had an unexpected effect. The sea, unable to wash over the dune during storms, eroded the shore in front of it, thus narrowing the beach.

When the dune was built up, marine geologists did not know what they do now about the dynamics of barrier islands. Normally, storm waves often washed over the dune at the lowest and weakest points, carrying sand across the narrow land and into the sound beyond. Sometimes, they cut a channel, which might subsequently fill in or might widen and deepen into a new inlet. At least twenty new inlets have formed within historic times, connecting the ocean to the sound, and as many old ones have closed. The Park Service, wiser now, has given up efforts to stabilize the sandy shore.

Every few miles along Route 12, there is an access route to the beach for off-road vehicles. Nothing is more dear to the hearts of surf casters, who constitute a high proportion of the beach users, than the right to drive an ORV along the sand to a point where the blues or the red drum are thought to be biting that day. Conservationists, however, complain that the ORVs are not good for the health of the numerous, though often invisible, creatures of the foreshore, notably the pale, nocturnal ghost crabs that live in burrows under the sand. Ghost crabs do not have enough friends in Congress to prevail over the ORVs, but some of the shorebirds do.

A bird to contend with is the piping plover. A small gray cousin of the terns, it lays its eggs in the dunes above the beach, anywhere between Maine and Georgia. By the latest count, only about four hundred pair are left on the Atlantic Coast. Like the snail darter and the northern spotted owl, it derives its clout from the federal Endangered Species Act.

Under the law, if even a single pair of piping plovers is found to be nesting on the shore, the area must be closed off until the end of the nesting season. That happened in Massachusetts, where six miles of beach on Plum Island were closed until July, and also in Rhode Island, where Moonstone Beach, the only recognized nudist beach in the state, was closed for good. At Indian River Inlet in Delaware, where I had stopped to see the station that pumps sand from one side of the inlet to the other, I learned that the engineers who built it had their fingers crossed for fear that a pair of plovers might force them to shut it down. So far, I was assured, none of the little birds had chosen that particular nesting place.

On the Outer Banks, a confrontation became inevitable when fourteen pair of plovers, the only ones known to be living in the National Seashore, were found to be nesting in the path used by ORVs. As required, the superintendent of the Seashore closed the area to traffic—a clear victory for bird lovers but, as it turned out, a dubious one. Over the following months, grass reclaimed the area, sand filled in the ORV tracks—and the plovers disappeared. Naturalists could only conclude that the birds had chosen the area in the first place because the ruts left by dune buggies gave them shelter from the wind.

Conflict of interest is built into the basic conception of the national parks and seashores. The Park Service's mandate from Congress is to manage the parks "for the enjoyment of [the people] in such manner and by such means as will leave them unimpaired for the enjoyment of future generations." That charter has been compared to the commandment given by God to Man in Genesis: "Be fruitful and multiply, and replenish the earth and subdue it." How to subdue the earth and replenish it at the same time? How to let the public enjoy the parks and still preserve them?

The Park Service has carried out its balancing act with such success that it consistently gets the highest marks among government agencies. On the Outer Banks, the Hatteras Seashore has its special problems, as I learned from Thomas L. Hartman, the superintendent. One of them is the water table. All of the Outer

Banks share a single aquifer, which is being drawn down by the steadily increasing demands of new building.

"If the water table falls too far, it will affect the vegetation that grows on the surface," Hartman says, "and if the habitat changes—if different kinds of trees and grasses take over—the birds and animals will be affected. We could see the loss of many species."

Hartman worries that a shortage of funds will damage what he calls "the infrastructure" of the park. "I sometimes contrast it with a manufacturing enterprise," he says. "A business can put up a factory and then, if it wants to, let it run down, abandon it, and build another, more modern one. The Park Service can't do that. We have to maintain what we have because, if we let it deteriorate, it cannot be replaced."

Earlier that day, I had asked a local businessman if he had any complaints about the Park Service. The only thing that came to mind, he said, "was that time last year when they closed the Seashore."

That, Hartman explained, was the weekend of October 1, when Congress and the White House had not been able to agree on a federal budget. When the deadline passed, the President shut down the government, except for essential services. Hartman got his orders from Washington: "Close the Seashore"—at least those areas that required attendants.

Although all personnel automatically went off payroll, Hartman worked overtime for the next three days, trying to calm down the visitors. "I knew there would be a lot of angry people," he said, "and there were. I was called everything from 'the Jane Fonda of 1990' to 'Saddam Hartman.' " One old geezer in a motor home gave him an especially hard time, shouting, "I want to make a complaint." "And I'd listen to you if I were being paid for it," Hartman replied. The man stomped off to call the White House, where he got a recording: "This is the Complaint Desk. We are sorry. We are closed."

The policy of the Park Service nowadays is to let the forces of nature have their way. It is a policy that sometimes puts the Service at odds with the Corps of Engineers, which, in response to local demands for public improvements, often tries to subdue those forces. One place of difference in recent times has been the two-mile Bonner Bridge, which spans Oregon Inlet between

Hatteras and Bodie islands ("Bodie," some say, because of the bodies that washed up on it years ago after shipwrecks). Before it was built in 1963, marine geologists warned that the inlet was extremely unstable, having shifted two miles from north to south in little more than the century since it had opened up, and that no bridge would last long. Sure enough, the sands continued to move beneath the bridge and it was already in trouble when in 1990 a barge broke loose in the swirling waters of the inlet and knocked out a central section of the span. At the time we drove across it, the bridge had just been reopened after almost a year of work.

I asked Hartman how long it would last.

"I give it about eight years," he replied.

Ten miles north of the bridge, the National Seashore ends. Abruptly, we came into Nags Head, where the Outer Banks first flourished as a vacation resort, more than a century ago. Well-to-do families came by ferry from the mainland to Roanoke Island, by carriage across the island, and then by sailing vessel to Nags Head. At first, the visitors stayed at the old Nags Head Hotel, but after the Civil War they began to build their own cottages. Some of the early cottages are still to be seen, but they have been overwhelmed by rampant development since World War II. Nags Head is a classic example of a seaside town that apparently did not think of zoning controls until it was too late.

"It's worse than the Jersey shore," said Jane, my traveling companion, calling up her most damning comparison. She did not cheer up until we had turned west and crossed the bridge to Roanoke Island, which lies within the shelter of the Outer Banks, between Pamlico and Albemarle sounds. There we found tall trees, attractive houses, a restored waterfront with shops and restaurants, and the Fort Raleigh National Historic Site.

Roanoke Island was the site of the colony planted by two of Sir Walter Raleigh's captains in 1587. We know how the land and its resident Indians, the Croatans, looked from the drawings of John White, the artist who was also governor of the colony. There had already been trouble with the Indians, but White painted them as tall, handsome children of nature, planting their fields and feasting on the bounty of the sea. Too trusting, he sailed back to England for more colonists and supplies, leaving a colony of 112, including his daughter and his newborn granddaughter, Virginia Dare, the first white child born in America. He had meant to return at once, but the impending threat of the Spanish Armada brought English shipping to a halt, and he did not get back to Virginia until three years later. The colony had vanished, leaving no clue to its fate except for the letters *CRO*, carved on a tree, and the word *CROATOAN* on a palisade.

Whether the colonists had been killed or carried off by the Indians, no one could discover. In later years, travelers reported seeing some Indians with light complexions and gray eyes in the region, but the mystery lived on. It has drawn people each summer for the last fifty years to a musical play, *The Lost Colony*, performed in an open theater by the shore.

To finish our tour of the Outer Banks, we returned to Nags Head and drove north through Kill Devil Hills to Kitty Hawk. When the early explorers sailed past this shore, they saw here the highest hills and tallest trees on the Carolina coast. The trees were cut down by early colonists and the ground cover withered away, leaving hills of sand that move constantly over the landscape with the never-ceasing wind. It was the combination of sand hills and steady wind that brought the Wright brothers here in 1900 to carry on their initial experiments with flight. Today, the hills are dotted with the bright wings of hang gliders. I talked to Francis Rogallo, the aeronautical engineer who invented the flexible wing used for hang gliding and who now lives a few miles away. Having seen hang gliders mostly in the mountains of Vermont and Colorado, I asked him why these low hills were so attractive.

"Because it's the best place to learn," he replied. "If you are just starting, you don't have far to fall and you land in soft sand. And there's always wind."

North of Kitty Hawk, everything is new. The houses are built mainly in developments, with dead-end streets and landscaped grounds. Yet they have ties to the past. In our journey up the chain of islands from Cape Hatteras, through settlements of increasing affluence, we had observed that the Outer Banks have a distinctive architecture. Along the shore, the basic design is that of the beach cottage or shack, set upon piles to keep it above the storm tides. With time and money, the shacks have been heightened to two or even three stories, wrapped around with exterior staircases, embellished with gables, turrets, verandas, and sometimes at the top a sky platform that would, in New England, be called a widow's walk. At their most extravagant, they look rather as if Piranesi had drawn a vision of a seaside villa and a bemused architect had tried to realize it in Carolina wood.

At Corolla, we reached the end of the road. This northern section of the barrier chain is not an island but a spit, and if you could follow it north you would find yourself at Virginia Beach. You cannot, however, because you run up against a wildlife refuge. Even the few people who live north of there can reach their houses only by driving along the beach in ORVs.

Almost at the end of the public road, we finally saw a sight for which the Outer Banks were once famous: the wild horses. We had seen a few in a fenced-off area of the National Seashore, but here were four of them running loose. Actually, they were grazing by the side of the road on lush green grass—grass that surely never grew wild on the Outer Banks. If these were really wild horses, they were not the galloping stallions seen in early photographs. Though obviously unconfined, they appeared to be cherished survivors of a wilder time, at ease with passing humans and quite happy to have found so comfortable a habitat.

CHAPTER FIFTEEN

HURRICANE HUGO

"WHAT would a hurricane do to this coast?"

That was a question I had often asked myself while driving along the eastern edge of the United States. I had read about hurricanes past and seen pictures of the damage they had done. Old people remembered the big blow of 1926 that struck Miami and brought an abrupt end to the Florida land boom of the twenties. Some recalled the 1935 hurricane that destroyed the railroad to the Florida Keys. I, like many people in the Northeast, had lived through a series of hurricanes, beginning in 1938 and extending into the fifties, that wrecked houses and boats on the New England coast.

Since that time, there had been a lull. A National Hurricane Center was established in Miami, and the hurricanes were given women's—and later, to be fair, men's—names. Hazel, Donna,

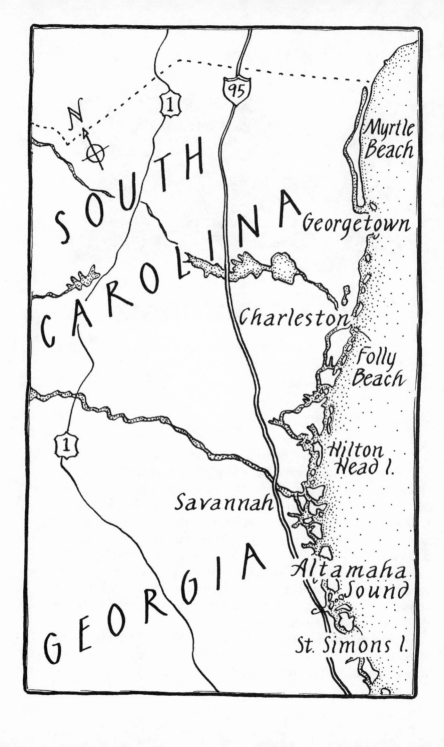

David, and others were severe blows, but overall they were not as devastating as the one in 1938. A lot of people began to forget.

Meteorologists warned that sooner or later the Big One would strike, and the destruction would almost certainly be greater than ever before, because now there was much more on the coast to destroy. In the years since World War II, almost every mile of shorefront, except for parks and wildlife refuges, had been developed and built upon. Many more houses and many more boats lay in the path of any future hurricane.

On the other hand, the science of weather prediction had been greatly upgraded. People would have more notice to save themselves and any movable property. And some coastal residents, learning from previous storms, had built houses that they hoped would be better able to withstand wind and water.

Now it had happened. During the night of September 21, 1989, Hurricane Hugo had made a direct hit on Charleston, the chief city and historic jewel of the South Carolina coast.

I approached Charleston, three months later, from I-95, just as it was getting dark. The highway was clear, but on either side trees were blown flat, signs knocked askew, buildings left without windows, walls, or roofs. I was lucky to get a room at my favorite hotel, the Vendue. During the hurricane, its roof had been blown off and its ground floor flooded, but after three months it was back in business, still smelling strongly of paint and varnish.

The next morning when I walked around the old city—the whole place is an official historic district—I thought at first how good it looked. The streets and yards had been cleaned up, the fallen trees cut up and taken away. But along the Battery, I saw that the fine old houses had been almost up to their second floors in water. Crews were working to gut and rebuild the basements, strengthen the foundations, and repair the rooms above. Although the Battery is protected by a high seawall, the storm surge had flooded Charleston's proud waterfront.

For an assessment of the hurricane's effects, I went to the South Carolina Coastal Council, the agency charged with protecting the coast from damage by erosion, storm, and other perils. I found it in temporary quarters because, embarrassingly, its own roof had been blown off. The commission's office is several miles inland, and quite outside its governmental jurisdiction, but the building would provide some lessons in how to design a roof to withstand hurricanes.

One thing I learned was that the warning system had worked extremely well. Three weeks before Hugo struck South Carolina, the National Hurricane Center had picked it up as a tropical storm in the Atlantic off the coast of Africa. As it spun across the ocean, it gathered force and on September 14, it was upgraded to a hurricane and given a name. Three days later, it struck the island of Guadeloupe, then laid waste St. Croix and a corner of Puerto Rico before turning northwest. As it bore down on the mainland, the Hurricane Center issued a warning for the entire coast of South Carolina and part of North Carolina. On Wednesday, September 20, the governor ordered the evacuation of South Carolina's barrier islands. Thanks in large part to radio and television, almost everyone got the message in plenty of time, and most of them, though not all, heeded it. By the early evening of Thursday, September 21, the Hurricane Center narrowed its prediction of the impact point to the vicinity of Charleston. Said Mayor Joseph P. Riley, Jr.: "It's a killer, and we're staring it right in the eye."

During the night, the eye passed over Sullivans Island, outside Charleston harbor and just north of the city. Police Chief Jack Lilienthal, the last to leave, looked in his rearview mirror, just as he reached the mainland, and saw the bridge collapse behind him. The wind was clocked at 135 miles an hour.

The storm revealed some of the area's vulnerable points. Trailers were especially hard hit, being knocked about and piled in heaps. Roofs, especially flat ones without strong connections to the walls, were blown off a good many houses and some public buildings, including the Charleston city hall. Windows were often a peril because they popped when the pressure dropped in the hurricane's eye. At the Medical Center of South Carolina, a nurse grabbed two children just in time to save them from being sucked out.

The system of refuge centers worked well, giving emergency shelter to thousands of evacuees. Sometimes, though, there were close calls. At McClellanville, thirty miles up the coast, more than four hundred refugees were crowded into a school cafeteria. As the water came in, they climbed onto tables and, as it continued to rise, punched out the ceiling tiles in order to raise the children a foot or so higher. All of them survived. (Hugo's death toll was twenty-six in South Carolina, seventy-one including the Caribbean islands and all of the mainland.)

Although the eye of the storm passed over the Charleston area, that was not the place of maximum impact. Hurricanes in the northern hemisphere whirl in a counterclockwise direction. The winds to the north of the eye have the greatest impact because they come directly off the water, while the winds on the southern side are somewhat slowed by passage over land. Hugo dealt its strongest blow to the coast north of the city. Fortunately, that is a region of light population, composed mainly of the Cape Romain National Wildlife Refuge and the Francis Marion National Forest. What was lucky for people was unlucky for wildlife. Among other endangered species, the forest had the only growing population of Southern red-cockaded woodpeckers. Fewer than half of them survived and, with much of the forest leveled, more were likely to die of starvation. During nesting season, the forest also had the largest colony of bald eagles on the East Coast. Because it was not nesting season, the eagles had not arrived, but most of their old nests were gone, along with tall trees in which they might build new ones. The eagles would have to find a new habitat—if they could.

McClellanville, a fishing and shrimping port, took the hardest hit of all, with a storm surge of eighteen feet as compared with Charleston's ten. The most striking photograph of hurricane damage, played on the front pages of papers across the country, showed the pileup of boats on the shore of McClellanville harbor. Most of the boat owners had rigged double lines and extra anchors and taken refuge ashore, but the captain of one of them decided to ride it out. When the storm surge came, he says, his boat was driven right over the roof of a house.

On the morning after the hurricane, Charleston called for help, and it came from many quarters. I talked with Gene Guydosik, who had led a convoy dispatched by the city of Pompano Beach, Florida. Consisting of five trucks and ten men, it carried emergency supplies and heavy equipment for clearing the streets of fallen trees and debris. They started out in the evening, drove through the night, with only three hours out for rest, and reached Charleston the next day. "There were problems we never thought of," Gene said. "The roofing material that blew off the houses was full of nails. You couldn't drive through without getting a flat tire. So we had to clear the streets as we went." In five working days, the Pompano Beach crew cleared more than three miles of city streets, hauling 235 loads of debris to dump sites. By the time I saw Charleston three months later, the cleanup job had been completed and reconstruction was well under way.

The same could not be said for the barrier islands. To see some of the worst damage, I drove across a causeway to Folly Island, which lies just outside and to the south of Charleston harbor. In the town of Folly Beach, a road runs the length of the island, between one row of houses on the ocean and another row—or in some places several rows—behind. In the front row, some houses appeared to be totally destroyed, while others had roofs blown off, walls blown down, floors collapsed, and household goods strewn over the landscape. Here and there, an elevated walkway, built across the dune, still stood, while the house it served was in ruins. Everywhere, seawalls were knocked down or broken up. Trucks were carrying loads of debris to a smoldering dump at one end of the island, but piles still stood in backyards and along the road.

Folly Beach is exactly the kind of shore that, in the view of modern coastal experts, should never have been built upon. The houses on the ocean side are only a few feet above sea level. For years, the beach has suffered serious erosion. The island's exposed position makes it a sitting target for both hurricanes and northeast storms.

Nevertheless, Folly Beach has been built up for seventy years. Indeed, the front row of houses was not always the front row. Until 1938, there was a line of houses seaward of those that are there today. In a series of storms that eroded the sand, that whole front row was wiped out. All that remained of it for Hugo to destroy was the Atlantic House restaurant, built out of what was left of two of the old houses. It stood on piles in the ocean, and now that was gone.

I stopped in at the mayor's office to ask how things were coming along. "Pretty slow," said Mayor Tom Linville. "People have had to wait a long time for their insurance payments. And even then it's hard to get a good contractor." After the hurricane, a lot of outside contractors showed up in South Carolina.

The mayor was worried about the quality of the work they would do.

"You take Aunt Nellie," said the mayor. "She probably inherited her place a long time ago. She never sees it except at vacation time. She doesn't know a thing about building or repairing a house. She's likely to be an easy mark for some fly-by-night contractor."

In the aftermath of Hugo, the owners of damaged houses had something new to face: the South Carolina Coastal Zone Management Act, passed originally in 1977 and strengthened by amendments in 1988, just fifteen months before Hugo struck. Its purpose was to regulate the kind of shorefront building—and rebuilding—that has made Folly Beach a recurrent disaster area. It reflected the new gospel of coastal management, as developed by geologists and environmentalists and preached most vigorously by Professor Pilkey of Duke University. The South Carolina Coastal Commission, set up to administer it, was still working out its regulations when Hugo struck. "We didn't expect it to be tested so soon," I was told by Christopher Brooks, the deputy director.

The commission had begun its work by identifying the dune line all along the coast. In places where the dunes were gone, it established an "ideal dune line" where the dunes would be if they were still there. Within a twenty-foot zone behind the baseline, no new structures could be built and none that was very badly damaged could be repaired. Behind that "dead zone" was a zone of varying width (depending on the local rate of erosion) where construction was strictly limited as to size and type.

Even before Hugo, the law had been challenged. One property owner on the Isle of Palms, denied permission to rebuild, sued the state for an unconstitutional taking of private property. The court that heard the case (*Lucas* v. *South Carolina Coastal Commission*) accepted his argument and awarded him $1,200,000, but the state supreme court reversed that verdict. (Almost three years after Hugo, the United States Supreme Court overturned the ruling of the South Carolina Supreme Court. Without saying yes or no to the question of compensation in the case at issue, it ordered South Carolina to consider more carefully whether the legislative regulations applying to waterfront property were justified by the established principles of land-use law. Lower courts were admonished also that "changed circumstances or new knowledge may make what was previously permissible no longer so." One thing seemed clear: Coastal law was evolving and many more cases would probably be heard before its principles were settled.)

After the wholesale destruction by Hugo, a crucial question in the case of many houses was the exact degree of damage. According to the regulations, a building that was more than two-thirds damaged could not be rebuilt. But just how to measure the damage? If the foundation of the structure was still there, the inspectors counted that as 25 percent of the house. A standing wall, no matter how shaky, added more percentage points. The upshot was that if the "footprint" of the house still existed, it would probably pass the one-third-intact test. Virtually all of the houses at Folly Beach were approved for rebuilding, the only exceptions being a few flimsy structures that had been totally washed away.

In other places, the conflict between coastal law and property law was not so easily resolved. In the great resort area of Myrtle Beach—the so-called Grand Strand—cottages, motels, and swimming pools had been built out almost to the water's edge. Some of the owners, denied permission to rebuild, were already in court challenging the law.

One thing that Hugo had demonstrated was that houses built to withstand hurricanes did, in fact, suffer much less damage. The ones worst hit were those with weaker foundations, weaker joints, and walls that took the full brunt of the storm surge. Those that came through best were securely anchored in the ground, held together with "hurricane clips" at the joints, and were either set up on stilts or built with "breakaway" first-floor walls. Rebuilt houses would be better for all those features.

The main reason why Folly Beach has suffered so much erosion is that it lies just south of a jetty built along the channel into Charleston harbor. Here, as elsewhere on the Atlantic Coast, the greatest erosion occurs where such jetties interrupt the longshore current, causing sand to accumulate on the shore up-current from the jetty and to wash away on the shore down-current. Mayor Linville thought that the Army Corps of Engineers, which built the jetty, should repair the damage. "They owe me a beach," he said. The Army Corps of Engineers did not deny that the jetties made things worse but it figured it was responsible for only 57 percent of the loss. The mayor had some independent engineers look at the situation. "They tell me," he said, "that it's more like one hundred percent."

Seawalls are another problem. The South Carolina Coastal Zone Management Act embodies the doctrine that the best way to preserve a beach is not to armor it with walls and groins but to replenish it with new sand when erosion occurs. But that is not the accepted view at Folly Beach. Having fought erosion for many years and lost a whole row of houses, the homeowners put their trust in hard, defensive works. At the time the act was being written, Folly Beach won an exemption allowing it to keep its seawalls and revetments, in return for giving up state aid on beach replenishment. Even after Hugo knocked some of the walls to pieces, the owners were glad they had them. "It's the only thing that saved me," one owner told me. Now the walls would be rebuilt, though under the new regulations they would have to be built at a backward slant instead of straight up.

One reason that Folly Beach would be rebuilt, as would all the others areas hit by Hugo, is that the insurance setup gives homeowners every incentive to do so. Most of them had flood insurance issued by the Federal Emergency Management Agency (FEMA). Congress authorized the program in the 1960s because private flood insurance was prohibitively expensive (naturally so, because the only people who wanted it were people in special danger of flood). The federal bill for Hugo was expected to be something more than $3 billion. For some owners, that would not be the first time they had collected federal insurance and perhaps not the last. Critics of the program cite instances where a structure has been destroyed, rebuilt, destroyed again, rebuilt again, destroyed yet again, and would be rebuilt a third time—all at government expense.

FEMA now denies insurance to new buildings in areas of great flood risk, but most such areas are already built up and insured. FEMA even offers to pay 110 percent of value to any property owner who does not rebuild, but it gets few takers. Generally, the shorefront space is worth a lot more than the house itself, but only if something can be built on it. (Three years after Hugo, Congress was still trying to amend the law to discourage risky building.)

Some of those who had prophesied the damage that a hurricane like Hugo would do to places such as Folly Beach were inclined to say "I told you so." Professor Pilkey, the arch-prophet, did not win many friends in South Carolina when he called Hugo "a most timely hurricane."

"If this was an undeveloped shore," said Mayor Linville, "I would say sure, you shouldn't have all these houses so close to the water. Build them back on higher ground. But these houses were here before most of the people who own them were born."

Hugo had proved the experts right in their warnings. It had destroyed all they said it would destroy. It had proved the worth of the early-warning system and the evacuation procedures. It had taught some valuable lessons about the dangers posed by roofs and windows and the special vulnerability of motor homes. But one thing it had not done was to dissuade people from building or rebuilding on low, open shores. Come hell, high water, or Dr. Pilkey, people would not give up their places on the sea.

THE SEA ISLANDS

HEADING south from Charleston, I soon passed out of the hurricane's track and followed the marshy coast to the old city of Beaufort. (In North Carolina, by the way, the town of the same name calls itself BO-fort, but here in South Carolina it is BYEW-fort.) Like Charleston, on a smaller scale, Beaufort grew rich and elegant before the Civil War as a shipping port for the rice and cotton grown on surrounding plantations. All of that ended abruptly on November 7, 1861, when a Union amphibious force knocked out the Confederate forts on Port Royal Sound and occupied the coast. By the time federal troops reached Beaufort, the white population had left. According to the Union commander, the slaves had "flocked into Beaufort on the hegira of the whites, and held high carnival in the deserted mansions."

For almost a century, the fine old houses settled and weathered, their roofs leaking and paint peeling. Crab and shrimp boats kept the place alive, as did the U.S. Marines training center at nearby Parris Island. Not until the middle of this century did tourists, vacationers, and waterfront home buyers bring new money to the area. Most of the old houses have been fixed up, and some of them restored as historic landmarks. Not all, however. From the looks of one grand, deserted mansion, walled away in an overgrown garden, I judged that it was not too late for some antique-house buff to spend half a million dollars restoring it to its antebellum glory.

That kind of money would not faze the property owners at Hilton Head, an island just to the south, across Port Royal Sound. When Beaufort was a citadel of wealth and culture, Hilton Head was planted with rice and cotton. During the Civil War, it became the base for a Union army of thirty thousand soldiers, but after the war, the island was left to subsistence agriculture.

Then in the 1950s, Charles E. Fraser, a young Harvard graduate with some family money, conceived the idea for a new kind of resort community. At the end of the island, behind guarded gates, there came into being a carefully planned enclosure called Sea Pines Plantation, made up of private houses, apartments, golf links, tennis courts, and a small harbor prized by travelers on the Intracoastal Waterway. It was such a success that other "plantations" were developed on the rest of the island, all attracting wealthy vacationers and permanent residents. By 1990, there were twenty-three golf courses, too many tennis courts to count, and growing problems with water and traffic. By then, even Fraser was lobbying for a freeze on growth. As for the blacks who had seen it all happen, what galled them most was that many of them had sold out when the land was cheap and now had to get a pass to visit the places they had owned.

The pattern of life that Hilton Head established has been copied at resorts all along the coast. I had passed some of them on my way from Charleston and saw more of them before I reached Savannah.

Savannah owes its famous charm to its founder, General James Oglethorpe. When he laid out the city in 1733 on a bluff above the mouth of the Savannah River, he provided for twenty-four squares, or small parks, much like those of London, at the intersections of streets. In the prosperous times before the Civil War, many of the little parks and the streets around them were lined with fine houses, graced by carved woodwork and wrought-iron grilles. They had a narrow escape in December of 1864 when General Sherman's army, having burned Atlanta and pillaged the countryside, headed straight for Savannah. To save the city, the Confederate defenders moved out, and Sherman was amused to present Savannah, intact, to President Lincoln as a Christmas present.

Other Colonial cities had started off with handsome plans, but in many cases the industrial boom that followed the Civil War rode roughshod over them. Savannah was spared the destruction, along with the boom; by the time things picked up, the Historic Savannah Foundation had enough clout to save the squares. Later on, the old cotton warehouses and docks at the foot of the bluff were turned into a promenade with shops and restaurants. Savannah does not have the hands-off near-perfection of Charleston's historic district, but it has the grateful charm of a genteel old lady who has known hard times but has finally come into some money.

South of Savannah, the Georgia coast dissolves into an intermingled sea and landscape, made up of estuaries, marshes, and islands. Some major rivers flow down to this coast, rising in the uplands, cascading over the fall line, and moving on across the coastal plain. The Altamaha, for one, pours a greater volume into the Atlantic than any other waterway on the eastern coast of the United States expect for Chesapeake Bay. Some of the rivers run brown with silt from the Piedmont; others are black with acids from decomposing organic matter on the bottomlands. By the time the rivers have crossed the floodplain, they are flowing so slowly that there is no clear dividing line between river and marsh. If you are in a boat, it is hard to tell marsh from dry land, easy to get hopelessly lost in the maze of islands and grass-grown channels.

Under the bright sun of midday, the marsh is a sweeping expanse of waist-high grass, swaying gently with the breezes and currents. As the day ends, it turns to gold and then silver, fading into an eerie night. Sidney Lanier was its poet:

Oh, like to the greatness of God is the greatness within
The range of the marshes, the liberal Marshes of Glynn.

And the sea lends large, as the marsh; lo, out of his plenty
  the sea
Pours fast; full soon the time of the flood-tide must be;
Look how the grace of the sea doth go
About and about through the intricate channels that flow
          Here and there,
              Everywhere,
Till his waters have flooded the uttermost creeks and the
  lowlying lanes
And the marsh is meshed with a million veins,
That like as with rosy and silvery essences flow
In the rose-and-silver evening glow . . .

And I would like to know what swimmeth below when the
  tide comes in
On the length and the breadth of the marvelous Marshes of
  Glynn.

What swimmeth and crawleth and burroweth below is a gargan-
tuan biomass of living creatures—worms, snails, crabs, turtles,
alligators, and numberless species of small crustaceans. This is
where egrets and herons and other wading birds come to probe
the bottom. This is where the food chain that supports the fishery
has its base.

Lanier, the troubled poet, forever worrying about his frail
health and his failure to make a living, came to stay for a time,
shortly after the Civil War, with his father-in-law, at Brunswick.
He liked especially to walk along the edge of the marsh that
lies between the mainland and St. Simons Island. Often, he sat
beneath a certain great tree, inviting his muse and listening to the
melodious repertoire of the mockingbird, "yon trim Shakespeare
in the tree."

The tree is still there, an ancient live oak with five diverging
trunks, but now it is on the median strip of Route 17, the coastal
highway, with streams of traffic on either side. It is no place to
look for the muse, or even for the mockingbird. While I was
there, I spotted a dark-colored bird of about the right size among
the leaves of the tree, but when it gave voice it turned out to be
a grackle.

Among and beyond the marshes, stretching along the coast of Georgia from Savannah to Florida, are the Sea Islands. These are true barrier islands with older, higher, more stable cores, and less striking shapes than the far-flung outriggers of North Carolina's Outer Banks or the thin offshore strips of eastern Florida. Some of them, such as Sapelo, Wolf, and Blackbeard, stand apart at sea, unreached by bridges, while others, such as St. Simons and Jekyll, are tied, for better or worse, to the mainland. Smaller alluvial islands nestle in the mouth of the Altamaha, between the several channels through which that river empties into the sea.

Two of those channels, lent status by the names of Butler River and Champney River, embrace the fifteen hundred acres of Butler's Island. This was the rice plantation made infamous by Fanny Kemble in her book *Journal of a Residence on a Georgian Plantation in 1838–1839.*

The daughter of a noted English theatrical family, Fanny had made a brilliant debut on the stage of Covent Garden at the age of nineteen in the role of Juliet. Lovely, magnetic, and "sometimes sublime," she arrived in New York in 1832 to begin an American tour. In Philadelphia, she met a young man named Pierce Butler, who followed her from city to city and eventually persuaded her to marry him. Fanny saw him as a handsome, social, wealthy suitor who gave her flowers, played the flute, and liked to ride horseback as much as she did. She did not know, or did not give much thought to the source of his wealth, which came from plantations acquired by his grandfather, Maj. Pierce Butler. The major had been a delegate to the Constitutional Convention and a senator, and had married into the great, landed Middleton family of South Carolina.

After four years of marriage, during which she gave up her stage career and bore two daughters, Fanny Kemble Butler prevailed upon her reluctant husband to take her and the little girls on one of his periodic trips to the plantation. They traveled by train, coach, and steamboat to Darien, Georgia, and then were rowed in two small boats to Butler's Island. Their reception took Fanny by surprise. The landing was "crowded with Negroes, jumping, dancing, shouting, laughing and clapping their hands . . . to express their ecstasy at out arrival." She was not taken in. The slaves, she divined, were only hoping that their absentee master would bring them relief from the harsh rule of his overseer.

The next morning, Fanny set out to explore the domain of which she was now "the Missus." Most of the plantation was divided into rice fields—paddies, as they would be called in Asia—and these were surrounded by dikes. Because the river level was governed by the tide for many miles inland, the fields were under the water level for hours every day. A system of gates and ditches let in fresh water from the river on the outgoing tide and kept out salt water on the incoming tide. Here the slaves worked through the daylight hours, often up to their ankles in water. " 'Tis neither liquid nor solid," Fanny wrote of the plantation, "but a kind of mud sponge floating on the bosom of the Altamaha."

On a slightly higher stretch of ground, Fanny passed the rows of slave cabins and stopped to inspect the infirmary. Her *Journal* records what she saw:

> Many of the sick women . . . were cowering, some on wooden settles, most of them on the ground, excluding those who were too ill to rise; and these last poor wretches lay prostrate on the floor, without bed, mattress, or pillow, buried in tattered and filthy blankets, which, huddled round them as they lay strewed about, left hardly space to move upon the floor. And here, in their hour of sickness and suffering, lay those whose health and strength are spent in unrequited labour . . . to buy for us all the luxuries which health can revel in, all the comforts which can alleviate sickness.

Fanny was particularly appalled by the dirty condition of several sick babies. When she remonstrated with an equally sick mother, a slave named Harriet, the woman explained that within three weeks of giving birth the women were sent back into the fields. They went out at daybreak and did not get back until evening, too tired to do anything but throw themselves down and sleep. That night, Fanny protested to the overseer. On her next visit to the infirmary, Harriett told her that she had been flogged for complaining to "the Missus."

Life on the plantation was not all horror. Since there was no place to ride a horse, Fanny learned to row a boat and went on fishing trips, sometimes alone, sometimes with her young black manservant, Jack. When they saw her at the oars, the other slaves shrieked with astonishment at the sight of a white woman using her muscles.

Fanny stepped onto dangerous ground when she asked Jack whether he would like to be free. His face lighted up but he quickly answered, "Free, missis? What for me wish to be free? Oh, no, missis, me no wish to be free, if Massa only let me keep pig!" Fanny could not even arrange the pig because, she was told, a slave would not have anything to feed it.

As planters went, Pierce Butler was not an especially cruel one. He accepted slavery as an inescapable part of the economic system into which he was born. And being an absentee owner, he hesitated to second-guess his overseers. He was not unmoved by the impassioned pleas of his troublesome young wife. Their most bitter confrontation came when Fanny learned that Pierce had given a slave named Joe to a former overseer who now owned a plantation in Alabama. Joe was the husband of Fanny's housemaid, a pretty mulatto named Psyche, who would be left behind with their two small children. Pierce met Fanny's furious protests with stony silence, but the next day she learned that he was keeping Joe.

After seven weeks on the rice island, the family moved, by boat and barge, ten miles downriver to another plantation on St. Simons Island. There, on higher, dryer land, Butler and his brother grew the fine, long-fiber sea island cotton that brought top prices on the English market.

Fanny was able to ride horseback again, but she did not lose her new love for boating. Sometimes, on trips over open water, she was rowed by a crew of eight oarsmen and a steersman, who sang boating songs and improvised verses about the charms of "Old Massa's darling"—herself. One day as they were rowing into a stormy wind, Fanny heard one of them say something to which the others loudly agreed. What was it? she asked.

The steerer said they were pleased because there was not another planter's lady in all Georgia who would have gone through the storm all alone with them in a boat—i.e. without the protecting presence of a white man.

"Why," said I, "my good fellows, if the boat capsized, or anything happened, I am sure I should have nine chances for my life instead of one."

At this there was one shout of "So you would, missus; true for dat, missus"; and in unusual great good humour we reached the landing at Hampton Point.

Spring had come, bringing with it a great blooming of roses and honeysuckle but also mosquitoes, as well as the prospect of fever and of the oppressively humid Sea Island summer. It was time to leave, but first Fanny wanted to see how an island looked in a natural state of wilderness. One day, she had her men row her across the Hampton River to Little St. Simons, where the Butlers had some cotton fields and a penal swamp to which they exiled unruly slaves. It was a hard trip, with the men hacking a path through the woods while Fanny covered her little girls' faces with veils and handkerchiefs against the swarms of mosquitoes and sand flies. By the time they reached the other shore, Fanny was in no mood to appreciate the "fearful-looking stretch of dismal, trackless sand."

Fanny was not sorry to leave the Sea Islands. She had done what she could for the slaves. She had managed to get the infirmary furnished with beds and mattresses. She had taught the women to keep their houses and their babies clean. She had begun teaching one of the house slaves to read—a serious transgression of the law, for which anyone except the master's wife could have been flogged or imprisoned. Now her husband had refused to hear any more of her incessant petitions for better treatment of "his people." Fanny felt there was nothing more she could do to lift the burdens of slavery. In fact, there was—and she did—but not until many years later.

The Butler marriage drifted on for another ten years, but Fanny spent long periods in England, where she found a new career giving readings of Shakespeare's plays. Finally, in 1848, they were divorced, Pierce getting custody of the two girls under Pennsylvania law. Eleven years after that, having squandered his fortune in gambling and in affairs with women, he saved himself from bankruptcy by selling all his slaves. In what they always remembered as "the weeping time," 440 of them were auctioned, family by family, in the slave market at Charleston. The Butler plantations were left with an equal number owned by the estate of his brother, Charles.

When the Civil War began, just two years later, and Union gunboats blockaded the coast, the planters evacuated the Sea Islands, moving their able-bodied slaves far inland. In June of 1863, a young Union colonel named Robert Gould Shaw (the white commander of a black regiment in the 1989 movie *Glory*) rode out to see the place where Fanny, an old family friend from the Abolitionist movement, had spent a winter. The few aged slaves still living on the abandoned plantation told him they wished the massa were back ("Massa Butler was good Massa"), and when he said he knew Mis' Fanny, they "looked most pleased."

Although Fanny had published two other journals, one of her American travels and one of her Italian visit, she had put away her Georgia journal, presumably reluctant to stir up more family trouble. But, living in England during the war, she was alarmed to find English sentiment hardening in favor of the South. She gave her publishers a go-ahead and the *Journal* was published in May of 1863, shortly before the battle of Gettysburg. It opened some influential English eyes to the horrors of slavery, and may have had some effect in forestalling a British loan to the Confederacy. At any rate, it fulfilled Fanny's determination to do what she could to end slavery.

Fanny never went back to the Sea Islands, but her younger daughter, Frances Kemble Butler, did, hoping to revive the plantation with paid labor. She found it in about the same condition that Scarlett O'Hara found Tara. Some of the former slaves had returned, but many of them balked at the hard work of rebuilding the dikes. Moreover, the rice market had fallen, in the face of competition from Louisiana. After five frustrating years, Frances Kemble Butler left for England, where she married a clergymen who became dean of Hereford Cathedral.

For the freed slaves and the ruined planters alike, the economy of the Old South was finished. Fanny was not surprised. Perceptive as always, she wrote:

It seems to me most probable that, like other regions long cursed by the evil deeds of their inhabitants, the plantations will be gradually restored to the wild treasury of nature, and the land "enjoy its Sabbaths" as a wilderness, peopled with snakes, for perhaps a good half century yet.

And so it happened. The old cotton and rice fields lay untilled. Most of the freed slaves drifted away, leaving only a few to scratch a living from the soil. Decades passed before some of the Sea Islands were picked up, for a fraction of their former value, by rich Northerners who used them as hunting preserves. In the 1920s, Sea Island, just off St. Simons, was turned into a posh resort. Jekyll Island became a millionaires' retreat for Rockefellers, Morgans, and Goulds. On some low-country plantations, certain trappings of the Old South were preserved, as I witnessed in the late 1930s on a chance visit to a South Carolina plantation then owned by Nelson Doubleday, the New York publisher. After dinner, the black servants—gardeners, chauffeurs, cooks, and the like—gathered to sing spirituals for the guests, ending with "Good night, Massa Doubleday." It had all the authenticity of a parade in eighteenth-century costumes by the guides at Colonial Williamsburg.

Butler's Island, as I found on my trip along the Georgia coast, is now a waterfowl refuge maintained by the state. Its most striking feature, just a few yards from Route 17, is a seventy-foot brick chimney—all that remains of the mill that ground the rice. The house where Pierce and Fanny stayed is long gone; the slave settlement is now an open field. The dikes are still maintained, to keep out the Butler River, and the rice fields, overgrown with rushes and water lilies, are home to thousands of shorebirds. I knocked at the door of what appeared to be a caretaker's house, but it was Sunday morning and no one answered.

St. Simons Island, on the other hand, is greatly changed. In the last few decades, most of the old plantations have been turned into residential developments, with expensive houses, golf courses, and guarded gates. At the north end of the island, nothing remains of the Butler plantation but some fragments of walls made of tabby, the low-country mixture of lime, shells, sand, and water. Near the point where the old dock stood, there is now a marina where, by invitation, you can get a boat for Little St. Simons.

Of all the Sea Islands, none is closer to its natural state than Little St. Simons. It was bought in 1908 by Philip Berolzheimer, a pencil manufacturer who intended to make pencils out of the red cedar trees. Most of the cedar turned out to be too gnarly for the purpose, but Berolzheimer kept the island as a vacation home, and his family has preserved it untouched. Except when the cedar hunting lodge is being used for reunions in November and December, it takes paying guests.

Boarding the island boat at Butler Point, we churned down the Butler River at waterskiing speed, leaving a brown wake, and landed just about where Fanny must have on her visit to the island. We were greeted warmly by Debbie McIntyre, our attractive hostess, who told us that the lodge is run "like an adult camp." There are three ways to see the island—by foot, on horseback, or by pickup truck. Our guide for the tour was Debbie's husband, Kevin, who knows all there is to know about the flora and fauna of Little St. Simons. As we drove over ridges in the forest, Kevin explained that we were crossing old coastal dunes, now hundreds of yards inland. By the luck of the longshore currents, Little St. Simons has been steadily gaining sand. What used to be frontal dunes are now covered with full-grown pine, cedar, and live oak, offering shelter for great numbers of fallow deer. The marshy parts are home to alligators, snakes, turtles, and flocks of waterfowl. As we walked the wide beach—a fine, sparkling one, despite what Fanny said—I commented to Kevin how fortunate it was that the owners had kept the island pristine. "I don't know," he replied, "whether anyone really owns a place like this."

Except for Little St. Simons, all of Georgia's large Sea Islands have passed from the hands of the wealthy families who owned them, and most have escaped developers. Sapelo, which belonged to R. J. Reynolds, is a wildlife refuge and the site of a marine research institute. Cumberland, once mostly owned by the Carnegie family, is now a National Seashore. Except for Ossabaw and for St. Catherines, where an archaeological study of ancient Indian settlement is under way, most of the islands can be reached by ferry or by private boat, for day trips or overnight camping. On Cumberland, for a price, visitors can stay overnight in the old Carnegie mansion, now called the Greyfield Inn.

In Fanny Kemble's day, the plantation slaves spoke Gullah, a dialect that may have gotten its name from Angola, the place from which many of them came. It was a kind of basic English, spoken with the rhythms and accents of Africa—a useful lingua franca for communicating with their masters. Today, on some of the Sea Islands, where isolated settlements of slave descendants survive, one may still hear traces of the Gullah speech. It is about the only living link with the Sea Island life of Fanny's time.

CHAPTER SEVENTEEN

ON BARTRAM'S TRAIL

AFTER crossing the Florida border and cir-
cling the busy port of Jacksonville, I regained the coast at the
beautiful Ponte Vedra Beach. I was now on one of the long string
of sandy barriers—islands and spits—that stretch down the east
coast of Florida, almost all the way to the end of the peninsula.
Between the coastal barriers and the mainland are long, narrow
waterways, variously called rivers, sound, lakes, and bays. This
is the route of the Intracoastal Waterway, used by all but the
biggest boats that move along the Florida shore. Down the mainland coast run Interstate 95 and old Route 1. Route A1A runs
down the barrier chain, detouring back to the mainland when it
has to get around a break in the coastal barrier.

Americans have been told often enough that St. Augustine
was the first European settlement in what is now the United
States. But they do not quite accept that historic fact, continuing

177

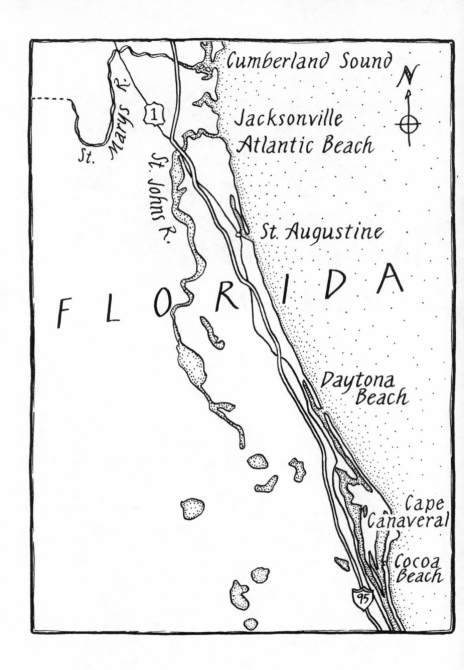

to think of Plymouth, or perhaps Jamestown, as the starting point of our history. That, no doubt, is because St. Augustine never led to much of anything, as the English colonies did. The fact remains that St. Augustine was the first. Because it remained such a dead end for so many centuries, some of the early buildings still stand. In recent times, St. George Street has been restored as a pedestrian mall with historic exhibits, shops, and restaurants.

When I turned on the TV in my motel room I was surprised to find that "Good Morning America" was broadcasting from the old city, only a mile away. The heart of the restoration is the Spanish Quarter, where the life of the eighteenth-century city is recreated in meticulous detail. By the time I got there, the TV show was over and the staff people of the Spanish Quarter were getting back to their regular work. In one shop, the blacksmith, whom I had just seen on TV, was demonstrating to the first visitors how he made tools and guns, but not horseshoes, which were made by the farrier; not until a later time, he explained, when the other work had been taken over by machines, did the blacksmith fall back on horseshoes.

In the director's office, I found an old friend, Earle Newton, who has made the Spanish Quarter one of the country's truly authentic restorations. Newton had turned out his guides in costume at five o'clock for "Good Morning America," but when the producer wanted to borrow some of them for a scene outside the sugar mill at the nearby Fountain of Youth, he had drawn the line. A mill needed running water, Newton pointed out, and there was no natural river at the site of the mill, which uses well water to turn its paddlewheel. Not every exhibit in St. Augustine meets Newton's standards.

On my way to the Fountain of Youth, I was sidetracked by its neighbor, the Tragedy in U.S. History Museum, which advertised "President Kennedy's Car" and the car in which Lee Harvey Oswald carried the assassination gun. The President's car, it turned out, was not the open one in which he was shot but a limousine he had used in Washington. The really grisly exhibit is "Jayne Mansfield's Death Car," a smashed-up Buick Electra in which the actress was decapitated in 1967.

I continued on to the Fountain of Youth, a privately owned historical attraction on the site of an ancient Indian village.

According to the proprietors, this is where Ponce de León landed in 1513 and discovered the magical fountain. A pretty girl in Spanish dress offered me a cup of the restorative water and showed me a large cross, cut out of the rock, supposedly by the explorer's men. On a pedestal beside the cross stands a blackened silver cellar in which, she said, was found a document attesting that this was the place where Ponce de León had claimed a continent for the King of Spain.

"Where is the paper now?" I asked.

"I don't know," she replied. "I guess they have it somewhere."

Historians are not so sure they know where Ponce de León landed. Samuel Eliot Morison, the leading authority on the explorer's voyages, concluded that the probable landing spot was fifty miles south, at what is now called Ponce de León Inlet. As for the cross, it was not revealed until 1904. In any case, it seems unlikely that Ponce de León thought he had found the fabled Fountain of Youth, because he went on looking for it in other parts of Florida.

There is no doubt, however, that this was the site of an Indian village called Seloy. It belonged to the Timacua people, whose homeland included most of northeast Florida. From them, we have our first images of Native American life in what is now the United States. When the French sent a fleet to seize the territory from the Spanish in 1564, the company included an artist named Jacques LeMoyne, who made sketches and paintings of the Indians. In the ensuing rout of the French expedition, LeMoyne lost all his artwork, barely escaping with his life. Later in London, he repainted the scenes from memory, and those paintings became the source for a book of engravings published with LeMoyne's notes by Theodore DeBry. They show a race of tall, handsome people, the men dressed in loincloths and the women in skirts of finely woven grass. They lived in round, palm-thatched huts within a log palisade. They raised maize, beans, and pumpkins, played a ball game that looks something like lacrosse, worshiped the sun and moon. LeMoyne shows the chosen bride of a tribal chief, or *cacique*, being carried in a litter to her wedding. She is adorned with feathers, pearls, and tattoos, and is attended by flutists, warriors, and maidens bearing fruit.

Once the Spanish had given up their hopes of finding either gold or youth in Florida, they settled into their capital at St. Augustine, where they built a fort, the Castillo de San Marcos, which is now a National Monument. The Indians had the rest of the peninsula pretty much to themselves, but, chiefly because of the white man's diseases, they were reduced to a small fraction—perhaps a tenth—of their former numbers. Only a handful of travelers from the north—trappers, pirates, fugitives, runaway slaves, and the like—found their way to Florida, and they left little record.

Then, in 1763, when Spain ceded Florida to England, in return for Havana, the frontier opened and Colonial Americans began moving in. Few trekked down the sandy coast. Instead, they went up the St. Johns River from Jacksonville and moved south through the forest, looking for timber, furs, and likely land for plantations. Among those early venturers were John Bartram, the leading botanist of the colonies, and his son, William, a young man with a talent for painting plants and animals. The St. Johns is almost unique among the rivers of North America in that it flows from south to north (the only other one of any size being the Red River of the North). Rising more than halfway down the state, just inland from Fort Pierce, it flows through a string of lakes and swamps, seldom more than twenty or thirty miles from the coast, at such a slow pace that it seems hardly to move at all. In the course of 280 miles, it falls only twenty feet, and the last half of it is tidal. It was, in Bartram's day—and, wherever man has let it alone, still is—a great place for wildlife.

Instead of following the coast, I did as the Bartrams did and turned inland, picking up their trail at Palatka. The Bartrams, in a shallow-draft boat rowed by four slaves, had traveled slowly up the river, studying the trees and plants. When it came time to turn back, William said that he wanted to remain and set up an indigo plantation. To his purposeful father, botanist to the king, friend of Franklin and Jefferson, William was a problem. In earlier tries at agriculture and cotton trading, he had failed. But Bartram senior agreed and bought him enough slaves to clear and plant a tract of land (a compromise of the Bartrams' Quaker principles, in compliance with British policy on the Florida frontier: no slaves, no land grant). Three years later, Henry Laurens, another of John Bartram's friends and later president of the Continental Congress, stopped by and sent Bartram senior a report on ". . . that poor young man. His situation on the river is the least agreeable of all places that I have seen . . . on a low stretch of sandy pine barren, verging on the swamp—water almost stagnant, exceedingly foul, and absolutely stank when stirred up by our oars." Of the six slaves only four could handle an ax properly and of those one had been "exceedingly insolent." Laurens concluded, "Possibly, sir, your son, though a worthy, ingenious man, may not have resolution, or not the sort of resolution, that is necessary to encounter the difficulties incident to, and unavoidable in his present state of life."

William Bartram had failed again, but now he knew what he really wanted to do: to combine his knowledge of wildlife with his talent for drawing, in the career of a naturalist. In 1766, he got a commission from an English collector to gather botanical specimens.

This time, Bartram started up the river alone in a small boat, with oars and a sail that doubled as a tent at night. He spent his days collecting seeds and plants, identifying birds, insects, and animals, and bestowing names on those not recorded before. He had an eye for the beauties of primeval nature and a gift for describing them in vivid, not to say rapturous, prose. Here is his description of one campsite:

> How happily situated is this retired spot of earth! What an elysium it is! where the wandering Seminole, the naked red warrior, roams at large, and after the vigorous chase retires from the scorching heat of the meridian sun. Here he re-clines, and reposes under the odoriferous shades of Zan-thoxilon, his verdant couch guarded by the Deity; Liberty and the Muses inspiring him with wisdom and valour, whilst the balmy zephyrs fan him to sleep.

The river basin of the St. Johns is a thoroughly water-logged country, underlain with a deep aquifer and bubbling with springs. Bartram left the river to look at one now known as Salt Springs. He was amazed by what he found:

Just under my feet was the inchanting and amazing crystal fountain which incessantly threw up, from dark, rocky caverns below, tons of water every minute, forming a bason, capacious enough for large shallops to ride in. . . . The waters are thrown up in such abundance and amazing force, as to jet and swell up two or three feet above the common surface. . . .

Innumerable bands of fish are seen, some cloathed in the most brilliant colours . . . whole armies descending into an abyss, into the mouth of the bubbling fountain, they disappear! are they gone forever? is it real? I raise my eyes with terror and astonishment. . . . I looked down again to the fountain with anxiety, when behold them as it were emerging from the blue ether of another world, apparently at a vast distance, at their first appearance, no bigger than flies or minnows, now gradually enlarging, their brilliant colours begin to paint the fluid.

The publication of Bartram's *Travels* in 1791, during the Romantic movement in English literature, gave the poets, especially Coleridge and Wordsworth, just what they needed for their pictures of a primeval world. Bartram's description of the crystal fountain was the inspiration for the first lines of Coleridge's *Kubla Khan*:

> In Xanadu did Kubla Khan
>   A stately pleasure-dome decree;
> Where Alph, the sacred river, ran
>   Through caverns measureless to man
> Down to a sunless sea.

The spring is still there, within what is now the Ocala National Forest, but its wonder is gone. The natural forces that govern the pressure of water beneath the ground have reduced the "amazing ebullition" to a gentle bubbling. The spring has been enclosed on three sides by a concrete wall, with a walkway for visitors. Looking into the pool, I could see lots of fish, but they were all gray and were just swimming around, neither descending into deep caverns nor erupting out of them. A young man with a snorkel who was in the pool, trying to spear a mullet, told me that he had probed the openings in the bottom and none was more than a few feet deep. Alas, I had come two hundred years too late to see the spring as Bartram had.

Farther up the river, at the entrance to Lake Dexter, Bartram rowed into a vast congregation of alligators—"in such incredible numbers, and so close together from shore to shore, that it would have been easy to have walked across on their heads, had the animals been harmless."

> Two very large ones attacked me closely, at the same instant, rushing up with their heads and part of their bodies above the water, roaring terribly and belching floods of water over me. They struck their jaws together so close to my ears as almost to stun me, and I expected every moment to be dragged out of the boat and instantly devoured.

From his campsite on the edge of the lake, he witnessed an alligator's epic battle:

> Behold him rushing forth from the flags and reeds. His enormous body swells. His plaited tail brandished high, floats upon the lake. The waters like a cataract descend from his opening jaws. Clouds of smoke issue from his dilated nostrils. The earth trembles with his thunder. When immediately from the opposite coast of the lagoon, emerges from the deep his rival champion. They suddenly dart upon each other. The boiling surface of the lake marks their rapid course, and a terrific conflict commences. They now sink to the bottom folded together in horrid wreaths. The water becomes thick and discoloured. Again they rise, their jaws clap together, re-echoing through the deep surrounding forests. Again they sink, when the contest ends at the muddy bottom of the lake, and the vanquished makes a hazardous escape hiding himself in the muddy turbulent waters and sedge on a distant shore. The proud victor exulting returns to the place of action. The shores and forests resound with his dreadful roar, together with the triumphing shouts of the plaited tribes around, witnesses of the horrid combat.

To find the site on Lake Dexter, I enlisted the help of the obliging naturalists at the Lake Woodruff National Wildlife Refuge. My guide, Bud Wilcoxson, took me by motorboat across Lake Woodruff and through the river channel into Lake Dexter. At a small rise known as Idlewilde Point in Bartram's day, we found the site of Bartram's camp. It looked much as it must have looked in the eighteenth century, with a heavy growth of oak, gum, and water hickory trees. On the trip across the lake, however, we had seen only two alligators, sunning themselves on the bank. In Bartram's day, there had been bears, wolves, and panthers, which caused him to sleep with a loaded rifle. There were none left, Bud said, but there were deer and an oversupply of raccoons, swollen in numbers by the absence of large predators and the ban on steel traps. Despite some pollution from the river water, there were still enough fish—mostly bream, with some mullet—to attract the dozens of fishing boats we saw on the lake. There were lots of birds, although no one would say, as Bartram did, that they filled the sky.

As elsewhere in the springs country, there were mounds of shells, left long ago by the Indians, who feasted on shellfish. There were also the remains of more recent refreshments, especially beer and cola bottles. "We put out trash cans," said Bud, "and they won't even use them."

Except for some deer hunters, who are allowed to hunt with bow and arrow or "primitive" guns in a brief season, the visitors to Lake Woodruff are either fishermen or bird-watchers. It is the fishermen who leave the trash, said Bud, a fisherman himself. The birders take theirs out with them.

Bartram was not the last great naturalist to visit this country. On the lake, we passed a place called Audubon's Island. John James Audubon came here in 1831, in a very bad humor. The federal government had given him the use of a boat for his journey up the St. Johns River, but he had quarreled with the captain and gone ahead on his own. Armed with a rifle for collecting specimens, he had found few that he did not already have. He did shoot an ibis, which he wanted, but the bird was only wounded and got away. To his wife, Audubon wrote:

Here I am in Florida, thought I, a country that received its name from odours wafted from the orange groves, to the boats of the first discoverers, and which from my childhood I have consecrated in my imagination as the garden of the United States. A garden where all that is not mud, mud, mud is sand, sand, sand; where the fruit is so sour it is not eatable, and where in place of singing birds and golden fishes, you have a species of ibis that you cannot get when you have shot it, and alligators, snakes, and scorpions.

Grumpily, he told her of the island where he and some companions had stopped for lunch. "It was determined *nolens volens* that it should be called Audubon's Island, on the St. Johns River Lat. 29° 42!"

On the way back, Bud told me something about the human habitat in what I had taken to be a fairly backwoods part of Florida. The road on which he had commuted for years between his home and the wildlife refuge was also the road that led to Orlando, the ever-expanding home of Disney World. Finally, the traffic got so bad that he and his wife gave up their home and moved into a cabin they had on a lake near the refuge.

At the refuge headquarters, the others agreed that Florida's overriding problem is too many people. "They are coming across the border at the rate of a thousand a day—coming to stay," said the refuge manager, Leon Rhodes. Neil Carper, his assistant, laid some of the blame on Mickey Mouse: "They should have stopped that rat at the border."

In the years before the building of the Florida East Coast Railway, when the St. Johns River was the chief route of travel south, steamboats were common on the river and its chain of lakes. One passenger boat, the *Princess Ann*, still takes visitors like myself on excursions out of Sanford. Here, the river snakes through a wide expanse of swampy ranch land. Captain Harley P. Hoy, the skipper, has a tricky job of navigation because, when the river is low, as it was on our trip, the average depth is only eight inches. When the river is high, the whole basin is one big puddle, with cattle standing up to their knees in the flood, munching the water hyacinths.

We passed Marina Isle, a kind of maritime shantytown, made up of fishing boats, houseboats, and trailers. I wondered what the fishermen caught there.

"Some of them catch black eels," said the captain. "They're sold to Japan, where they bring ten dollars a pound."

What used to be trash is now treasure. In the days of empire, I reflected, the British on their little offshore island imported delicacies from faraway lands—dates, oranges, pineapples, curry, and Bombay duck. Now the Japanese on *their* little off-shore island send out agents to bring back *their* favorite gourmet foods—sea urchins from Maine and black eels from the Florida swamps.

I had followed the St. Johns as far as William Bartram could be my guide. The next morning, I cut back, north and east, to regain the coast at Daytona Beach.

ON THE FLYWAY

DAYTONA Beach had the feeling of a city awaiting barbarian invasion. The defending forces had been put on alert, reserves called up, sentries posted. Residents had seen to their food supplies. Shops and inns had put away their breakables.

Daytona had already withstood the assault of the motorized cavalry—four thousand cyclists roaring through town to the International Speedway. Now it was waiting for the infantry attack—four *hundred* thousand college students, more or less, coming from all across the East and Midwest for Spring Break.

No relief was expected from sister cities. Fort Lauderdale, long famous as the place "Where the Boys Are" (and the girls, too), had turned them away by enforcing laws against drinking on the streets and all-night carousing. Key West, alarmed by rumors that it might be next on the hit list, had sent out pleas to the campuses, warning (quite truthfully) that its motel rates were the highest in the state. Daytona was in for it.

Not that the partying hordes lacked allies within the city. Motel keepers had come to depend on spring break for a third of their annual business. Pizza parlors, bars, and T-shirt stores were hoping for peace with profit.

"This year," said a policeman, "we're ready for them."

I did not stay to see the invasion. Some weeks later, I learned that Spring Break had not been as bad as the year before. Only 6,085 collegians had been arrested. Only six had fallen off motel balconies. None had died.

As I drove out of town, I wondered at the sight of automobiles cruising over the broad white beach. There was a time, not beyond memory, when goggled and helmeted drivers with names such as Barney Oldfield and Sir Malcolm Campbell raced their cars over the hard-packed sand. Perhaps in another fifty years, visitors will think it just as strange that the beach was still open to motorists in the 1990s.

Fifty miles farther down the coast, I came to Cape Canaveral. Here, the string of long, thin coastal barriers is broken by a landform akin to Cape Hatteras and Cape Fear, the outflung banks of North Carolina. Cape Canaveral is shared by the John F. Kennedy Space Center and the Merritt Island National Wildlife Refuge. When NASA took what it needed of the cape in the 1960s, it turned over the rest to the management of the Fish and Wildlife Service. Later, a twenty-four-mile beachfront received added protection as a National Park—the longest stretch of undeveloped beach in Florida.

The juxtaposition of a rocket-launching station and a wildlife refuge works surprisingly well. At the refuge visitors' center, I saw a film in which ospreys in their lofty nests were feeding their young, quite unconcerned by a rocket making its fiery ascent a mile or so away. Some creatures get a special break. The tortoise, one of nature's slowest creatures, is easy prey for a car or truck when it tries to cross a road, but it has a fighting chance against one of man's slowest vehicles, the giant mover that conveys rockets to the launching pad. In the film, at least, the tortoise won the race.

The manatee is another slow-moving creature that has found a refuge at the space center. A big, gray, bulbous mammal, related more closely to the elephant than to anything else, the manatee has long been a familiar sight in Florida's coastal waters, cruising slowly, grazing on sea grass, or just floating the day away. Over the years, it has suffered from hunting, pollution, and the dredging of sea grass, but its worst enemy is the powerboat. When manatees are brought ashore, most of them bear propeller scars. By the best estimates, there are only about fifteen hundred manatees left in Florida waters and there are more than 700,000 powerboats.

In the last few years, Florida has begun to impose strict limits on the speed of powerboats in waters where the manatees are most at risk. But such laws are hard to enforce, and the fate of the manatees is still uncertain. Meanwhile, they have found one haven in the barge canal at the space center, where vessels proceed carefully to avoid hitting them. Last year about 250 of them—a sixth of the whole Florida population—were counted at the space center.

Merritt Island is not only the largest wildlife refuge on the East Coast, it also has the greatest number of endangered and threatened species—nineteen of them, counting four kinds of turtles and two of snakes. Among the birds in trouble are the southern bald eagle, the wood stork, the peregrine falcon, the scrub jay, and the magnificent frigate bird.

One bird that has recently been removed from the list is the dusky seaside sparrow. Its only habitat, the open savannas of the St. Johns River floodplain and the brackish marshes of Merritt Island, was effectively destroyed in the 1960s by construction and by mosquito-control projects. By 1978, only seven duskies were left, all male. In an effort to save something of the species, six were captured and mated with females of a closely related species, Scott's seaside sparrow from the Gulf Coast. Although a few young were hatched, it was too little and too late. The last dusky seaside sparrow died on June 16, 1987.

"That's the way it always is," I was told by Wes Biggs, ornithologist of the Florida Audubon Society. "Every species that has become extinct has been the victim of something man has done."

On the brighter side, things are looking up for the southern bald eagle. The eagle's dilemma is that it likes to nest in tall trees near the edges of salt or fresh water—the same places where humans like to build houses. Because the eagle is our national bird, it commands more public concern and more stringent legal protection than other species. Recently in Florida, a multimillion-dollar bridge-building project was brought to a halt for at least the duration of the nesting season, after an eagle's nest was discovered nearby. Florida counts about one thousand pairs of eagles now, up from a third that number since the banning of DDT. So, while the eagles took a hit from hurricane Hugo in South Carolina, they are making up for it in Florida.

The role of the federal government in the protection of endangered species had its origin at the beginning of this century on a little island in the Indian River, twenty miles south of Cape Canaveral. In those days, sportsmen traveled the coastal waterway by steamboat, and when they passed the island they got their kicks by standing at the rail and shooting broadside at the brown pelicans. When a German boat builder named Paul Kroegel, who lived across the river, started a campaign to stop the slaughter, he found a sympathetic ear in the White House. In 1903, Theodore Roosevelt, our first environmentalist President, issued an executive order creating the Pelican Island wildlife sanctuary. It was the first of more than 450 areas that now make up the National Wildlife Refuge System.

For some birds, including such stately waders as herons, egrets, and ibis, the Merritt Island refuge is a permanent home. Others fly in for the winter from all over the eastern and central states and Canada. Still others, following the Atlantic Flyway, use it as a stopping place on flights between their summer ranges in the north and winter ranges in the Caribbean and South America. In recent years, the incoming flocks from the north have held their own, but those from the west have been smaller. Refuge managers attribute the decline to the loss of habitat in the prairies, woodlands, and wetlands of the western states.

Walking along Playalinda Beach, on the ocean side of the cape, I chanced upon a little flock of sandpipers running along the tide line, darting down after each retreating wave to pick up whatever edible morsels had been brought in. I wondered whether these might be the same sandpipers I had seen the previous summer on the beaches of Cape Cod. The answer is yes, as I found out when I talked to C. Dwight Cooley, the staff biologist of the refuge, but it is not as simple a matter as I had supposed. After an hour's conversation, I had a better understanding of the life and times of this little bird.

The sandpiper I had asked about is the sanderling, known to ornithology as *Crocethia alba*. It is not actually white but is pale sandy in color, with a white stripe on the wings. It is the lightest colored of sixteen sandpipers listed in Roger Tory Peterson's *Field Guide to Eastern Birds*. The reason it is so familiar to beach walkers is that it feeds on the open beach rather than in marshes, as other sandpipers do.

A sanderling seen in early March at Cape Canaveral has been on his winter range since fall. Within the next month or so, something in his glands will tell him that the mating season is approaching, and something presumably in his genes—some "biological clock"—will tell him it is time to start north. He does not want to start too soon, however, because then he might outrun the advancing line of spring. Well before he leaves, he will start to consume more food, building up his body weight for the long journey. By the time he is ready to take off, numerous flocks of sandpipers and many other birds will have already left. Other flocks will be coming in from wintering places farther south, pausing at Cape Canaveral on their way. If the sanderling starts north in the second week of April, he will be in about the middle of the spring migration.

Whitey—to give him the name by which some people call him—leaves about an hour after sunset in a flock of thirty or forty birds. They will travel mostly at night, when they are generally safe from hawks and other predatory birds, especially the peregrine falcon, which can swoop down out of the sun and make a meal of a little sandpiper.

Storms have always been the greatest peril to migrating birds, but now there are other dangers. Soon after takeoff, the sanderlings confront the bright beacon at Ponce de León Inlet. Programmed perhaps by nature to fly by the light of the moon and stars, migrating birds become confused by other lights, especially in rain and fog. Sometimes after a foggy night, the ground around the lighthouse has been littered with dead birds. Luckily, it is a clear night, and the flock gets safely by the lighthouse, but all along the coast it will have to contend with the lights of cities, houses, signs, and automobiles.

In migration season, the night is filled with hundreds of

thousands of birds, most of them flying at heights of several hundred or a few thousand feet, while some, like the Canada geese, may be as high as five miles up. Few are ever seen by humans, but there is always a chance that an all-night bird-watcher, with his powerful telescope trained on the moon, may see our little flight of sandpipers cross its face.

The first night's trip takes Whitey and his flock to a beach in northern Florida, after a flight of some 250 miles at a speed of about thirty miles an hour. The greatest advantage of flying at night is that the birds have the daylight hours in which to forage, rest, and build up their strength for another flight. Migration is not as hard for sanderlings as it is for birds that depend on marshes and uplands for their roosting and feeding places. Along a coast that once was wild and wooded but is now built-up, migratory birds may have a hard time finding an empty marsh or a patch of forest. That is why the wildlife refuges— federal, state, and private—are so important to their survival.

It is only within fairly recent times that the mysteries of bird migration have been unraveled. For centuries, many people believed, with Aristotle, that they hibernated. Some thought that they dived into ponds and buried themselves in the mud. The author of one treatise in 1703 believed that they flew to the moon.

Now, ornithologists know where they go in winter, but they cannot say for certain how they get there. It may be that they navigate mainly by the moon and stars. It may be that they make their first flight with older birds and retain a memory of landforms along the route. It may be that they are guided by some genetic compass still unknown.

Four flying days take Whitey and his flock to Cape May at the mouth of Delaware Bay, where they alight in the greatest congregation of birds to be found anywhere on the Atlantic Flyway. Birds flock to the Delaware shore in May as Texans do to a barbecue. The feast they turn up for is the annual egg-laying frenzy of the horseshoe crab. As the multitudes of female crabs come crawling out of the sea to deposit their eggs—as many as fifty thousand apiece—the multitudes of birds are waiting to gulp them down. So prodigal is nature that even though only a tiny fraction of the eggs ever hatch, those are enough to keep the crabs coming every spring, as they have for millions of years.

After gorging themselves on the bounty of Delaware Bay, the sanderlings fly on north, some of them to Cape Cod, where I have seen them or others like them in earlier years, never realizing that they were only stopping off on a long migration. They may stay for a few days or even a couple of weeks, and when they leave they will be replaced by other sanderlings that look just like them.

The sanderling is luckier than others because his habitat—the sandy shore—is still there. Things have changed, however, as I learned from Wes Biggs of the Florida Audubon Society. "It may look," he said, "as if the sanderlings are undisturbed by people. They run along the water's edge, probing for food, and if people come along they just fly up and land a little farther down the beach. But if a child chases them or if they cannot find a quiet place in the dunes to rest, they are stressed. Most of all they need 'loafing time' to renew their strength."

In New England, the sanderlings' journey is not half over. From there, they will follow the coast north to the Bay of Fundy and then cut northwest across Canada. Whitey must now change his diet, giving up marine worms, sand fleas, and small crustaceans for tiny plants, buds, and moss. It is early June when he reaches his breeding ground on an island halfway between the Arctic Circle and the North Pole. Others of his kind have fanned out across the Arctic, nesting from Alaska to Greenland.

Whitey selects a patch of ground that will be his own and begins courting one of the female sanderlings. In a shallow depression on the open tundra, they make a nest of withered grass and leaves, in which the female lays four speckled brown eggs. As soon as the chicks are hatched, the parents are busy from dawn to dusk, stuffing them with food. It is clear now why nature directed these little birds to a far north feeding ground. For one thing, the summer explosion of plants and insects on the tundra provides a bountiful source of food for the insatiable appetites of newly hatched chicks. For another, the harsh winter climate makes predatory animals scarce.

Within about two weeks, the baby birds are able to fly and to forage for themselves. Whitey and his mate linger for a time, shedding their old feathers and growing new ones, rebuilding their weight and strength for another long trip. By the end of July, some of the sanderlings who flew north first have already started back south. In the middle of August, Whitey and his companions form a flock once more and take off, following the same route back, taking their time now and lingering at favorite stopping places such as the Bay of Fundy. One day in early October, they are back at Merritt Island.

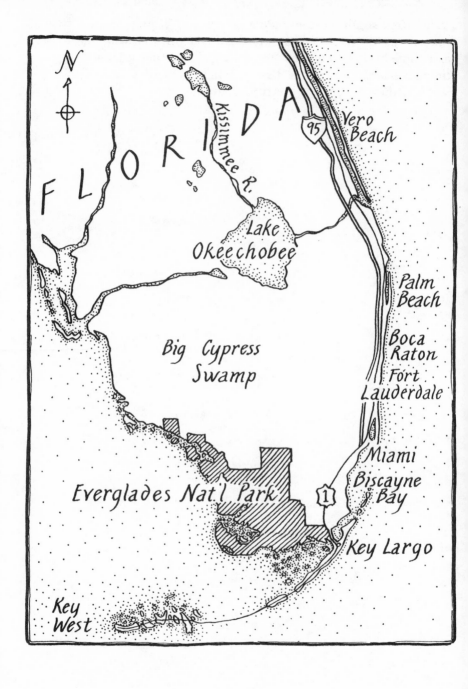

THE TREASURE COAST

PROCEEDING south on I-95, on my way to
Jane's place in Stuart, I came to the first of the Garbage Mountains. If those landforms were in Vermont or Colorado, they
would seem no more than low, rounded hills, but in Florida they
are the tallest things in sight. Little bulldozers scramble up and
down their sides, leveling the loads of trash and covering them
with dirt to hold them in place and foil the gulls. Floridians have
always had a talent for creative landscaping. They think nothing
of converting a swamp into house lots or dredging a grid of
canals through an island in order to give every lot its own waterfront. Now, in a state where a new development may be called
Hibiscus Highlands because it is twenty feet above sea level, they
are building what seem by comparison to be artificial Alps. At

197

the rate things are going, Florida may end up with a whole Garbage Range to puzzle future topographers.

This part of the Florida coast was slower to develop than sections to the north and south, but in the last twenty years it has been making up for lost time. Orange groves have been turned into subdivisions and fishing villages have blossomed into expensive resorts. Most of the new residents have come down from the north, but recently some have come back up from the south to escape the increasingly urban problems of West Palm Beach and Miami.

It is easy to see why this coast is so attractive. From Cape Canaveral south, the Indian River runs parallel to the ocean shore, between the mainland and the barrier islands. It begins as a river but then, for about eighty miles, it is a saltwater lagoon, the route of the Intracoastal Waterway. Thus there are three shores instead of one on which to build waterfront houses, ranging in style from cottages to mansions.

The prevailing pattern of building here, as in much of Florida, is the development—sometimes called a plantation, ranch, or estate—consisting of individual houses or condominiums, generally built in a single architectural style. Sometimes there is a community center with restaurant or swimming pool. The more expensive ones are often laced with the fairways of private golf courses. One on the water may include a marina or individual docks. Most of these developments have walls or fences, and the fancier ones are likely to possess gates, guards, and patrolling security police. There is a hint of fear in paradise.

I observed that the residents of these compounds had much in common with the birds I had seen in the wildlife refuges. Some of them live there all year. Some migrate spring and fall. Some of them indeed come in small flocks from empty nests in New Canaan or Short Hills or Shaker Heights. Their migrations, like those of certain birds, are often precise to the day. Quite a few arrive on the last day of October and leave on the first day of May, thus serving out the six-month stay that qualifies them to be Florida residents. (No income tax! No inheritance tax!)

Residents of the fancier enclaves do not have much reason to leave them, except to go to stores, restaurants, banks, and doctors' offices. It is important to play golf and bridge or to have a boat. Tennis is good, too, but it does not take up enough time. Pity the hostess, a friend of mine, who was expecting a houseguest: "She doesn't play golf or bridge. What will we do after shopping?"

The development, rather than the town or neighborhood, is the operative social unit. Voices are raised and sides taken over such issues as the length of a dog's leash, the time of day or night when the lawn sprinklers should be turned on, the height of artificial bumps to slow down traffic. Two such controversies made the front pages of the local papers while I was there. One centered on a woman who had sought to beautify her road by planting petunias around a hydrant. That, it seemed, was contrary to the bylaws of the condominium, which frowned on departures from the decorative norm. After months of wrangling, the dispute ended up in court, where a weary judge ruled that the petunias must go.

The other, more long-standing controversy concerned an elderly woman who had her grandson living with her. Since she lived in an adults-only development, there was no doubt that she was in violation of the rules. The grandmother pleaded in court that the boy was essential to her well-being, not only for his help in taking out the trash and driving to the grocery but also for protection against the ever-present threat of intruders. Her lawyer called into question the constitutionality of bylaws that discriminate on the basis of age. By the time the case came to trial, the boy was only a year and a half short of adulthood. Nevertheless, the court ordered him to leave.

Those who choose to live on the ocean have the same problems that residents of other barrier beaches face. One day, Jane and I were walking along the shore of Hutchinson Island with a friend who was thinking of buying a waterfront condo. When we came to a building that was just being finished, directly behind the dune, she decided to see what it had to offer. We were shown a ground-floor condo, priced about $100,000 more than it would have cost anywhere except on the ocean. But that was $50,000 less than apartments on the two floors above, and for good reason. While it faced the ocean, you could not actually see the water because its windows were below the top of the dune.

The dune was offering protection from the ocean, but for

how long? When we crossed back to the beach, we saw that on the ocean side the dune rose only about five feet above beach level and it was eroding at the base. It is not the nature of a dune to stay in place. As I had seen on other shores, its nature is to retreat, rolling over on itself when high waves strike it and maintaining its form by moving landward. If something blocks its path—something such as a building—it slowly disintegrates and moves sideways along the beach. We wondered how long it would be before the condo lost whatever protection the dune offered.

A nearby structure was already in trouble. It had relied on a seawall for protection, and when the wall was undermined, the owners had not been allowed to rebuild it. A terrace was already falling into the sea and the building itself stood only a few feet back.

In recent years, the state and local authorities who set the rules for coastal building have been learning fast. Heeding the cautions of geologists and ecologists, many of them now require that buildings be set back from the dune line, that they be anchored deep in the sand, that vegetation be left in place, and that buildings be raised so that, in the event of a severe storm, the water can flow under them. Unfortunately, many of the towers that now line parts of the shore were built before those regulations were in effect. In the worst cases, the builders bulldozed the dunes away, thus improving the ground-floor views but leaving no protection from high water.

The threat of a hurricane hangs over all of the Florida coast, but nowhere more than it does on this barrier beach. Except for a few hummocks here and there, Hutchinson Island rises only five or ten feet above sea level; hurricane tides, on the historical record, have run seven to eight feet above normal. In the authoritative handbook of Florida's east coast, written by Orrin H. Pilkey, Jr., and his team of coastal scientists, almost all of the shore, from the Georgia line to Biscayne Bay, is designated FLOOD RISK—EVACUATION DIFFICULT. Sailfish Point, the site of an expensive resort developed by Mobil Oil at the tip of Hutchinson Island, has the distinction, rivaled only by Fisher Island in Biscayne Bay, of being marked EVACUATION VERY DIFFICULT.

Of course, as Jane pointed out, the geographic conformation that worries the coastal scientists is just what makes this coast so desirable as a place to live. At Stuart, the St. Lucie River comes in from the west and runs parallel to the Indian River until both of them connect with the ocean at St. Lucie Inlet. If that means you have to cross two bridges to get from Hutchinson to the mainland, it also means that there are five waterfronts, counting the banks of both rivers and the ocean shore.

"Up north," Jane said, "you were always complaining that the beaches were closed. Here you have Hutchinson Island, which is one long, beautiful beach, and anyone can get to it easily." Of course she was right about that.

Behind the island barrier, the lagoons offer protected water for sailboats and motorboats, for waterskiing, windsurfing, jet skiing, scuba diving, and whatever new water sports may come along. White herons stalk the shallows, cattle herons roam the golf courses, and pelicans compete with fishermen for the day's catch. And what's more, as Jane pointed out, nothing beats the sunsets from her place on the Indian River.

This part of Florida's eastern shore is known as the Treasure Coast because it has yielded gold, silver, and emeralds from the wrecks of Spanish galleons. The source of the treasure is the great lost flota of 1715.

It was the Spaniards' custom, in their time of empire, to assemble each year at Havana the precious metals and jewels that they had seized or mined in the New World. From there, a fleet of heavily laden ships set sail, following the Gulf Stream up the coast of Florida before turning east to Europe. It was a slow passage, made perilous by hidden reefs and sudden storms. In 1715, the flota of twelve ships sailed on July 24 and six days later was struck by a savage hurricane. One by one, eleven ships foundered, leaving a trail of wrecks for fifty miles along the coast, from Stuart to Sebastian.

In the centuries that followed, the ships rotted away and their cargoes were buried by sand. Sometimes Spanish coins were found on the beach after storms and occasionally a fishing captain caught his net on a cannon. That was all until 1943, when the aqua-lung was invented.

The man who opened the modern treasure hunt on the Florida coast was Kip Wagner, a contractor who lived at Wabasso. In 1951, he assembled a team of divers and brought up, on their first day of exploration, two blackened lumps containing four thousand eight-*real* silver coins—the famous "pieces of eight."

Later, Mel Fisher, who had been running a dive shop in California, arrived on the Treasure Coast, bringing two more important aids to the search. One was the discovery, in the Archive of the Indies at Seville, of the records of the Spanish fleets, including their manifests and the location of wrecks. The other was a method of directing the wash of a boat's propeller downward, so as to blow away the sand that covered the wrecks. Fisher made his great strike when he found the *Nuestra Señora de Atocha*, not on the east coast but in the Gulf of Mexico, sixty miles west of Key West. From that single galleon, divers have brought up gold, silver, and jewels worth hundreds of millions of dollars.

To see how the hunt was going, Jane and I drove up to Fisher's building at Wabasso, where divers bring their finds to be cleaned and restored. There, we found his daughter, Taffi, looking after the family enterprise. Taffi began diving, she told us, when she was five or six years old, and has spent a lot of her time underwater ever since. Tall, blond, and slender, she would have looked at home in a wetsuit or a mermaid's skin, but in fact she was wearing blue jeans. From her back pocket, she took out a foot-long bar that she used as a pointer to show us coins, guns, necklaces, and miscellaneous artifacts that lined the shelves. The faintly gleaming pointer, I realized, was a gold bar—not rectangular like the ones in the mint but long, thin, and slightly crooked, and worth about fifty thousand dollars at auction.

The Treasure Coast has yet to yield a trove to match that of the *Atocha*, but the finds continue. Every year, dozens of dive boats, working under license from the Fisher organization, can be seen on the Treasure Coast. With ever more sophisticated instruments of detection, they hope any season now to find the mother lode.

Driving back through the towns of the Treasure Coast, we had a good lesson in the traffic problems suffered by towns that grow too much too fast. The scenes of congestion are no different from those on other sections of the Atlantic Coast, except that one at Stuart affords some comic relief. At a point known to the natives as Confusion Corner, Route A1A and another thoroughfare cross each other at odd angles, while the tracks of the Florida

East Coast Railway (which believes only in grade crossings) cut right across both of them. The scene is one of tentative starts and stops, since the average motorist cannot figure out who has the right of way. The resulting automobile ballet has provided hilarious footage for television shows.

With all the waterways along the Florida coast, there are many bridges, and almost all of them are too low for even a medium-sized sailboat to get under. Hence, they are always going up and down to allow boats to pass. Because of a long-standing prejudice that boats are somehow morally superior to automobiles, I have always taken a secret satisfaction in seeing long lines of cars held up while a drawbridge rises to let a little sailboat through. But that prejudice is tested by frequent waits in heavy traffic. With ever more boats on the water and ever more automobiles on land, there is a smoldering war between boaters and drivers.

There are traffic problems on the water, too. At Coconut Creek, the marine police, as I read in the paper, had just issued the latest of nineteen summonses to the speed-loving skipper of the *Bad Attitude*. It was not his fault, he said. "I'm good-looking. I have three or four gorgeous women with me. I've got long hair and a lot of jewelry."

As any harbormaster will attest, the great increase in the number of boats and the horsepower of their motors has not been matched by any increase in the skill and experience of those who drive them. At Port Salerno, I talked with Billy Mason, the black-bearded lockmaster at the entrance of the Okeechobee Waterway. This is the point where boats coming down the Intracoastal can take a short cut across Florida to the Gulf of Mexico. In the thirteen years he has managed the lock for the Corps of Engineers, Mason has opened the lock for vessels of all sorts, from ten-foot runabouts, to grand yachts with helicopter pads, to barges carrying sections of submarines. Some of the pleasure boaters, he said, are so lacking in skills or so infused with holiday spirits that once they get into the lock, they don't know which way is out. "And the first thing they do," he said, "is to blame it on their wives."

Jimmy Haluska, who runs the C. and W. Fish Company at Port Salerno, has a special complaint against the sportfishing boats. "Every year there are more of them," he says. "When they go out the channel, they spook the fish, and the fish stay away." At the same time that the stocks of many species have been declining, the sportfishermen have been taking an increasing share of the catch.

"Commercial fishermen come from fishing families," Haluska says. "And now many of the younger ones don't go into fishing. With all the regulation and the competition, the fishermen will just go out of business. Then maybe there'll be plenty of fish, but no one to catch them."

From Port Salerno, I drove on south to Juno Beach, looking for Loggerhead Park. One evening a little earlier, at a restaurant on Hutchinson Island, I had found on our table a sign that read:

KEEP SEA TURTLES IN THE DARK
Minimize Beach Lighting in the Summer

Upon looking into the matter, I found that the beaches along this central Florida coast are a great breeding ground for several species of sea turtles, especially the loggerheads, which may weigh up to 350 pounds. One of the dangers they encounter is the increasing presence of artificial lights along the shore.

Sea turtles spend most of their lives in the open ocean. When the females come ashore in late May or early June to lay their eggs in the sand, they seem to be guided by the light of the moon and stars, especially by the reflection of natural light on the water. If they are confused by artificial light, they may not nest at all. If they do nest, and the eggs hatch, the baby turtles may also be confused. Mistaking the artificial lights for the shimmer of light on the ocean, they may wander inland and never get to the sea.

Even in a purely natural environment, baby sea turtles face appalling risks. Each buried turtle nest contains about one hundred eggs and, as they hatch, the baby turtles work their way up through the sand, almost to the surface. Then, sometimes all at once, they erupt from the sand and head instinctively for the sea. Depending on where they are, they must run a gauntlet of various predators—dogs, foxes, coyotes, ghost crabs, buzzards, and, in Florida, especially raccoons. In his classic book on the sea turtle, *So Excellent a Fishe*, the naturalist Archie Carr described the scene:

Their trip across the sand to the surf is both fast and direct. So, for the turtles of each nest, this time of maximum peril in the whole life of the species is not really a long time at all. It is only a minute or two. . . . The little turtles come into a world anxious to eat them. They have simply to go fast and straight to the ocean, even though they can't see it, never saw it before, and know of its existence only as a set of signals to react to instinctively.

On many of their nesting beaches, even in the wild, most baby turtles are eaten up before they ever reach the sea. If they are distracted by artificial light, they have an even smaller chance of surviving. The sign I had seen in the restaurant was part of a campaign, inspired by naturalists and financed by the Florida Power and Light Company, to get the owners of oceanfront houses to dim their lights.

Once they reached the ocean and got away from the shore, turtles generally used to be safe, for they have no important enemies in the open sea. Except now for man. In other parts of the world, they are hunted for food and for their shells. In U.S. waters, their greatest peril comes from shrimp trawlers.

My inquiries about the sea turtle led me to the Florida turtle's best friend, Mrs. Lee Hallman, who runs the Marinelife Center at Loggerhead Park. When I got there, Lee was giving tender, loving care to some particularly ugly turtles that suffered from papilloma, a contagious disease that causes pink growths on their heads.

"I started out with dolphins," she said. "Dolphins are endangered, too, but they are so smart and playful that everybody cares about them. Then I discovered sea turtles. They are not little people dressed up in dolphin suits. They are cute but dumb. I've always been for the underdog."

Lee's greatest battle has been with the shrimpers, whose nets entangle and drown the turtles. Environmentalists invented a Turtle Exclusion Device (TED) which enables turtles to escape the nets, and Florida required shrimpers to use it. The shrimpers resisted angrily, claiming that the devices cut down the catch. Even when tests proved that, when properly mounted, the TEDs did not significantly reduce the catch, they still dragged their feet. Lee Hallman decided to take them on.

"The toughest bunch were in Key West," she told me. "They are saltwater cowboys—'conchs,' as they call themselves. Most of them grew up in shrimping families. They say, 'Daddy was a conch and Granddaddy was a conch, and I'm a conch.' They never had a boss and they don't want a boss coming in. I'd go down to the dock and hand out leaflets. They'd say, 'Oh, there are plenty of turtles out there. I see them all the time.' "

She told of one encounter: "I had my German shepherd with me, but one of them came at me cussing and waving a gun. He said, 'I'm gonna shoot you.' I happened to notice that his fly was unbuttoned. I told him so and he looked down. That gave us time to get away."

Lee received a lot of threatening telephone calls and nearly got beaten up, but in the end most of the shrimpers grumblingly accepted the TEDs.

At the Marinelife Center, Lee and her colleagues monitor five miles of Juno Beach, keeping count of the turtles, controlling lights, and keeping predators away from the nests. With such human help, she estimates that more than 90 percent of the baby turtles that hatch there reach safety in the ocean.

Whether such efforts can save the turtles in Florida and the whole Caribbean basin is still a question. From Lee, I heard the same complaint I had heard from other naturalists: "There are just too many people. That's not a popular thing to say, but if I had my way I'd put up a barrier at the Florida border and everyone coming in would have to take an environmental-awareness test. If they passed, I'd let them in."

CHAPTER
TWENTY

THE GOLD COAST

FIFTEEN miles south of Stuart, Jane and I crossed over Hobe Sound to drive down Jupiter Island. This is the domain of Mrs. Permelia Reed, who, with her late husband, Joseph Verner Reed, founded Florida's most exclusive resort. We were driving on a public highway but we had the feeling that we were passing through a private park. Hobe Sound was created for people who found Palm Beach too gaudy—Bush people, not Reagan people. One home owner was, in fact, the President's mother, Mrs. Prescott Bush.

Think twice before you buy a place here. You would not enjoy it much unless you belonged to the Jupiter Island Club, and you would not belong to the Jupiter Island Club unless Mrs. Reed and her friends invited you. We were told of a lady who rented a house for the season at Hobe Sound. She was invited to

207

the club as a guest and met the right people. But after she returned north, she received a sweater from Mrs. Reed—the subtlest of verdicts that she was out in the cold.

Lying just south of the jetties that keep St. Lucie Inlet open, Jupiter Island has suffered rather severely from beach erosion. In recent years, its property owners have spent $15 million to pump new sand onto the shore. They might have gotten the state to pay the cost, but only if they had been willing to allow public access and parking for a hundred cars every half mile. Perish the thought! They paid for their own sand.

While cherishing their private enclave, the Reeds and their friends have donated tracts of adjoining land to be kept forever wild. Here, as in other places along the Atlantic seaboard, we saw how a few wealthy individuals had played a major part in keeping sections of the coast unspoiled.

In traveling from Hobe Sound to Palm Beach, we moved backward in history, back to a time when the Big Rich liked to be seen for what they were. Palm Beach owes its foundation to Henry Morrison Flagler, the Standard Oil partner who extended his Florida East Coast Railway to Palm Beach in 1894 and built the Royal Poinciana Hotel. High Society arrived from the north by rail, often in private Pullman cars, with their personal maids and valets. At the Royal Poinciana, they dressed for fancy balls, played golf and polo, gambled, and took the air in "Afromobiles" pedaled by local blacks.

We passed through West Palm Beach, which Flagler described as "the city I am building for my help," and which now has seven times the population of Palm Beach itself. Crossing Lake Worth (another misnamed saltwater lagoon), we drove down an avenue of towering royal palms and entered a community frozen in one brief span of time—the 1920s.

Flagler left in Palm Beach a Victorian hotel of yellow clapboard and a Greek Revival mansion of white marble. But the architectural style that came to prevail was created later by Addison Mizner, with some help from Paris Singer, heir to part of the sewing machine fortune. In 1918, Singer, who thought he was dying, invited Mizner to be his guest in Florida, and Mizner, who was broke, accepted. Party animals both, they so cheered each other up that Singer put up the money and Mizner drew the plans for the Everglades Club, which has been the citadel of Palm Beach society ever since. After seeing it, Mrs. Edward T. Stotesbury, the reigning social leader of the colony, commissioned Mizner to build a thirty-seven-room house, and he was on his way. There is perhaps no community in the United States that owes its image so fully to one architect.

In the social world of Palm Beach, Mizner became an instant celebrity, known for his cavalier treatment of clients. It was said that he sometimes forgot to put in a staircase and had to stick it on the outside. The Harold Vanderbilt house (more recently owned by Yoko Ono) does indeed have such a staircase, in a circular tower by the front door. But it was not necessarily an afterthought. The likelier explanation is that Mizner liked to break up a facade with features that arrest the eye.

Another story is that a wealthy lady found him lying on the beach and reproached him for being so slow with her house plans. Mizner picked up a stick and drew a complete design in the sand. "Dearie, there it is," he said, and she accepted it.

It is hard to sort out fact from fiction because Mizner, who enjoyed the party circuit, earned his dinners by telling outrageous stories about himself. It is true that he had rather sketchy architectural training and that he tended to change his houses as they went up. To a client who pressed him for blueprints, he protested, "How can I give you blueprints when I haven't even built it yet?"

In his own mind Mizner's houses were constructs of reverie: "I sometimes start with a Romanesque corner, pretend that it has fallen into disrepair and been added to in the Gothic spirit, when suddenly the great wealth of the New World has poured in and the owner has added a very rich Renaissance addition."

The Mizner style was more Spanish than anything else, with lots of stucco walls, orange tile roofs, cypress paneling, and iron lanterns. But, as Mizner said, it was "Spanish turned inside out" to let the Florida light and air and flowers into the house. On summer forays to the Mediterranean, he brought back shipments of antique Italian furniture, tapestries, ironwork, and whole walls of carved paneling. But he also manufactured his own "antiques" in workrooms where chests were beaten with chains to give them scars and marble mantels were chipped with sledgehammers. Somehow the elements came together in houses that seldom failed to delight the eyes and raise the spirits of those who entered them.

Mizner's style was adopted by other Palm Beach architects, whose houses are so like his that it sometimes takes a scholar to tell them apart. To one of them, designed by Marion Sims Wyeth, we had the good fortune to be invited for cocktails. "I'm Wild Jean," our effervescent hostess said as she led us through a heavy wooden door and through a dark foyer to the great hall. "I suppose I'm crazy to live in a house like this. Even if you have the money, you can't get the servants to run it in the way it was meant to be run—and even if you could get them, nowadays you couldn't trust them. But I happen to love it." She took us through arches into a loggia that opened onto spacious gardens. "You can see," she said, "how the house was planned to draw guests from space to space as vistas opened up." We could very easily imagine the great hall filled with a hundred guests and the gardens festive with flowers, fountains, and the light of many candles.

For sheer sweep and opulence, the largest of the Mizner houses invite comparison with the marble mansions that Richard Morris Hunt built for the Vanderbilts at Newport. But whereas Hunt's "cottages" are imposing and cold, Mizner's are warm and inviting. On our journey down the coast, we had not found any seaside dwellings to compare with these except the best of the Shingle Style summer houses on the New England coast.

The next morning, we drove past the line of houses on Ocean Drive. On the landward side, almost nothing was changed since the 1920s, but on the seaward side the beach was almost gone. In their zeal to keep the beach for themselves, Palm Beach residents lined the shore with walls and groins that had the usual effect of causing the sand to wash away. Now the owners, as well as the county coastal commission, would like to get it back. Robert Clinger, the county coastal engineer, took me to see the latest experiment, an artificial reef of triangular concrete blocks, built underwater 170 feet off the shore of Willis du Pont's property. Mr. du Pont paid the $200,000 bill. "He hopes it will trap sand," said Clinger. "So do we."

Ocean Drive leaves the ocean just beyond the Bath and Tennis Club and jogs abruptly inland. Clinger pointed out to me some traces of the old pavement where it used to continue along the shoreline. Some years ago, through whatever political pressures, the waterfront was turned over to developers who built high-rise condos on it.

After lunch, we drove south on I-95. Even when the interstate is miles from the ocean, you can follow the line of the coast by the rows of tall buildings rising at intervals on the eastern horizon. Apartment towers are the highest things—the only high things—in sight. We turned off at Fort Lauderdale, the much-filmed beach city where the college students came for Spring Break until the police cracked down on the beer binge and drove the collegians up to Daytona. It was easy to see why Fort Lauderdale was such a favorite with visitors. The city fathers had the good sense to keep buildings back from the waterfront, providing miles of open beach and plenty of parking.

If Fort Lauderdale is no longer "Where the Boys Are," it is still "Where the Boats Are." From the air, the city looks like a collection of hay rakes—actually strips of land separated by finger canals. Those provide extra miles of waterfront for houses, and a dock at every house. The finger canals are not recommended for swimming because they tend to be stagnant, collecting whatever floats by. In Italy, Venice has the same problem.

The largest collection of boats is at Bahia Mar, one of the world's largest marinas, with slips for 350 boats, including some of the longest afloat. Having heard of this great flotilla, I wondered whether there might not be some congestion on the water, sort of a maritime gridlock. Not while we were there. Along the piers, not a slip was empty; in the channel, not a boat moved. Here and there, a young crewperson sipped a Coke or rubbed a cloth lazily along a rail. Granted, it was a weekday, and not in the height of the season, but it was a beautiful sunny day, ideal for boating and fishing. I wondered how much the somnolent fleet must be costing its owners. Later, a friend with a mathematical mind calculated that the value of the boats might come to something like $20 million. At that rate, the owners could be incurring an interest charge of more than $7,000 a day, to say nothing of maintenance, insurance, and depreciation. Clearly, not all of that came from the pockets of the individuals who used the boats. A fair number of the biggest vessels gave their home port as that corporate tax haven, Wilmington, Delaware.

Owners of big boats pay thousands of dollars a season to keep them in slips at marinas such as Bahia Mar. For owners of small boats, such as a friend of mine at West Palm Beach, there is another solution. His fourteen-foot runabout is parked on the fourth tier of a storage shed. When he wants to use it, a giant forklift truck picks it up, rolls to the edge of the dock, and lowers it into the water. No more stepping into a launch and running out to a mooring, as we used to do on Long Island Sound. It is more like retrieving a file from a filing case. There are far too many boats now to accommodate them on free-floating moorings. Nature is not providing any more safe little harbors, whereas manufacturers are turning out motorboats as if they were automobiles.

To boaters of an earlier time, the mooring fees may seem outrageous, but in fact many marinas are finding it hard to break even. Taxes on waterfront land have soared, especially where assessments are based on the "highest economic use." The highest potential use is seldom a boat basin or a marina. Generally, it is a hotel, a restaurant, or a condo.

Driving down the east coast of Florida, you have the feeling that you are passing through a land close to the border of unreality. This is not what we think of as a normal place where people work for a living (though of course most of the permanent residents do, or else the place would stop running). It is the disproportionate number of golfers, sportfishermen, shoppers, and miscellaneous idlers that create the ambience of a never-never land where Adam's curse has been repealed.

You feel rather like Dorothy journeying toward Oz. And Oz is Miami, the Sun City of the United States—or so it was proclaimed by the land agents who shaped its image. Nowadays, however, it is best to wear your green glasses when you approach this Emerald City. If you take them off, you will see the same roadside sleaze, the same seas of dreary little houses (more of them pink and yellow in Miami's case), the same rivers of traffic and convoluted highway interchanges that you see on the outskirts of most cities.

The last time I had approached Miami by road was many years ago, during a winter vacation from college. That was when strangers thought first of Miami Beach rather than Miami itself as their destination. That was before the skyscrapers and the Orange Bowl and the drug traffic. Before Miami had become the capital of Cuba-in-Exile. Before the boat people from Haiti.

We passed through Miami at rush hour and reached the shore of Biscayne Bay. It was here that the history of Miami as a winter resort began in 1896. Henry Flagler had opened the Royal Poinciana in Palm Beach just two years earlier, but during that first winter a cold snap had frozen oranges on the trees, and Flagler realized that the frost-free line lay a little farther south. For the sake of both vacationers and oranges, the two mainstays of his railway, he extended the tracks to the little settlement called Miami and built another grand hotel, the Royal Palm.

From their rooms in the Royal Palm, Flagler's guests could look across Biscayne Bay to an offshore strip of sand and mangrove swamp, inhabited by alligators, snakes, and wild pigs. It remained wild until just before World War I, when it caught the attention of Carl Fisher, the founder of the Indianapolis Speedway, who had come down to race speedboats on Biscayne Bay. Fisher completed a bridge across the bay, dredged up sand from the bottom to fill in the mangrove swamps, and began selling land for houses and hotels. The Miami Beach real estate boom was under way.

Unlike the history of other cities, which can be divided into political or economic periods, the history of Miami and Miami Beach can be told in terms of great hotels. As the Royal Palm was the symbol of the first era, the Roney Plaza was the focal point of the period between the two world wars. Its center stage was not the ballroom but the swimming pool. Its stars were not society ladies but bathing beauties. This was the turf of Steve Hannigan, the legendary press agent who flooded the desks of northern editors with pictures of pretty girls cavorting on the beach or basking by the pool. A permanent nonpaying guest was Walter Winchell, who conveyed to his readers the impression—not far from the truth—that the Broadway celebrities who peopled his syndicated column could be found during the winter in the cabanas and nightclubs of Miami Beach.

South of the Roney Plaza, Collins Avenue was lined with smaller hotels, built mostly of stucco, painted in pastel colors, and trimmed with the stripes and swirls that would one day be called Art Deco. After World War II, they were eclipsed by new, taller, far more extravagant hotels to the north. Of this new breed, the form-giver was Morris Lapidus, and its first monument was the Fontainebleau. From the outside, the Fontainebleau was a twenty-story structure with undulating pink walls, built around a marble pool and formal French gardens. Inside, it was a palace of marble columns, rosewood paneling, gold paint, and crystal chandeliers. Ada Louise Huxtable, architecture critic of *The New York Times,* shuddered at the sight and reported that it gave her the "Fountain Blues."

But Lapidus knew what vacationers who came to Miami Beach wanted. "A hotel has something to sell," he told one critic. "What is that something? A home away from home? Absolutely not." Perhaps Henry Flagler's friends, who lived in mansions, wanted the same surroundings on vacation. But the guests of the Fontainebleau wanted to get away from the house, the kids, the bills. The last thing they wanted was to feel at home.

Musing to John Margolies, the leading connoisseur of American roadside design, Lapidus asked, "Where are their tastes formulated? Do they study it in school? Do they go to museums? Do they travel in Europe? Only in one place—the movies." So Lapidus gave them a grand marble staircase like the one that Busby Berkeley's dancing girls came down in MGM musicals. It didn't lead to much of anywhere, but the guests liked to go up and down it.

There could be no doubt that the Lapidus style was a great success, for it was reproduced by him and others in the Eden Roc, the Americana, the Doral, the Deauville, and other castles of the beach. While the new hotels grew ever taller and fancier, the little old ones at the south end of the beach were looking ever older and seedier. Most of them had long since given up competing for tourists and instead offered shelter to permanent residents, many of them elderly Jewish couples from New York.

Then, in the late seventies, the unpredictable arbiters of historical fashion began to look at them in a new light. They were perceived as neglected jewels of Art Deco style, akin to such monuments of design as the Chrysler Building and the liner *Normandie.* The whole district was ensconced in the National Register of Historic Places, eligible for attention in works of art history, and for renovators' tax breaks. Many have now been restored to their original look on the outside and changed on the inside into restaurants, shops, studios, or gentrified apartments.

Time moves fast in a beach resort. If the Art Deco hotels have found a niche in architectural history, will the Fontainebleau be far behind? Evidently not. The new high priest of architectural design, Robert A. M. Stern, has pronounced Lapidus's work "a powerful embodiment of the same American dreams of escape and glamour that have inspired the resort builders since Saratoga to design some of the most original and inventive architecture produced in this country."

A strange thing about these seaside palaces is that they seem to have an aversion to the beach. In the 1950s and 1960s many of them were built out almost to the high-tide line, with concrete ramparts to defy the waves. Indeed, some extended beyond the tide line, and one of them twenty feet beyond it, making an impassable barrier to beach walkers. The hotels' message to their guests seemed to be: Bask on our sunny terraces. Paddle in our marble pools. But don't go near the ocean.

As generally happens when man erects obstacles to the natural movement of the beach, the sand began to wash away. The result was disastrous for the image that had brought visitors to Miami in the first place: bathing beauties, swaying palms, and rolling waves on a wide white beach. By the 1970s, visitors were asking, "Where's the beach?"

In the 1980s, Miami Beach was rescued from its folly by the greatest beach replenishment project ever attempted. At a cost of $68 million, most of it put up by the state and federal governments, a new beach, one hundred feet wide, has been laid down in front of the hotels.

There are some stretches where the general public can gain access to the new sand, but Miami Beach is not exactly hospitable to day visitors. One is reminded that this city was a creation of real estate developers, with building and zoning laws that were written to protect their interests. Miami Beach is managed for guests—paying guests.

Rather than search too hard for a gap in the wall of hotels, we committed trespass by walking through one of the grand lobbies, across the terraces, around the pool, down the steps, and onto the sand. The beach is there all right, with a walkway running its length, as well as benches and flower beds. The sand, dredged up from the bottom, did not have quite the fine texture of the old sand, but it was good enough. Whether it will stay, and how long, is anyone's guess.

THE KEYS

LESS than an hour after leaving Miami, travel-
ing alone now on Florida's Turnpike, I came to Florida City and
Mile Marker 126. Here begins the Overseas Highway, which
ends in Key West at Mile Marker Zero. Within a few miles, the
road left solid farmland and ran straight across a great empty
landscape of saw grass, the southeastern corner of the Everglades.

I could understand how the developers of Florida made such
a mistake about the Everglades. This was a wasteland, they must
have thought, just waiting to be drained, reclaimed, and turned
into dry land for cities, farms, and ranches. Private business
venturers began the work, with more than generous help from
the state politicians, and then, in 1930, the Army Corps of Engineers moved in. Over the years, they built a network of canals,
levees, and dams, attempting to control the flow of water and
diverting some of it to the swiftly growing cities of the East

217

Coast. As the natural flow of water from the north slackened, wetlands dried up, stranding animals and water birds and letting salt or brackish water push north from Florida Bay into the freshwater ecosystem.

The most damaging project of all was carried out in the 1960s when the Corps of Engineers turned the meandering Kissimmee River, which runs down the center of the state to Lake Okeechobee, into a straight concrete canal. The project made such a wasteland of the surrounding country that even the strongest boosters of the replumbing of the Everglades agreed that the Kissimmee should be turned back into a free-flowing river. So the Engineers—theirs not to reason why—are getting ready to move back in with their dredges and bulldozers to undo, so far as they can, what they did thirty years ago.

I was soon past the southeast corner of the Everglades. Fifteen miles below Florida City, the Overseas Highway leaves the mainland, crosses over a lacework of keys and shallow sounds, and reaches Key Largo, the first and largest link in the island chain.

The Keys are different, in their landforms and life-forms, from any other part of the Atlantic Coast. The upper Keys are old coral reefs, created during a time span of more than a hundred thousand years by tiny polyps living beneath the surface of the sea and leaving their skeletons to build the reef. When the sea level dropped in the last Ice Age, a string of coral islands, dead now, was left above water. The Keys and the waters around them are home to birds and animals found nowhere else, or hardly anywhere else, in the world, among them the little key deer, the bright-patterned tree snail, and the great white heron.

This fragile archipelago, unique in North America, if not in the world, does not put its best foot forward. Driving down Key Largo, I was disenchanted to find that the Overseas Highway is still Route 1, with its usual gamut of commercial come-ons. They do have some local flavor: Sunken Treasure, Shell Shock, Coral Castle, The Pink Junktique. The roadside signs are no different from those of any other commercial strip, but in that delicate landscape they seemed more jarring. It is foolish, I suppose, to think that the whole island chain could have been a national park.

Some sections, happily, have been saved from development. Turn off the highway at mile marker 102.5 and you come to the

John Pennekamp Coral Reef State Park, named for the onetime editor of the *Miami Herald* who led the campaign to establish it. The park includes a section of the new living reef that formed offshore when the Keys were left high and dry. From a glass-bottomed boat or with mask and snorkel, you can explore the shallower parts of the reef and its population of bright-colored fish. If you want to go deeper, using scuba gear, the Keys claim to have more dive shops than anyplace else in the world.

Deep-sea fishing is the mainstay of the tourist business in the Keys, but some of the establishments provide less common aquatic experiences. I passed up an offer to "Swim with the Dolphins" but stopped to investigate an invitation to "Dive, Dine & Dream at Five Fathoms." Jules' Undersea Lodge, it turned out, is a tanklike structure that was used in the Caribbean in the 1970s for experiments in undersea living. Sunk now in a lagoon just off the Overseas Highway, it offers motel accommodations for six people. Since it is thirty feet down, you must be a scuba diver to get to it. I was sorry I did not qualify.

At the western end of Key Largo, the Overseas Highway really takes off, leaping from one island to another over the shallow waters of Florida Bay. The old two-lane highway has been replaced in recent years by a four-lane model, but in some places the old bridges have been left standing. They make fine places to fish from. When I passed Duck Key, the rail of the old bridge was shared quite companionably by fishermen leaning against it and pelicans standing on top of it.

At Big Pine Key, I came to the Key Deer Refuge. This is the last remaining home of the little key deer, a subspecies of the Florida white-tailed deer, standing about as tall as a medium-sized dog. At the time the refuge was established in 1954, the key deer was on the verge of extinction. Under the shelter of the Fish and Wildlife Service, the herd grew from less than fifty to about four hundred, but now it is in decline again.

"It's the loss of habitat," said Deborah Holle, the attractive, outspoken manager of the Refuge. "We don't have a unified tract of wild land, but a patchwork of wild and developed areas, with the Overseas Highway cutting through the middle. Fragments of land won't do. The deer need a sizable place where they can live in peace." Initially, the Wildlife Service acquired what land it could, and since then it has added parcels when they came on the market. But its funds for acquisition dried up at the same time that more and more land was being snapped up by developers. In the last eight years, Deborah said, Big Pine Key has had a population growth of 43 percent, compared to 13 percent for the Keys as a whole.

Appealing as the little deer are to visitors and environmentalists, they do not get much active support from the local people. "It's the buccaneer mentality," Deborah said. "The people here don't like any kind of interference from the government."

Deer are killed every year by that great modern predator, the automobile, when they try to cross the highway from one section to the other. Deborah would like to see some underpasses built for them. Such underpasses, built under "Alligator Alley" (Route 84) in the Everglades, have helped save the Florida panther from extinction. But on Big Pine, the business establishment has been more interested in building a service road parallel to Route 1 for local use. The two projects conflict because a tunnel built under both roads would be too long; deer will not enter a tunnel unless they can see light at the other end.

At a public hearing, when Deborah told about the highway deer kill, a driver dismissed her figures, saying, "I haven't seen any dead deer on the road."

"Of course you haven't," she responded. "That's because we pick them up right away."

"I wonder how many dead pedestrians he has seen," she added later.

She was doing her best, but, unless more land were to be added to the Refuge, she feared it might be a losing fight.

Big Pine Key is the headquarters also of the Great White Heron Refuge. The Great White is the largest, most stately of all the North American shorebirds. It is most often seen alone, standing or slowly walking in shallow waters near mangrove islands, ready to dip its beak quickly, pick up a fish, and raise its neck straight up to swallow the catch. The heron is not in such imminent danger of extinction as the key deer because its numbers are greater, and smaller colonies exist on the Florida mainland as well as on other shores of the Gulf of Mexico. But it had a narrow escape in the 1930s when, after losses from hunters and hurricanes, only fifty birds were counted in the Keys. The refuge includes about 320 square miles of Florida Bay, between the Keys and the mainland, and includes some hundreds of low, mangrove-covered islands, many of them privately owned. On Big Pine Key, the herons have adapted to the presence of people, sometimes alighting in backyards in hope of handouts.

Even before the Keys were connected to the mainland, the flora and fauna suffered depredations. A century ago hunters almost wiped out the egrets in order to take their long, curving plumes for ladies' hats. But the great assault was launched in 1905 by Henry M. Flagler.

Having brought his Florida East Coast Railway down to Miami, Flagler could not resist the temptation to run it on to Key West. Except for that city, the Keys were very lightly inhabited (Key Largo had in its fifty-mile length only five hundred people, some of them growing limes and pineapples, some just subsisting on the natural bounty of fruit and fish. Construction was begun with gangs of workmen—Swedish, Italian, and Irish immigrants, blacks from the American South, drifters from the northern cities—four thousand of them before they got through. On Key Largo, the job was easy but the damage great. Sparks from a locomotive set fire to piles of logs and brush beside the tracks, and the fires laid waste the hardwood forests. From Key Largo on, the tracks were carried from island to island over embankments and bridges, including one of seven miles between Marathon and Duck Key. Two hurricanes washed out tracks and bridges and killed about seven hundred workers. Never mind, the line was built, and on January 22, 1912, at the age of eighty-two, Flagler rode triumphantly into Key West.

It was an industrial empire builder's last fling. Flagler had had some notion of connecting the line by ferry with Honduras on the other side of the Gulf, but nothing came of that. The line, someone said, was "a railway carrying nothing for nobody to nowhere."

Key West was an old city with a long history and a colorful reputation. Ever since the days of the Spanish treasure ships, it had been a port for buccaneers, smugglers, and pirates. Under U.S. rule, it became the thriving center of the "wrecking" trade, a perfectly legal, if not very inspiring, enterprise carried on by captains who raced one another to salvage any ship that ran onto the reef. So lucrative was the salvage trade that in the early nineteenth century Key West reported one of the highest per capita incomes of any city in the country.

That was not all. In the 1860s, Cubans settled in Key West, making it the cigar-making capital of the United States. Later, for a while it was the sponge capital, with a colony of Greek divers. But the good times did not last. The wrecking business petered out when lighthouses and marine engines combined to keep ships from running aground. The cigar business moved to Tampa, and the sponge center to Tarpon Springs. Despite a boost from the railroad, Key West slumped into deep depression, its population down from 22,000 to 12,000. Then the crowning blow: On Labor Day in 1935, a hurricane struck the Keys, knocking out great sections of the railroad. Once again, Key West was an island in the ocean.

Two things saved the decrepit old town. First, the federal government built a highway over the trestles of the ruined railroad. Then visitors began to come, attracted by the sun, the coral sea, the quaint houses. The tone of present-day Key West was already being set by Ernest Hemingway, who arrived in 1928, and by other writers and artists, both straight and gay, who followed him in the 1930s. Duval Street came alive after dark, with bars, restaurants, and nightclubs. "It was a place," observed Elmer Davis, the radio commentator, "where a man couldn't fall down in any direction without falling into a bar."

There is something special about places at the end of the line. People who come to such places have two choices. One is to turn around and go back; the other is to stay and take what comes along. In time, such a place accumulates a disproportionate number of loners, drifters, seekers, romantics, and fugitives from normal, boring, regulated life. Their philosophy generally includes a desire to be left alone and a willingness to leave others alone. Therefore, the community tends to be more tolerant and relaxed than most.

When I reached Key West, I drove on through until, at the corner of Whitehead and Fleming streets, I came to a sign that read, END OF ROUTE 1. Many tourists, seeing that sign, are inclined to say "Good riddance," but, having followed the frowsy, historic highway all the way from Maine, I was rather sad to see it end.

Just beyond was Mallory Dock, and the time was close to

sunset. Late every afternoon, I had been told, the people of Key West go down to the dock to watch the sunset. Indeed, there was a fair-sized crowd when I got there and, as advertised, there were "buskers"—several jugglers, a kilted bagpiper, palmists, fortune-tellers, acrobats, a man with cats that jumped through hoops of fire, a sword swallower, and vendors selling food, shells, and T-shirts. It did indeed look for all the world like old prints of a medieval fair in front of a cathedral.

There were only two things wrong with the scene. One was that most of the onlookers were not natives but tourists. "Down in front," they cried as a young woman with a camcorder stood on a fence to capture the scene. "*Achtung!*" chimed in a corps of German visitors. The girl held her ground.

The other thing wrong with the scene was that there wasn't any view of the sunset. The *Queen of Bermuda* had come in that day and, claiming some kind of mechanical trouble, had not left dock. A bearded old fellow in a T-shirt, who confirmed that he was indeed a local and that he did come there every day, looked bemused. The tourists stared up at the ship. The passengers stared down at the tourists. The sun set.

If Mallory Dock belongs to the tourists, the rest of the harbor belongs to the "conchs," so called, some say, because their ancestors consumed so many of the big, tasty mollusks. Many are shrimpers now. It was one of them who gave Lee Hallman, the turtle protector from Juno Beach, such a hard time over TEDs, the turtle exclusion devices. Fiercely independent, they still control the political climate of Key West. When I was at Big Pine Key, Deborah Holle, the refuge manager, had shown me a bumper sticker that she said epitomized the politics of the "Conch Republic." It had been issued in response to a federal government order to Key West to stop dumping raw sewage in the shallow waters of Florida Bay. The bumper sticker read:

KEYS STATEHOOD
DUMP THE MAINLAND

This might seem a rather reckless political platform, considering the fact that Key West gets almost all its water from the mainland by pipe and almost everything else by truck. But if it comes to a choice, the conchs want everyone to know that, like their fellow spirits in New Hampshire, they will take liberty over economic well-being.

The conchs would like to keep things as they were, but in fact things are changing fast. Ann Boess, the editor of a weekly paper called *Solares Hill* (named after the highest point in town), told me that she had seen great change in the four years she had lived in Key West. "There's a lot of new money," she said, "and a lot of new development. It has been too much, too soon, with too little thought. This is only a little place, and it is all one ecosystem. There's none other like it."

The combined effects of new outside money and plentiful native artistic talent are plain to be seen. Fine old falling-down houses, some of them relics of the prosperous wrecking days, have been restored with skill and taste. The result has been an escalation of both elegance and property values.

As historic houses go—quite stuffily on the whole—those in Key West are somewhat nonstandard. The "Audubon House" is one in which Audubon was a part-time guest for all of six weeks while he was stalking birds in the Keys; the house belonged to a captain who had made his fortune in the wrecking trade. As for the Hemingway house, it exhibits not only the rooms where he lived and wrote but the urinal that he and his fellow revelers brought back one night from the men's room at Sloppy Joe's bar.

Sloppy Joe's is still a must stop on the pilgrim's visit to Key West, but it now occupies a different building, at the corner of Duval and Greene streets. The old Sloppy Joe's, down the block a ways, is now Captain Tony's Saloon, owned and presided over by Tony Tarracino, a former ship captain and gunrunner. When I was there, Mr. Tarracino was also the mayor of Key West.

In Key West, it helps for even a developer to be somewhat offbeat. The biggest one in town is Pritim Singh, and his project is the Truman Annex. This was part of the old Navy Yard, where Harry Truman spent vacations in a cottage known as the winter White House. The federal government offered the property first to the state and the city; when neither wanted to buy it, Singh got 102 acres for a bargain price of $17.5 million. Singh is a French Canadian whose original name was Paul La Bombard and who spent two summers in the 1960s camping out at Key West before joining an ashram in Massachusetts. Emerging with a Hindu name, a beard, and a turban, he proceeded to make a small fortune in New England real estate before returning to Key West. His plans for the Truman Annex call for a complex of houses, condos, shops, and, on an offshore island where the navy kept oil tanks, a Ritz Carlton hotel reached by launch. As proof of his ecological sensitivities, he stopped construction for several weeks when some roseate spoonbills nested on the property.

Everywhere in the Keys, the pressures on the land are easy to see. The pressures on the coral reef are equally great but visible only to divers. On the waterfront, hard by the docks used by shrimpers and sportfishermen, I found the office of Reef Relief, a single-purpose environmental organization founded by the husband-and-wife team of Craig and DeeVon Quirola.

DeeVon sat in a clutter of paper and artwork, some of it related to the work of the Quirolas' commercial design studio and some of it related to the cause of saving the reef. With only five hundred members, volunteer help, and occasional grants to her organization, DeeVon has clearly been run pretty ragged. "We call ourselves Puppies," she said. "Poor Yuppies."

"People must realize," said DeeVon, "that the reef is a living organism, and a very delicate one." It can be badly damaged if a fishing boat drops its anchor on it. To prevent such damage, Reef Relief has installed a string of mooring buoys, so that boats can tie up to them. Divers, who used to break off hunks or sprays of coral for souvenirs, are warned not to let their hands or feet touch the reef.

DeeVon ticked off a list of other perils to the reef: discharges of oil or sewage from the ever-growing number of boats, effluent from sewers and seepage from septic tanks, oil from passing tankers. Worst of all is the threat that offshore drilling may be allowed nearby. "Even without a major disaster," she says, "there would always be small spills."

Some months later, I was glad to read that the efforts of Reef Relief and other environmental groups were beginning to bear fruit. President Bush, who knew the Keys from fishing trips out of Islamorada, put a twelve-year hold on plans to open the offshore waters to oil drilling. At about the same time, Congress designated the Keys as a National Marine Sanctuary, thereby improving the prospects for federal help in controlling pollution and overdevelopment.

In the long run, the Keys may have something else to worry about. Ever since the end of the last Ice Age, when the glaciers began to melt, the oceans have been rising. Along the mid-Atlantic Coast in modern times, the rise has been about a foot a century. Most oceanographers believe that it is rising faster now, though they do not agree on how fast. The wild card in all their calculations is the greenhouse effect of industrial gasses that trap the sun's heat within the earth's atmosphere. Dr. Stephen Leatherman, director of the Laboratory for Oceanic Research at the University of Maryland, is predicting a rise of four or five feet in the next century.

Such a rise would have serious effects on the Atlantic Coast, flooding the waterfronts of coastal cities and turning low shores into marshes or ocean bottom. Florida would be the hardest hit, losing a lot of its edges, where the population is greatest. The Keys, which have an average elevation of about six feet, would shrink or disappear.

In the Keys, that is too much to think about. There are too many more immediate perils: that a hurricane like that of 1935 will cut the archipelago off from the mainland; that the reef will die; that pollution will kill the fish; that developers and their political allies, sometimes known as the Concrete Coalition, will pave everything over. The spirit of the Keys is not attuned to perils that are measured in human lifetimes. Today, the sun is bright, the water is warm, and the fishing is still pretty good. *Carpe diem.*

I had one more thing to find at Key West. Having started my journey at the northernmost house on the U.S. Atlantic Coast (the keeper's cottage at West Quoddy Head Light in Maine), I wanted to see the southernmost house. Upon inquiring at the chamber of commerce, I was directed to a big Victorian mansion with pink brick, turquoise trim, and drawn shutters, at the end of Duval Street. I suppose that it used to be the southernmost house, but it wasn't anymore. I walked on past three more houses before I came to the corner of South and Whitehead streets. There, I found a brightly painted channel buoy bearing the words SOUTHERNMOST POINT. Tourists were taking one another's pictures in front of the buoy and buying shells from Julian Kee. He was clearly the southernmost merchant, having been at this corner selling shells for forty-nine years. The southernmost house, as I could see, was a white one just behind the fence and across a stretch of grass from the buoy. It belonged, Mr. Kee said, to Billie Ruff, the proprietor of Billie's Bar and Restaurant in the center of town. Billie was not at his restaurant, but I reached him by telephone in Miami. He confirmed with some pride that, no matter what the chamber of commerce said, he was the southernmost American, and the southernmost point of land was where the flagpole stood on his lawn.

So ends the Atlantic Coast of the United States.

BIBLIOGRAPHY

GENERAL

Bascom, Willard. *Waves and Beaches*. Garden City, N.Y.: Doubleday, 1964.

Edey, Maitland A. *The Northeast Coast*, New York: Time-Life Books, 1972.

Hay, John, and Peter Farb. *The Atlantic Shore: Human and Natural History from Long Island to Labrador*. New York: Harper & Row, 1966.

Kaufman, Wallace, and Orrin Pilkey. *The Beaches Are Moving*. Garden City, N.Y.: Doubleday, 1979.

Laskin, David. *Eastern Islands: Accessible Islands of the East Coast*. New York: Facts on File, 1990.

Leatherman, Stephen P. *Barrier Island Handbook*. College Park, Md.: Laboratory for Coastal Research, The University of Maryland, 1988.

Leonard, Jonathan Norton. *Atlantic Beaches*. New York: Time-Life Books, 1972.

Morrison, H. Robert, and Christine Eckstrom. *America's Atlantic Isles*. Washington, D.C.: National Geographic Society, 1981.

Ogburn, Charlton, Jr. *The Winter Beach*. New York: Morrow, 1966.

Reiger, George. *Wanderer on My Native Shore*. New York: Simon & Schuster, 1983.

Robinson, William F. *Coastal New England*. Boston: Little, Brown, 1983.

CHAPTER 1: WAY DOWN EAST

Jewett, Sarah Orne. *The Country of the Pointed Firs*. 1896.

Morison, Samuel Eliot. *Samuel de Champlain*. Boston: Little, Brown, 1972.

Rich, Louise Dickinson. *The Peninsula*. Philadelphia: Lippincott, 1958.

CHAPTER 2: THE MAINE ISLANDS

Caldwell, Bill. *Islands of Maine*. Portland, Maine: Guy Gannett Pub., 1981.

Conkling, Philip W. *Islands in Time*. Camden, Maine: Down East Books, 1981.

Island Institute. *The Island Journal*. Rockland, Maine: Island Institute, 1984.

McLane, Charles B. *Islands of the Mid-Maine Coast*. Falmouth, Maine: Kennebec River Press, 1982.

Porter, Eliot. *Summer Island*. San Francisco: The Sierra Club, 1966.

CHAPTER 3: THE ROCKY COAST

Beam, Philip C. *Winslow Homer at Prout's Neck*. Boston: Little, Brown, 1966.

Clark, Charles E. *Maine: A Bicentennial History*. New York: W. W. Norton, 1977.

CHAPTER 4: THE SANDY COAST

Slade, David C., Project manager. *Putting the Public Trust Doctrine to Work*. Washington, D.C.: Coastal States Organization, 1990.

CHAPTER 5: NORTH OF BOSTON

Garland, Joseph E. *Boston's Gold Coast: The North Shore 1890–1929*. Boston: Little, Brown, 1981.

Morison, Samuel Eliot. *The Maritime History of Massachusetts 1783–1860*. Boston: Houghton Mifflin Co., 1921.

Thaxter, Celia L. *An Island Garden*. Boston: Houghton Mifflin Co., 1894 and 1988.

Whitehill, Walter M. *Boston: A Topographical History*. Cambridge, Mass.: Harvard University Press, 1963.

CHAPTER 6: CAPE COD

Beston, Henry. *The Outermost House*. New York: Rinehart, 1928.

Hay, John. *The Great Beach*. New York: Doubleday, 1963.

Thoreau, Henry David. *Cape Cod*. 1865.

CHAPTER 7: OFFSHORE

Chamberlain, Barbara Blau. *These Fragile Outposts: A Geological Look at Cape Cod, Martha's Vineyard, and Nantucket.* New York: Doubleday, 1964.

Stackpole, Edouard A. *The Sea Hunters: The New England Whalemen During Two Centuries.* Philadelphia: Lippincott, 1953.

CHAPTER 8: THE FISHING GROUNDS

Kipling, Rudyard. *Captains Courageous.* 1896.

McCloskey, William. *Fish Decks.* New York: Paragon House, 1990.

Melville, Herman. *Moby Dick.* 1851.

Warner, William W. *Distant Water: The Fate of the North Atlantic Fishermen.* Boston: Little, Brown, 1983.

CHAPTER 9: THE SOUND

Cutler, Carl. *Mystic, the Story of a Small New England Seaport.* Mystic, Conn.: The Marine Historical Association, 1951.

Gleason, Sarah C. *Kindly Lights: A History of the Lighthouses of Southern New England.* Boston: Beacon Press, 1991.

Scully, Vincent. *The Shingle Style Today.* New York: George Braziller, 1974.

CHAPTER 10: LONG ISLAND

Caro, Robert. *The Power Broker: Robert Moses and the Fall of New York.* New York: Knopf, 1974.

Kouwenhoven, John A. *The Columbia Historical Portrait of New York.* New York: Doubleday, 1953.

Morris, James. *The Great Port.* New York: Oxford, 1955.

Payne, Robert. *The Island* (Gardiner's). New York: Harcourt, Brace, 1958.

CHAPTER 11: THE JERSEY SHORE

Bennett, D.W. *New Jersey Coastwalks.* Highlands, N.J.: American Littoral Society, 1981.

Pilkey, Orrin H., Jr. et al. *Living with the New Jersey Shore.* Durham, N.C.: Duke University Press, 1986.

Chapter 12: Chesapeake Bay

Barth, John. *The Tidewater Tales*. New York: Putnam's, 1987.

Horton, Tom. *Bay Country*. New York: Ticknor & Fields, 1987.

Horton, Tom, and William Eichbaum. *Turning the Tide: Saving the Chesapeake Bay*. Chesapeake Bay Foundation. Washington, D.C.: Island Press, 1991.

Michener, James A. *Chesapeake*. New York: Random House, 1978.

Warner, William W. *Beautiful Swimmers: Watermen, Crabs and the Chesapeake Bay*. Boston: Little, Brown, 1976.

Chapter 13: Past the Capes

Fisher, Allan C., Jr. *America's Inland Waterway*. Washington, D.C.: National Geographic Society, 1973.

Morine, David E. *Good Dirt: Confessions of a Conservationist*. Chester, Conn.: Globe-Pequot Press, 1990.

Plummer, Henry M. *The Boy, Me, and the Cat, 1912–13*. Reprint. Rye, N.H.: C. Chandler Co., 1961.

Chapter 14: The Outer Banks

Bailey, Anthony. *The Outer Banks*. New York: Farrar, Straus & Giroux, 1987.

De Blieu, Jan. *Hatteras Journal*. Golden Col.: Fulcrum Pub. Co., 1991.

Stick, David. *The Outer Banks of North Carolina 1584–1958*. Chapel Hill, N.C.: University of North Carolina Press, 1958.

Chapter 15: Hurricane Hugo

Tait, Lawrence S., Editor. *Beaches: Lessons of Hurricane Hugo*. Tallahassee, Fla.: The Florida Shore and Beach Preservation Association, 1990.

Chapter 16: The Sea Islands

Bell, Malcolm, Jr. *Major Butler's Legacy: Five Generations of a Slaveholding Family*. Athens, Ga.: The University of Georgia Press, 1987.

Conroy, Pat. *The Water Is Wide*. Boston: Houghton Mifflin Co., 1972.

Kemble, Frances Anne. *Journal of a Residence on a Georgian Plantation in 1838–1839*. London, 1863. Reprint. Athens, Ga.: University of Georgia Press, 1984.

Lanier, Sidney. *Poems*, 1884.

McKee, Gwen, Editor. *A Guide to the Georgia Coast*. Savannah, Ga.: The Georgia Conservancy, 1984.

Chapter 17: On Bartram's Trail

Bartram, William. *The Travels of William Bartram*. New Haven: Yale University Press, 1958.

Proby, Kathryn Hall. *Audubon in Florida*. Coral Gables, Fla.: University of Florida Press, 1974.

Chapter 18: On the Flyway

Bent, Arthur Cleveland. *Life Histories of North American Shorebirds*. New York: Dover, 1962.

Chapter 19: The Treasure Coast

Carr, Archie. *So Excellente a Fishe: A Natural History of Sea Turtles*. Garden City, N.Y.: The Natural History Press, 1967.

Derr, Mark. *Some Kind of Paradise: A Chronicle of Man and the Land in Florida*. New York: Morrow, 1989.

Karp, Walter. "Lost Galleons of the Spanish Main," in *Mysteries of the Deep*. New York: American Heritage Publishing Co., 1980.

Chapter 20: The Gold Coast

Curl, Donald W. *Mizner's Florida: American Resort Architecture*. Cambridge, Mass.: M.I.T. Press, 1984.

Jahoda, Gloria. *Florida: A Bicentennial History*. New York: W.W. Norton, 1976.

Stern, Robert A. M. *Price of Place*. Boston: Houghton Mifflin Co., 1986.